SHADOWS
ON SAPLINGS

Inspired by the classic manga
series **Lone Wolf and Cub** by
KAZOU KOIKE
and
GOSEKI KOJIMA

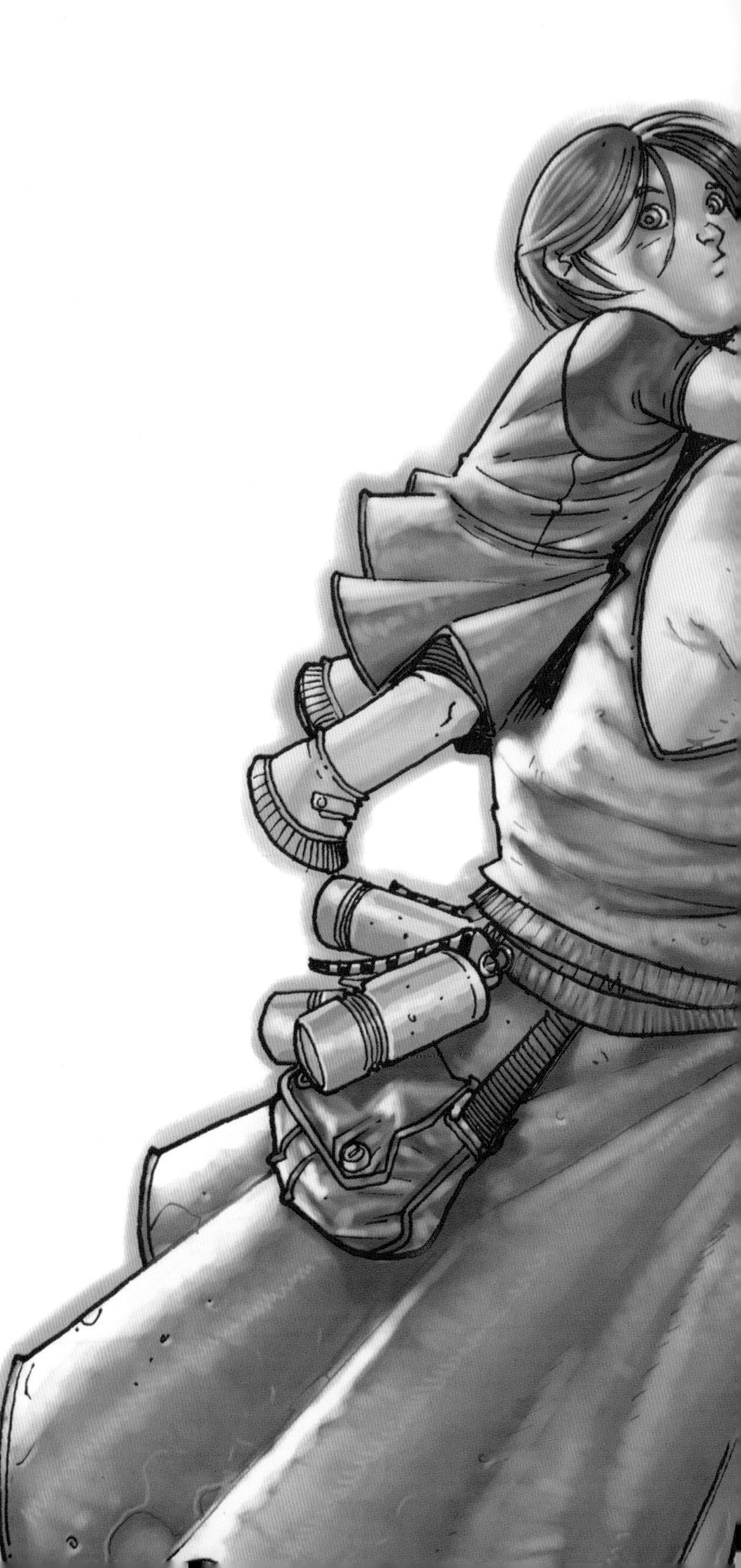

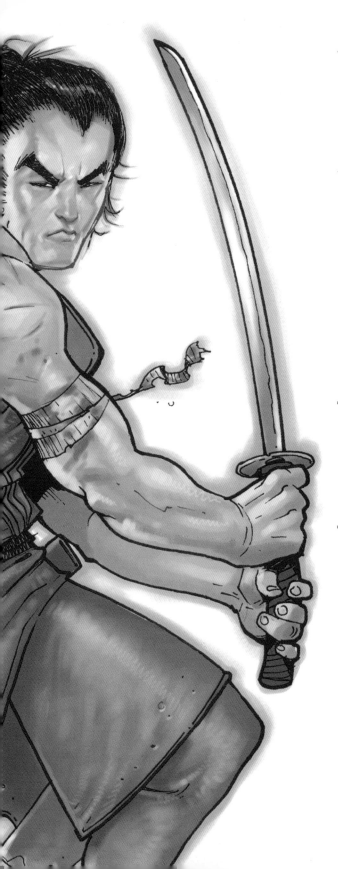

LONE WOLF 2100

子連水狼

SHADOWS ON SAPLINGS

written by
MIKE KENNEDY

art by
FRANCISCO RUIZ VELASCO
with additional coloring by Studio F

lettering by
DIGITAL CHAMELEON

Dark Horse Comics®

publisher
MIKE RICHARDSON

collection designer
DARIN FABRICK

art director
MARK COX

assistant editor
JEREMY BARLOW

editor
RANDY STRADLEY

special thanks to
Martin Takahashi

LONE WOLF 2100 Volume 1 — SHADOWS ON SAPLINGS
Lone Wolf 2100™ copyright © 2002, 2003 Dark Horse Comics,
Inc., Koike Shoin, and Liveworks. Dark Horse Comics® and the
Dark Horse logo are trademarks of Dark Horse Comics, Inc.,
registered in various categories and countries. All rights reserved.
No portion of this publication may be reproduced or transmitted,
in any form or by any means, without the express written
permission of Dark Horse Comics, Inc. Names, characters, places,
and incidents featured in this publication either are the product
of the author's imagination or are used fictitiously. Any resemblance
to actual persons (living or dead), events, institutions, or locales,
without satiric intent, is coincidental.

This volume collects issues one through four
of the comic-book series, **Lone Wolf 2100**.

Published by
Dark Horse Comics, Inc.
10956 SE Main Street
Milwaukie, OR 97222

www.darkhorse.com

To find a comics shop in your area, call
the Comic Shop Locator Service toll-
free at 1-888-266-4226

First edition:
ISBN: 1-56971- 893-8

1 3 5 7 9 10 8 6 4 2
Printed in China

FOREWORD

Chances are, many of you who pick up this book will already be familiar with the core concept of **Lone Wolf and Cub**: a lone samurai wanders the countryside with his son, seeking revenge on those who sullied his reputation and murdered his wife. Perhaps it was even your familiarity with the property that prompted you to purchase the book you hold in your hands. But some of you have never had the pleasure of experiencing the original **Lone Wolf and Cub**. Read on.

Created for Japanese comics in 1970 by writer Kazuo Koike and artist Goseki Kojima, **Lone Wolf and Cub** (**Kozure Okami** in Japanese) eventually filled nearly eight thousand pages – the epitome of a simple story told exceedingly well. The series' lean, visceral plots and stark, cinematic storytelling became a permanent benchmark in comics excellence, to this day inspiring a host of comics artists and writers around the world. But **Lone Wolf and Cub**'s influence didn't end with the printed page; it also served as source material for a series of feature films (popularly known as "the babycart films") and a television series in its native Japan, and was the inspiration for the graphic novel from which the recent American film **The Road to Perdition** was adapted.

Now, thirty-some years after its Japanese debut, the **Lone Wolf and Cub** saga is finally available in English, in its entirety — all twenty-eight volumes. Read one, and you'll be hooked by the power, the savagery, and the poignancy of the father and son's journey down the path to restoration, revenge, and ultimately to Hell. Run, don't walk, to your nearest library or bookstore and experience it for yourself.

How does **Lone Wolf 2100** fit into all of this? It is our hope (and belief) that this new saga can reside peacefully with its progenitor; that it can stand on its own merits — being neither a commentary on, nor a sequel to, the original series — and exist as a respectful re-imagining that borrows liberally from the original's core concept, but follows its own path to its own logical conclusion. For the freedom to explore this new territory, we are deeply grateful to Kazou Koike, whose permissions and enthusiasm paved the way for our efforts.

Randy Stradley
Portland, Oregon
November 2002

子連れ狼

2100

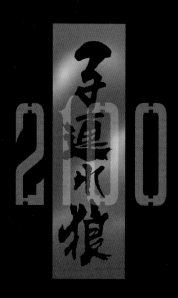

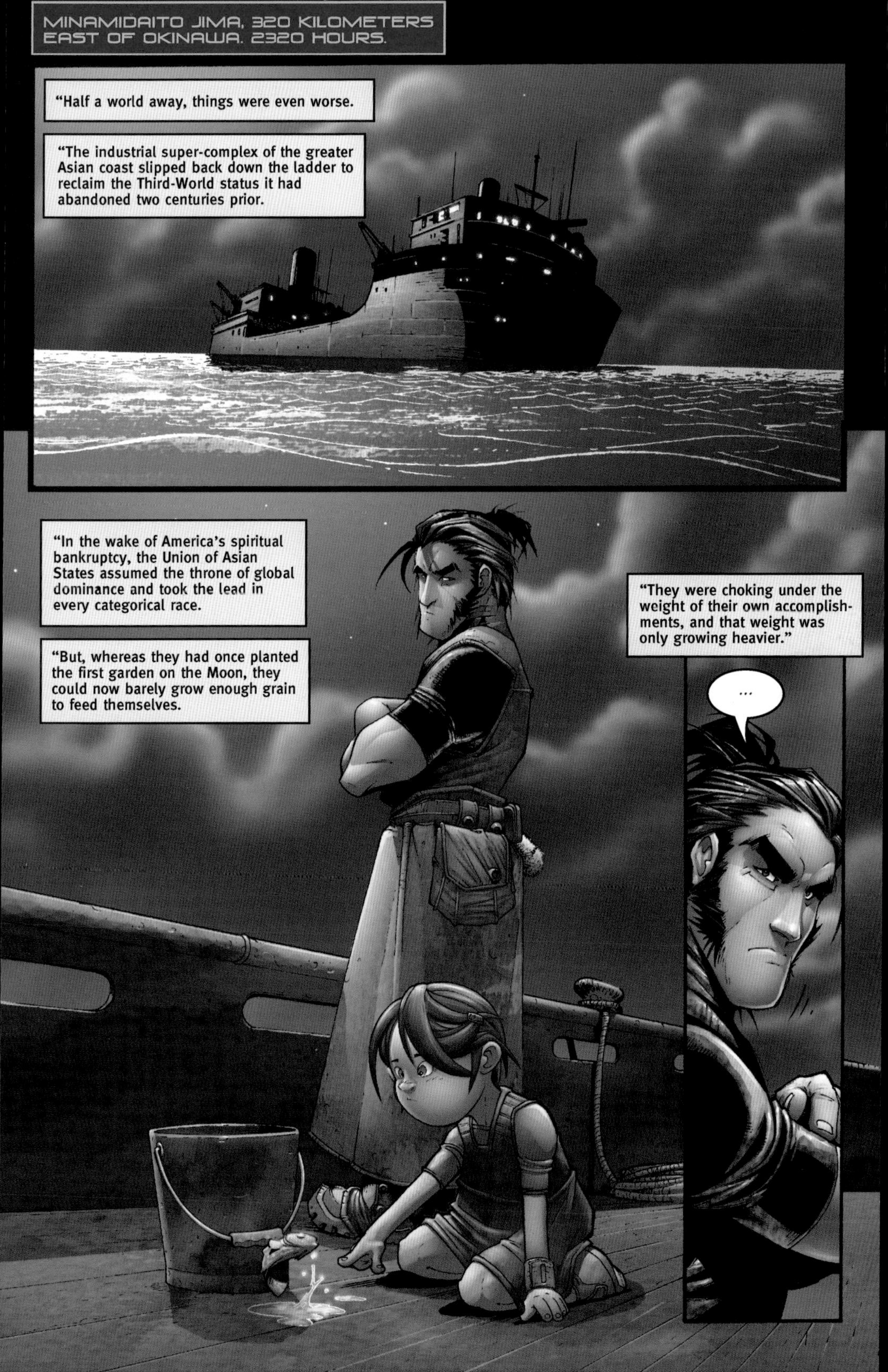
MINAMIDAITO JIMA, 320 KILOMETERS EAST OF OKINAWA. 2320 HOURS.
"Half a world away, things were even worse.
"The industrial super-complex of the greater Asian coast slipped back down the ladder to reclaim the Third-World status it had abandoned two centuries prior.
"In the wake of America's spiritual bankruptcy, the Union of Asian States assumed the throne of global dominance and took the lead in every categorical race.
"But, whereas they had once planted the first garden on the Moon, they could now barely grow enough grain to feed themselves.
"They were choking under the weight of their own accomplishments, and that weight was only growing heavier."
...

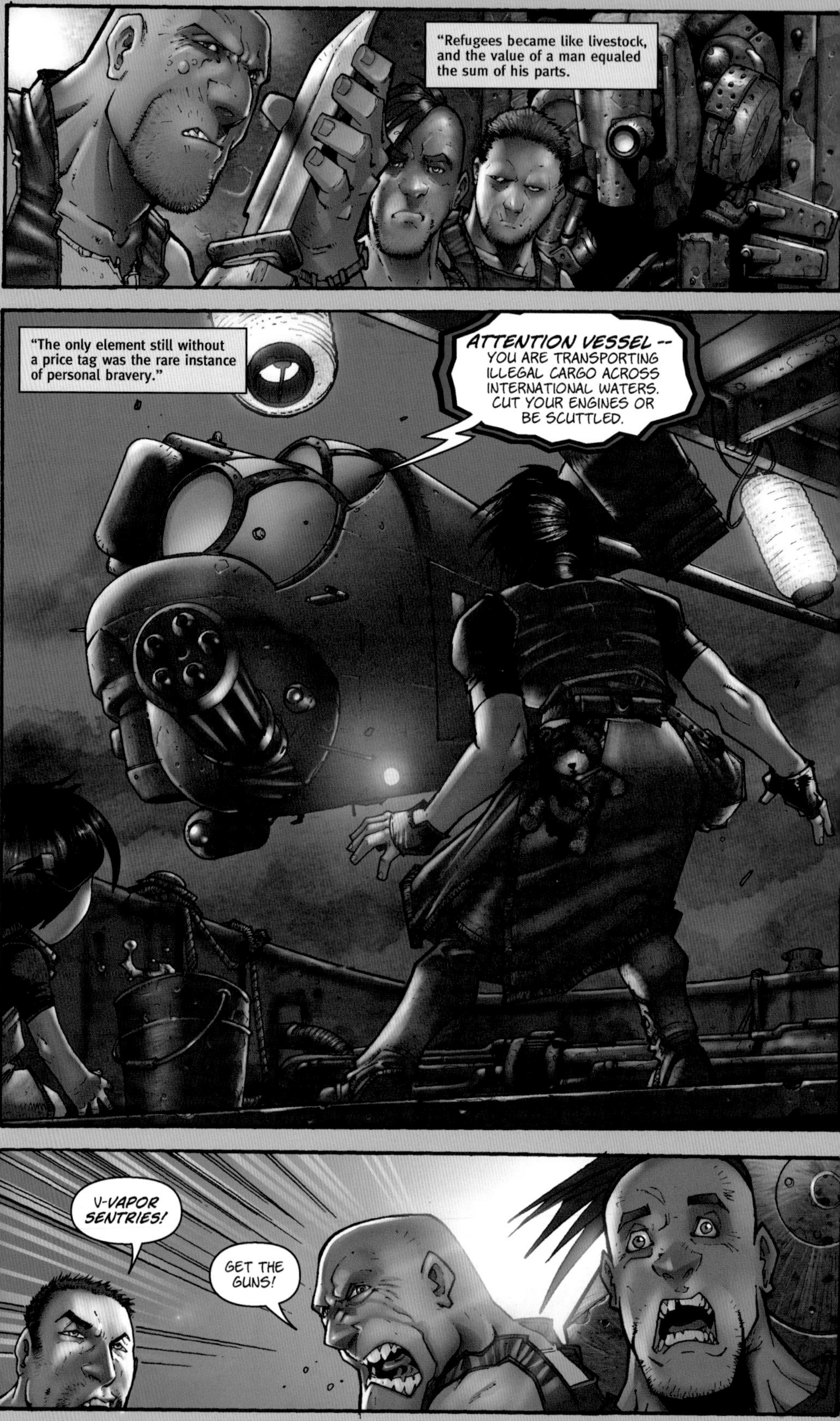
"Refugees became like livestock, and the value of a man equaled the sum of his parts.
"The only element still without a price tag was the rare instance of personal bravery."
ATTENTION VESSEL -- YOU ARE TRANSPORTING ILLEGAL CARGO ACROSS INTERNATIONAL WATERS. CUT YOUR ENGINES OR BE SCUTTLED.
V-VAPOR SENTRIES!
GET THE GUNS!

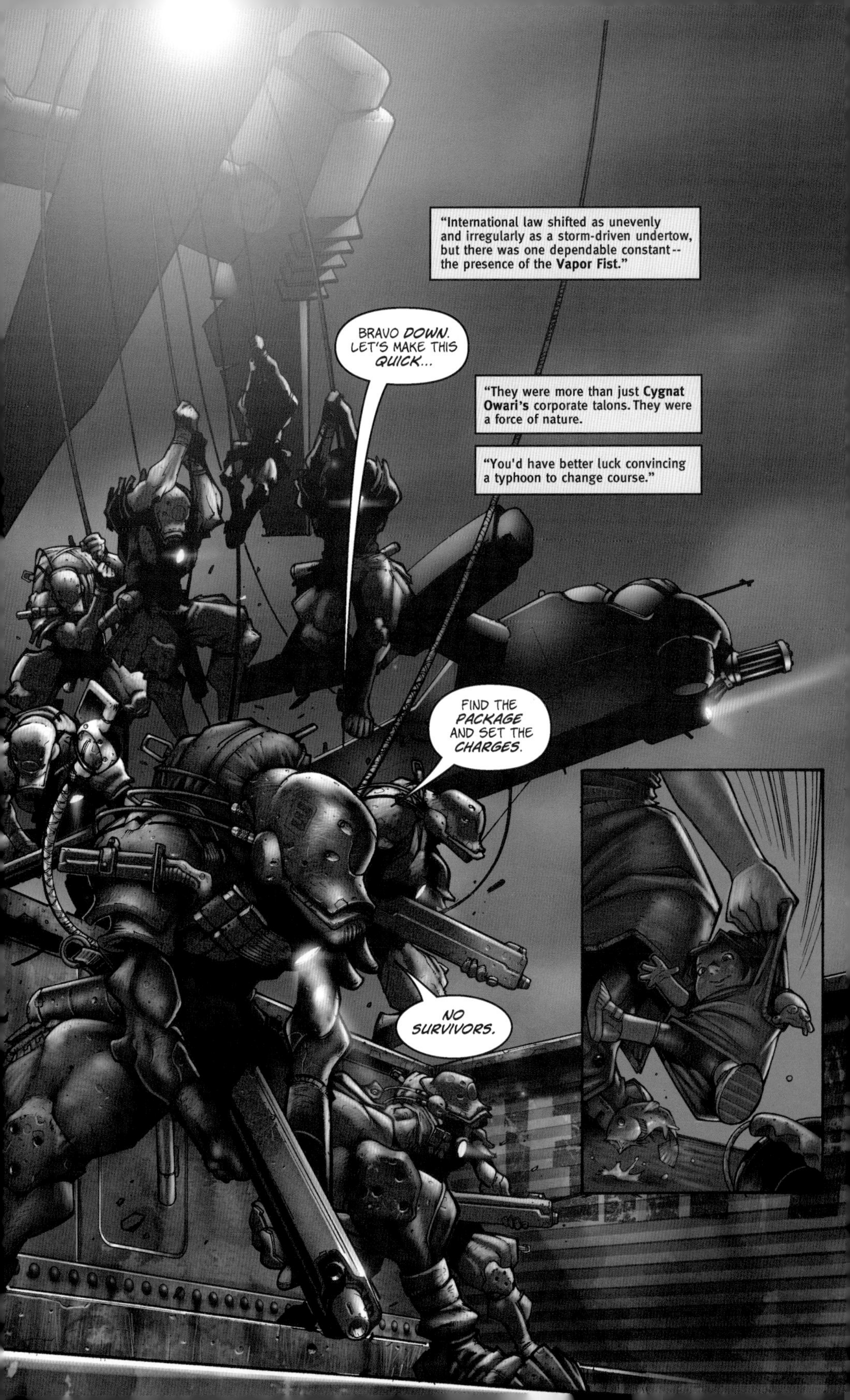
"International law shifted as unevenly and irregularly as a storm-driven undertow, but there was one dependable constant -- the presence of the **Vapor Fist**."
BRAVO *DOWN*. LET'S MAKE THIS *QUICK*...
"They were more than just **Cygnat Owari's** corporate talons. They were a force of nature.
"You'd have better luck convincing a typhoon to change course."
FIND THE *PACKAGE* AND SET THE *CHARGES*.
NO SURVIVORS.

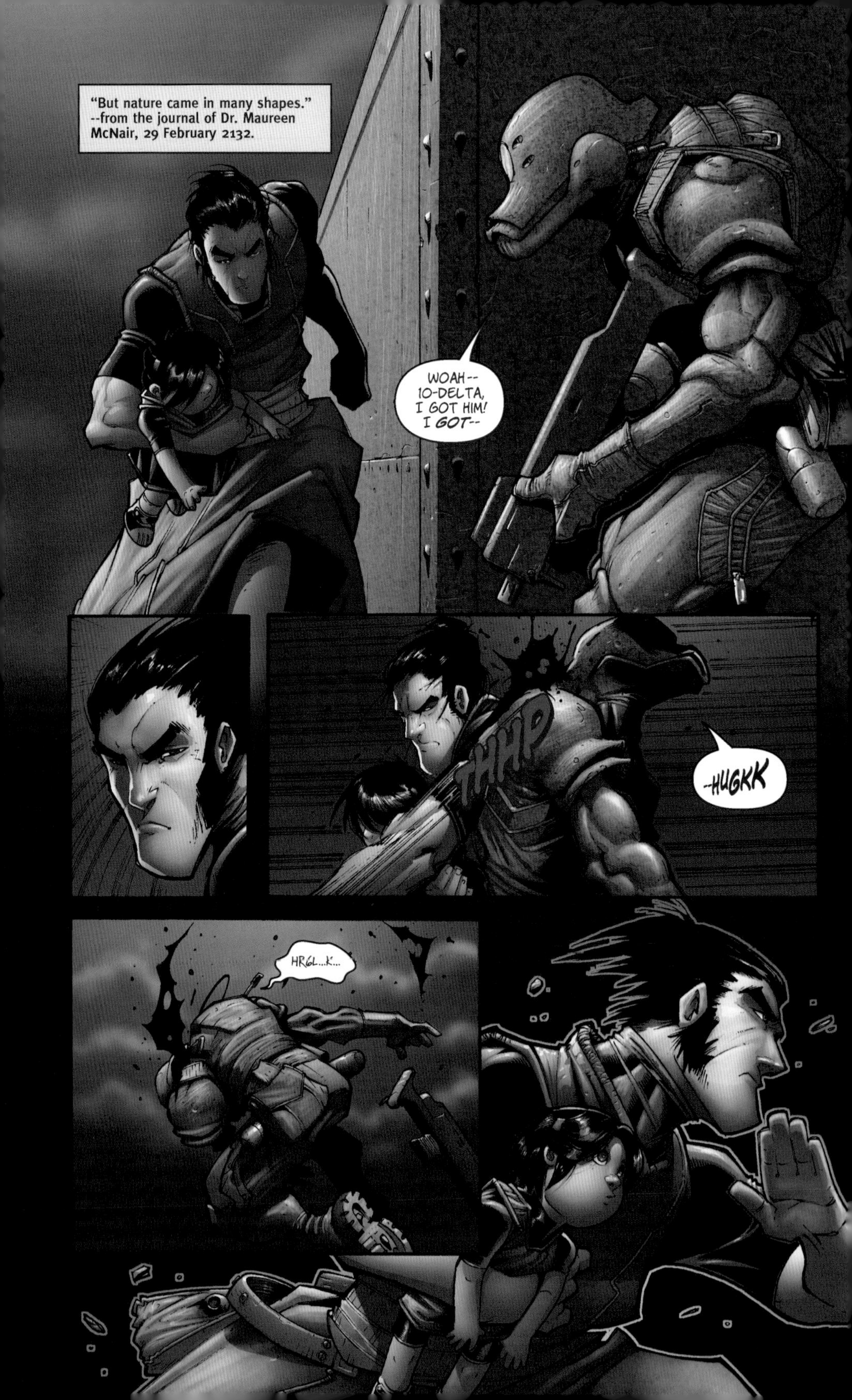
"But nature came in many shapes."
--from the journal of Dr. Maureen McNair, 29 February 2132.
WOAH-- 10-DELTA, I GOT HIM! I GOT--
THHP
--HUGKK
HRGL...K...

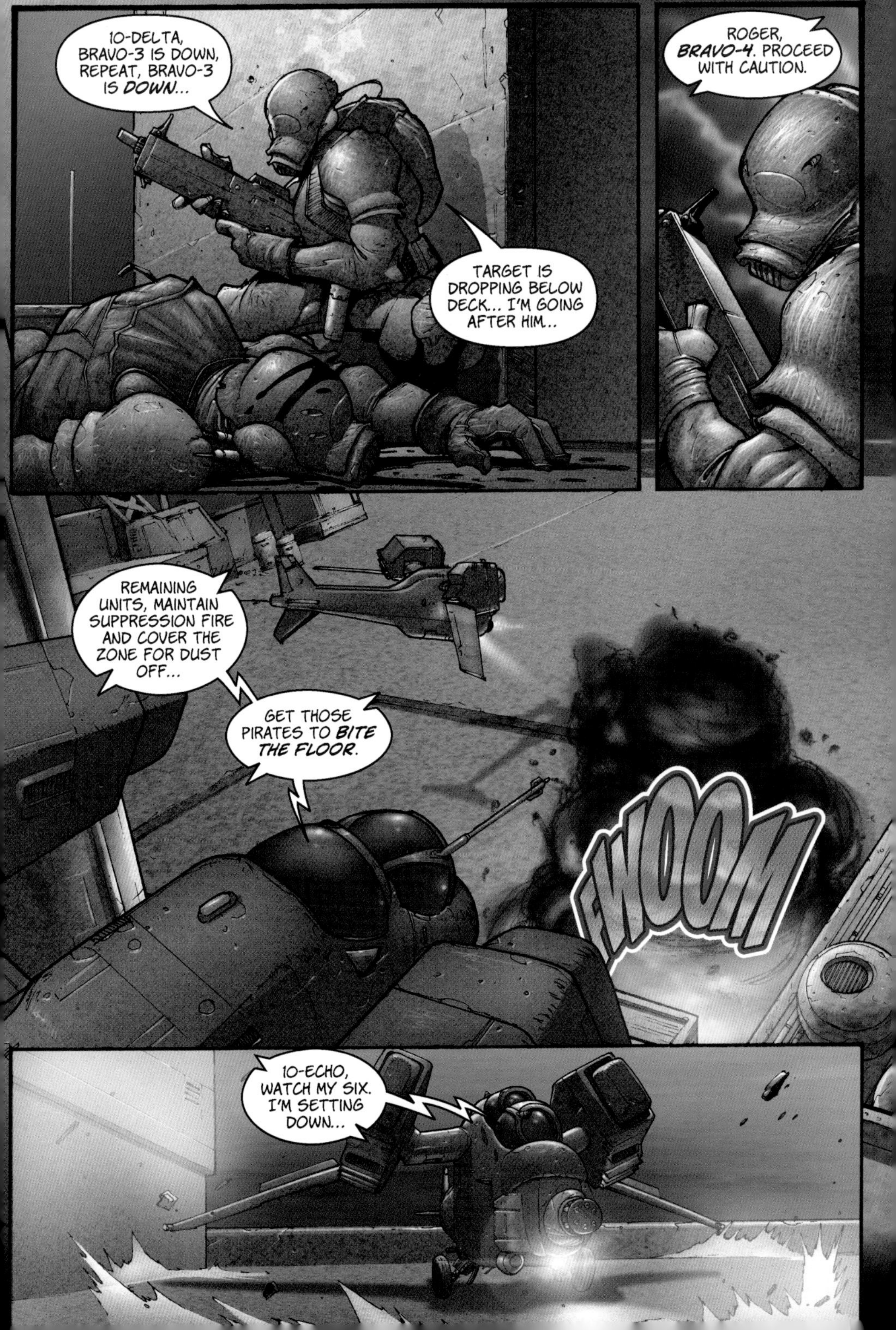
10-DELTA, BRAVO-3 IS DOWN, REPEAT, BRAVO-3 IS *DOWN*...
TARGET IS DROPPING BELOW DECK... I'M GOING AFTER HIM..
ROGER, ***BRAVO-4***. PROCEED WITH CAUTION.
REMAINING UNITS, MAINTAIN SUPPRESSION FIRE AND COVER THE ZONE FOR DUST OFF...
GET THOSE PIRATES TO ***BITE THE FLOOR***.
FWOOM
10-ECHO, WATCH MY SIX. I'M SETTING DOWN...

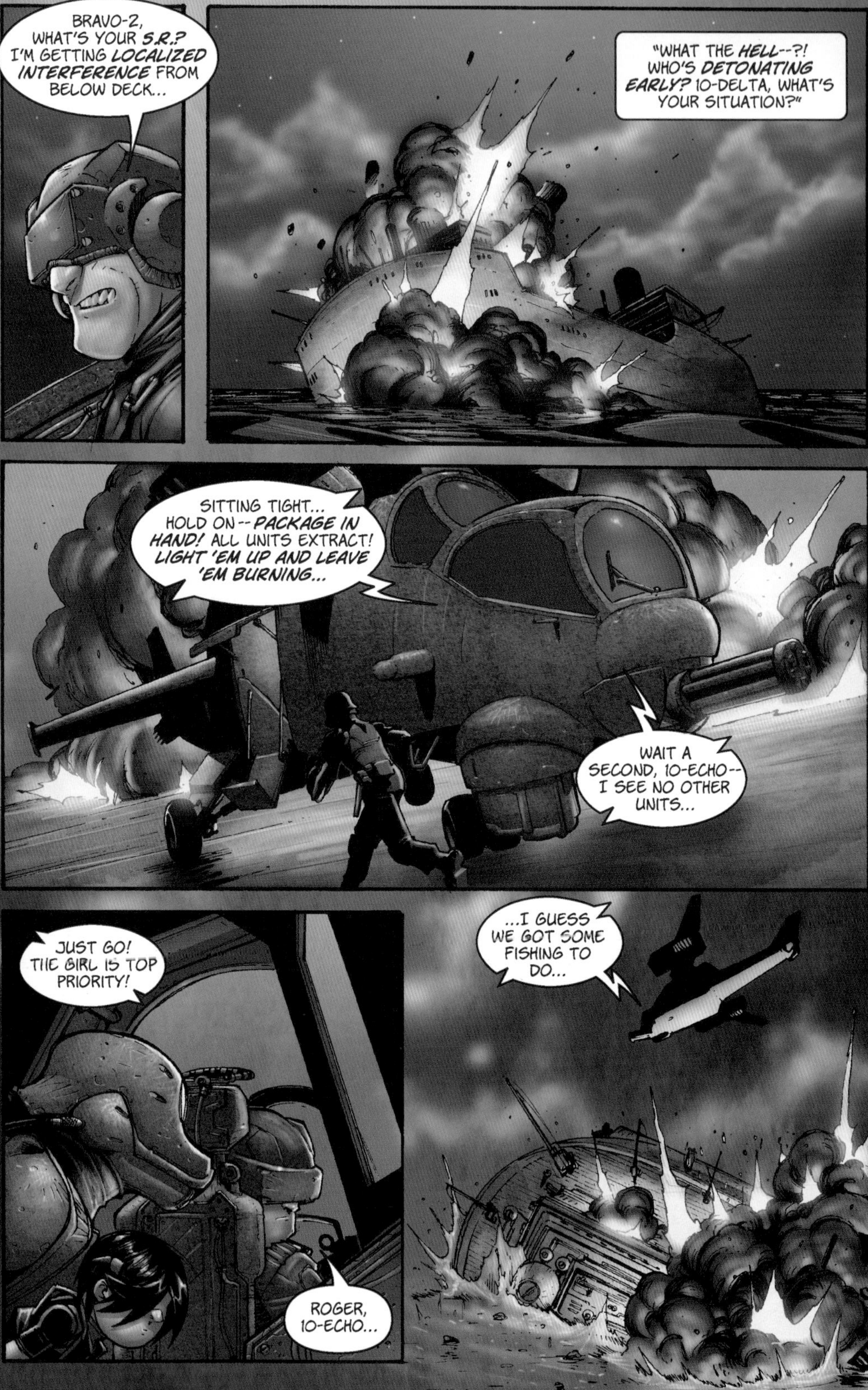
BRAVO-2, WHAT'S YOUR *S.R.?* I'M GETTING *LOCALIZED INTERFERENCE* FROM BELOW DECK...
"WHAT THE *HELL*--?! WHO'S *DETONATING EARLY?* 10-DELTA, WHAT'S YOUR SITUATION?"
SITTING TIGHT... HOLD ON--*PACKAGE IN HAND!* ALL UNITS EXTRACT! *LIGHT 'EM UP AND LEAVE 'EM BURNING...*
WAIT A SECOND, 10-ECHO-- I SEE NO OTHER UNITS...
JUST GO! THE GIRL IS TOP PRIORITY!
ROGER, 10-ECHO...
...I GUESS WE GOT SOME FISHING TO DO...

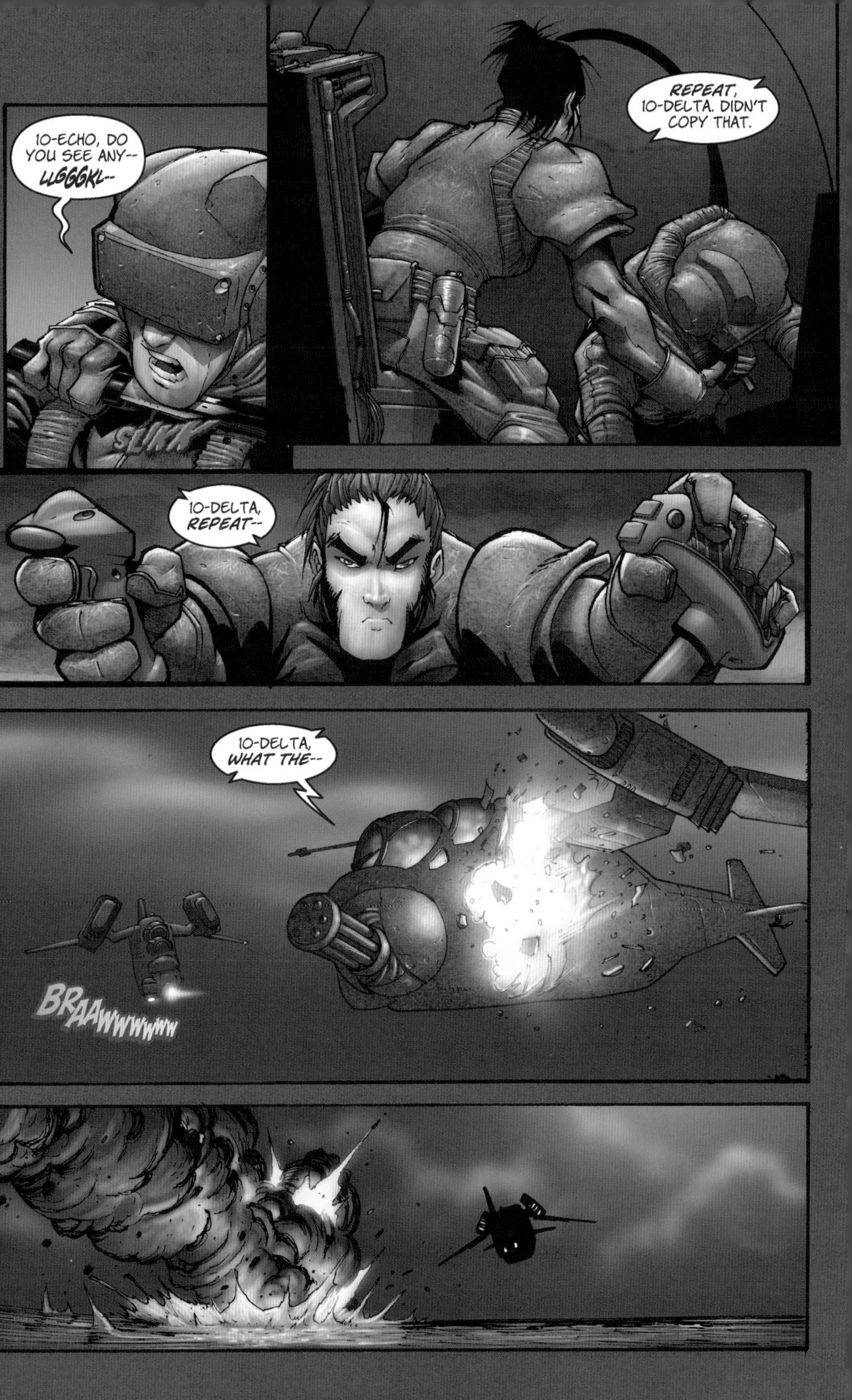
10-ECHO, DO YOU SEE ANY-- LLGGGKL--
SLIKK
REPEAT, 10-DELTA. DIDN'T COPY THAT.
10-DELTA, REPEAT--
10-DELTA, WHAT THE--
BRAAWWWWWW

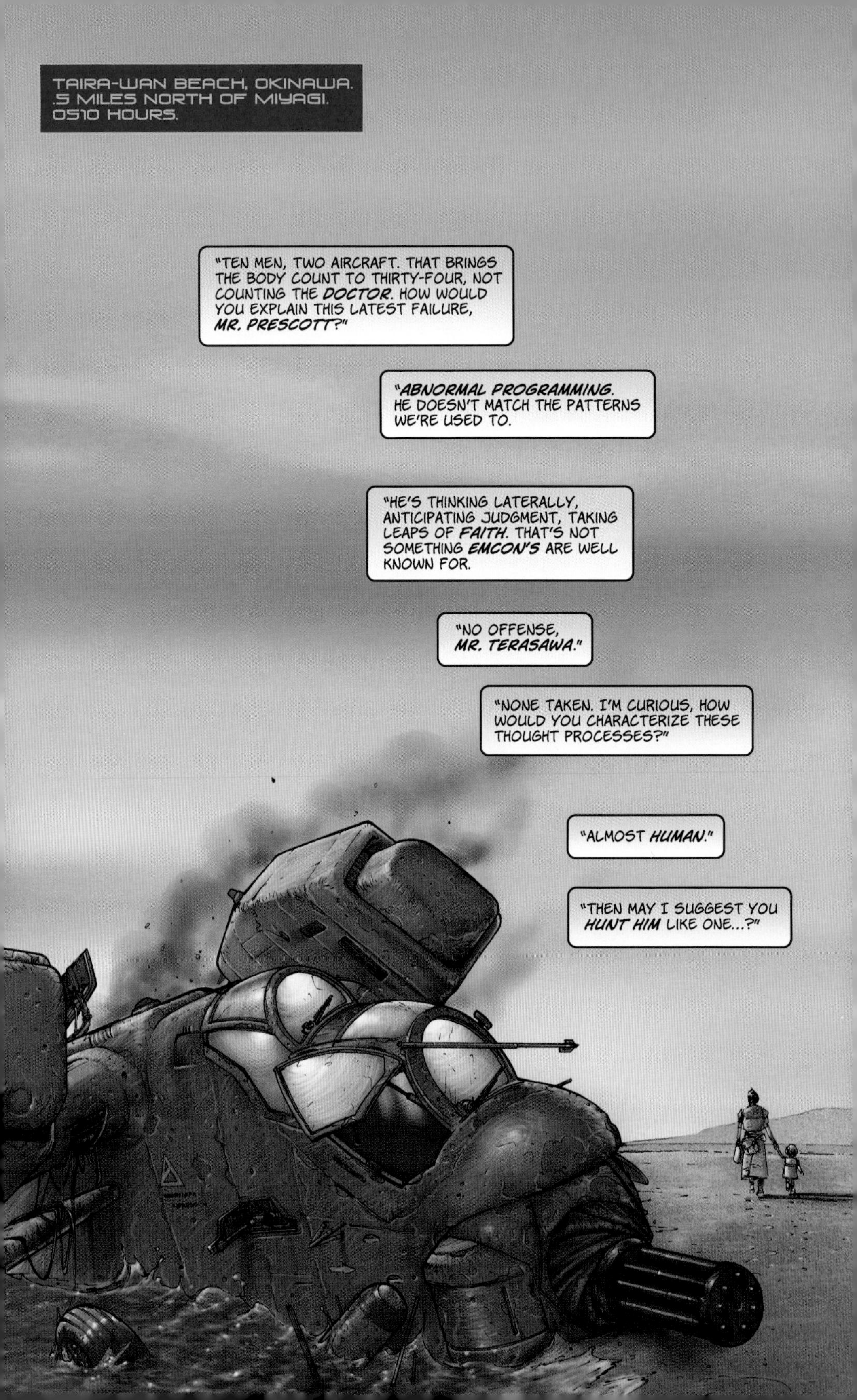
TAIRA-WAN BEACH, OKINAWA. .5 MILES NORTH OF MIYAGI. 0510 HOURS.
"TEN MEN, TWO AIRCRAFT. THAT BRINGS THE BODY COUNT TO THIRTY-FOUR, NOT COUNTING THE *DOCTOR*. HOW WOULD YOU EXPLAIN THIS LATEST FAILURE, *MR. PRESCOTT*?"
"*ABNORMAL PROGRAMMING*. HE DOESN'T MATCH THE PATTERNS WE'RE USED TO.
"HE'S THINKING LATERALLY, ANTICIPATING JUDGMENT, TAKING LEAPS OF *FAITH*. THAT'S NOT SOMETHING *EMCON'S* ARE WELL KNOWN FOR.
"NO OFFENSE, *MR. TERASAWA*."
"NONE TAKEN. I'M CURIOUS, HOW WOULD YOU CHARACTERIZE THESE THOUGHT PROCESSES?"
"ALMOST *HUMAN*."
"THEN MAY I SUGGEST YOU *HUNT HIM* LIKE ONE...?"

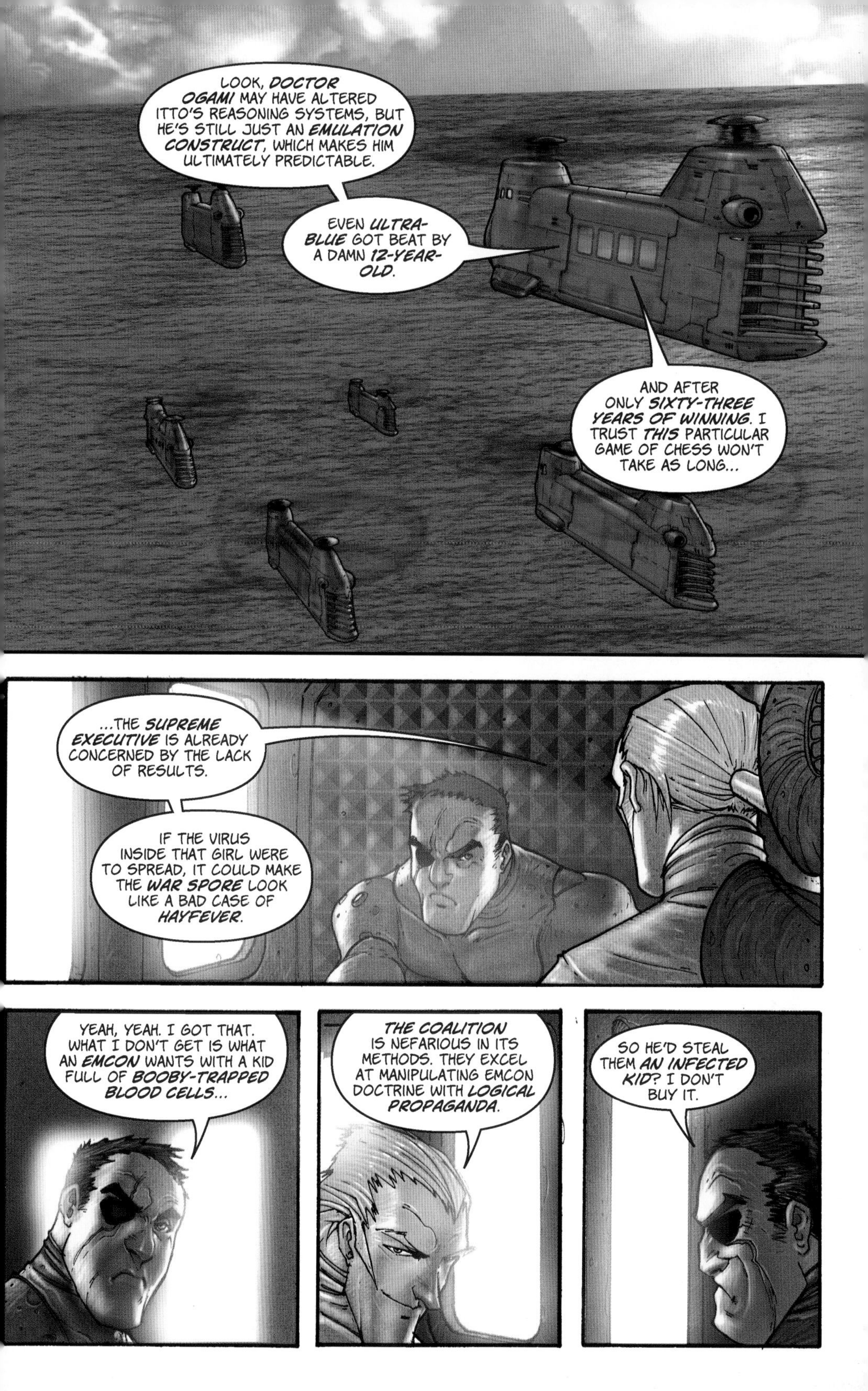
LOOK, DOCTOR OGAMI MAY HAVE ALTERED ITTO'S REASONING SYSTEMS, BUT HE'S STILL JUST AN EMULATION CONSTRUCT, WHICH MAKES HIM ULTIMATELY PREDICTABLE.
EVEN ULTRA-BLUE GOT BEAT BY A DAMN 12-YEAR-OLD.
AND AFTER ONLY SIXTY-THREE YEARS OF WINNING. I TRUST THIS PARTICULAR GAME OF CHESS WON'T TAKE AS LONG...
...THE SUPREME EXECUTIVE IS ALREADY CONCERNED BY THE LACK OF RESULTS.
IF THE VIRUS INSIDE THAT GIRL WERE TO SPREAD, IT COULD MAKE THE WAR SPORE LOOK LIKE A BAD CASE OF HAYFEVER.
YEAH, YEAH. I GOT THAT. WHAT I DON'T GET IS WHAT AN EMCON WANTS WITH A KID FULL OF BOOBY-TRAPPED BLOOD CELLS...
THE COALITION IS NEFARIOUS IN ITS METHODS. THEY EXCEL AT MANIPULATING EMCON DOCTRINE WITH LOGICAL PROPAGANDA.
SO HE'D STEAL THEM AN INFECTED KID? I DON'T BUY IT.

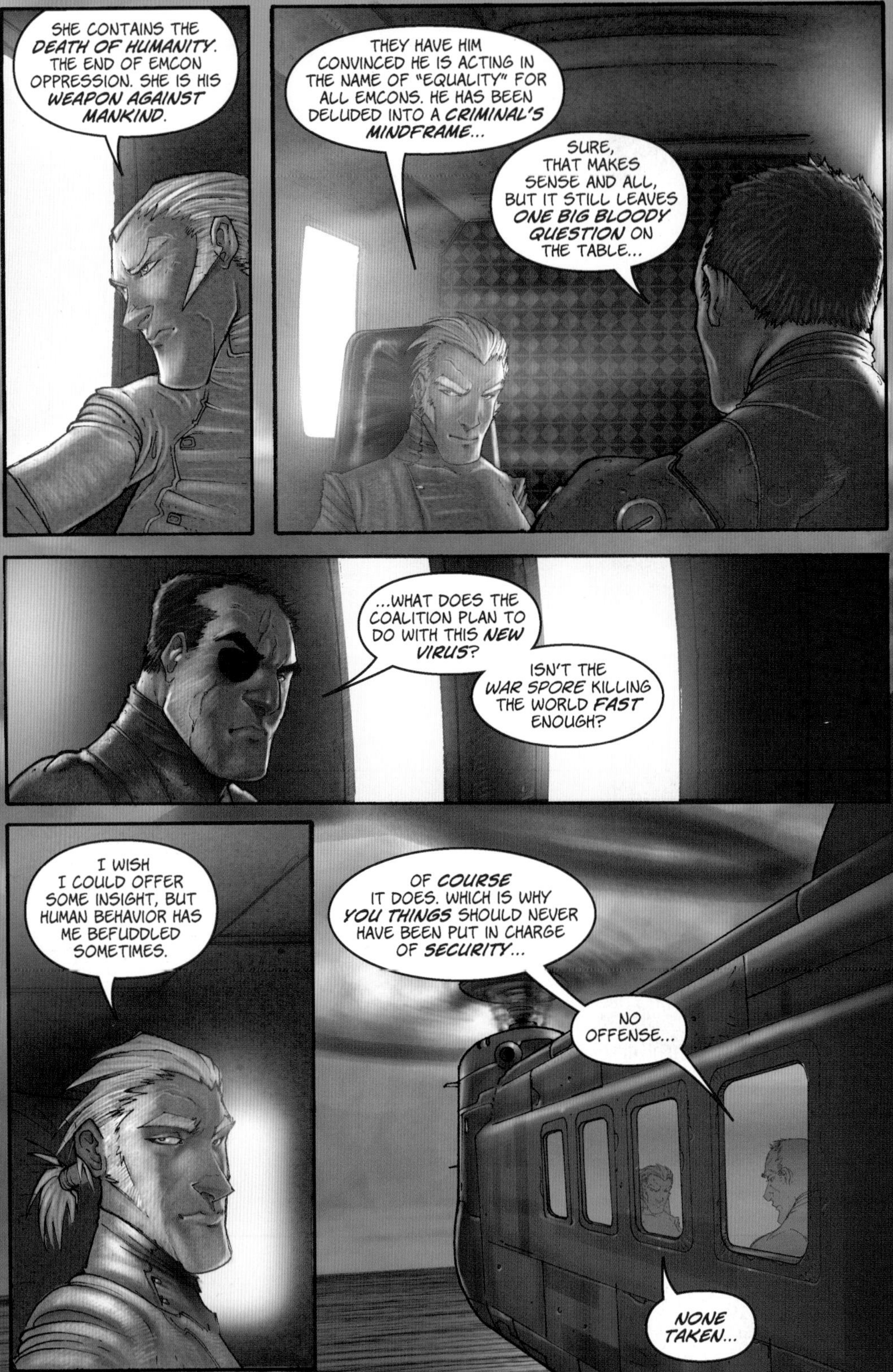
SHE CONTAINS THE DEATH OF HUMANITY. THE END OF EMCON OPPRESSION. SHE IS HIS WEAPON AGAINST MANKIND.
THEY HAVE HIM CONVINCED HE IS ACTING IN THE NAME OF "EQUALITY" FOR ALL EMCONS. HE HAS BEEN DELUDED INTO A CRIMINAL'S MINDFRAME...
SURE, THAT MAKES SENSE AND ALL, BUT IT STILL LEAVES ONE BIG BLOODY QUESTION ON THE TABLE...
...WHAT DOES THE COALITION PLAN TO DO WITH THIS NEW VIRUS?
ISN'T THE WAR SPORE KILLING THE WORLD FAST ENOUGH?
I WISH I COULD OFFER SOME INSIGHT, BUT HUMAN BEHAVIOR HAS ME BEFUDDLED SOMETIMES.
OF COURSE IT DOES. WHICH IS WHY YOU THINGS SHOULD NEVER HAVE BEEN PUT IN CHARGE OF SECURITY...
NO OFFENSE...
NONE TAKEN...

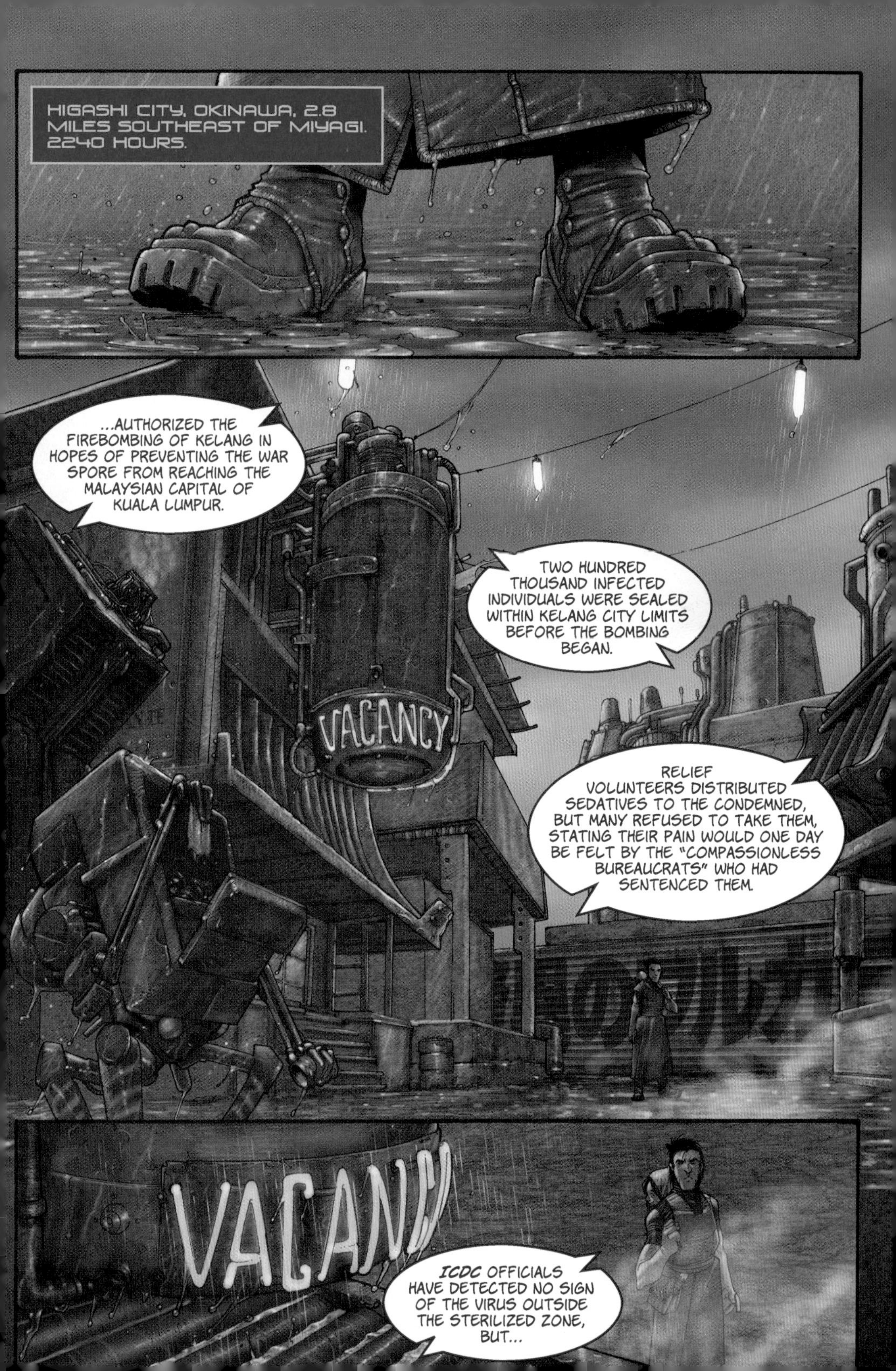
HIGASHI CITY, OKINAWA, 2.8 MILES SOUTHEAST OF MIYAGI. 2240 HOURS.
...AUTHORIZED THE FIREBOMBING OF KELANG IN HOPES OF PREVENTING THE WAR SPORE FROM REACHING THE MALAYSIAN CAPITAL OF KUALA LUMPUR.
VACANCY
TWO HUNDRED THOUSAND INFECTED INDIVIDUALS WERE SEALED WITHIN KELANG CITY LIMITS BEFORE THE BOMBING BEGAN.
RELIEF VOLUNTEERS DISTRIBUTED SEDATIVES TO THE CONDEMNED, BUT MANY REFUSED TO TAKE THEM, STATING THEIR PAIN WOULD ONE DAY BE FELT BY THE "COMPASSIONLESS BUREAUCRATS" WHO HAD SENTENCED THEM.
ICDC OFFICIALS HAVE DETECTED NO SIGN OF THE VIRUS OUTSIDE THE STERILIZED ZONE, BUT...

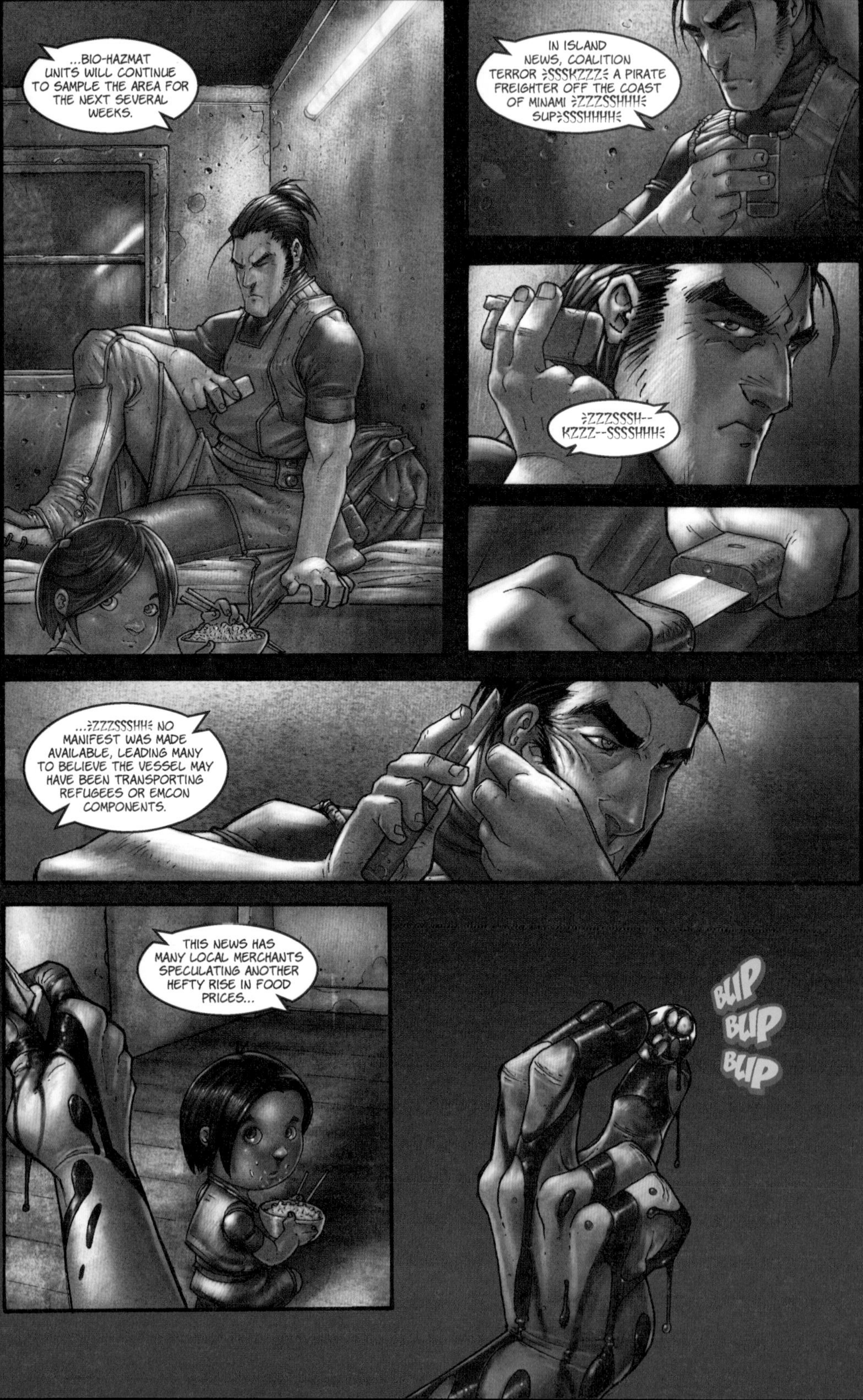
...BIO-HAZMAT UNITS WILL CONTINUE TO SAMPLE THE AREA FOR THE NEXT SEVERAL WEEKS.
IN ISLAND NEWS, COALITION TERROR ⩥SSSKZZZ⩤ A PIRATE FREIGHTER OFF THE COAST OF MINAMI ⩥ZZZSSHHH⩤ SUP⩥SSSHHHH⩤
⩥ZZZSSSH-- KZZZ--SSSSHHH⩤
...⩥ZZZSSSHH⩤ NO MANIFEST WAS MADE AVAILABLE, LEADING MANY TO BELIEVE THE VESSEL MAY HAVE BEEN TRANSPORTING REFUGEES OR EMCON COMPONENTS.
THIS NEWS HAS MANY LOCAL MERCHANTS SPECULATING ANOTHER HEFTY RISE IN FOOD PRICES...
BLIP
BLIP
BLIP

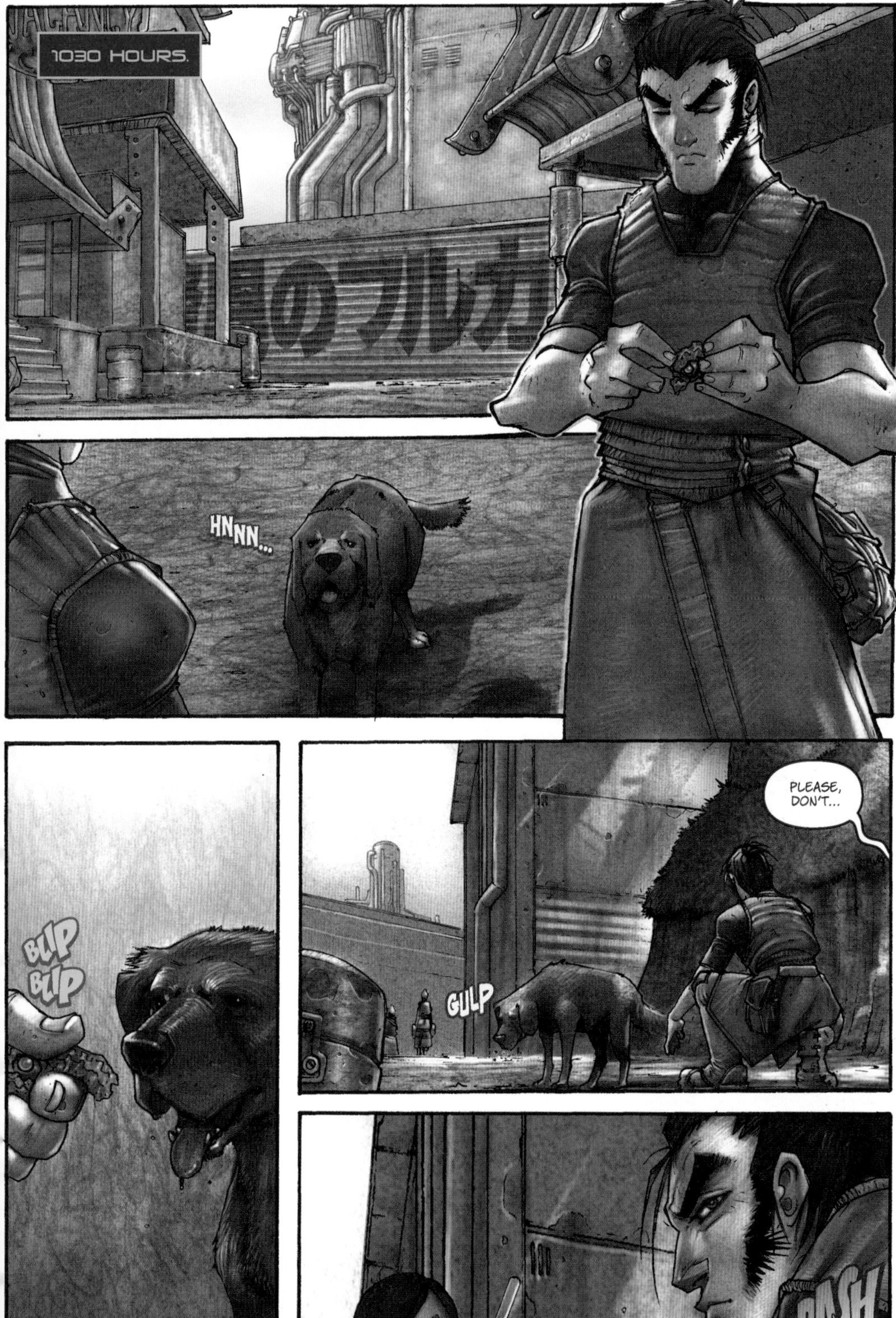
1030 HOURS.
HNNN...
BLIP
BLIP
PLEASE, DON'T...
GULP
CRASH

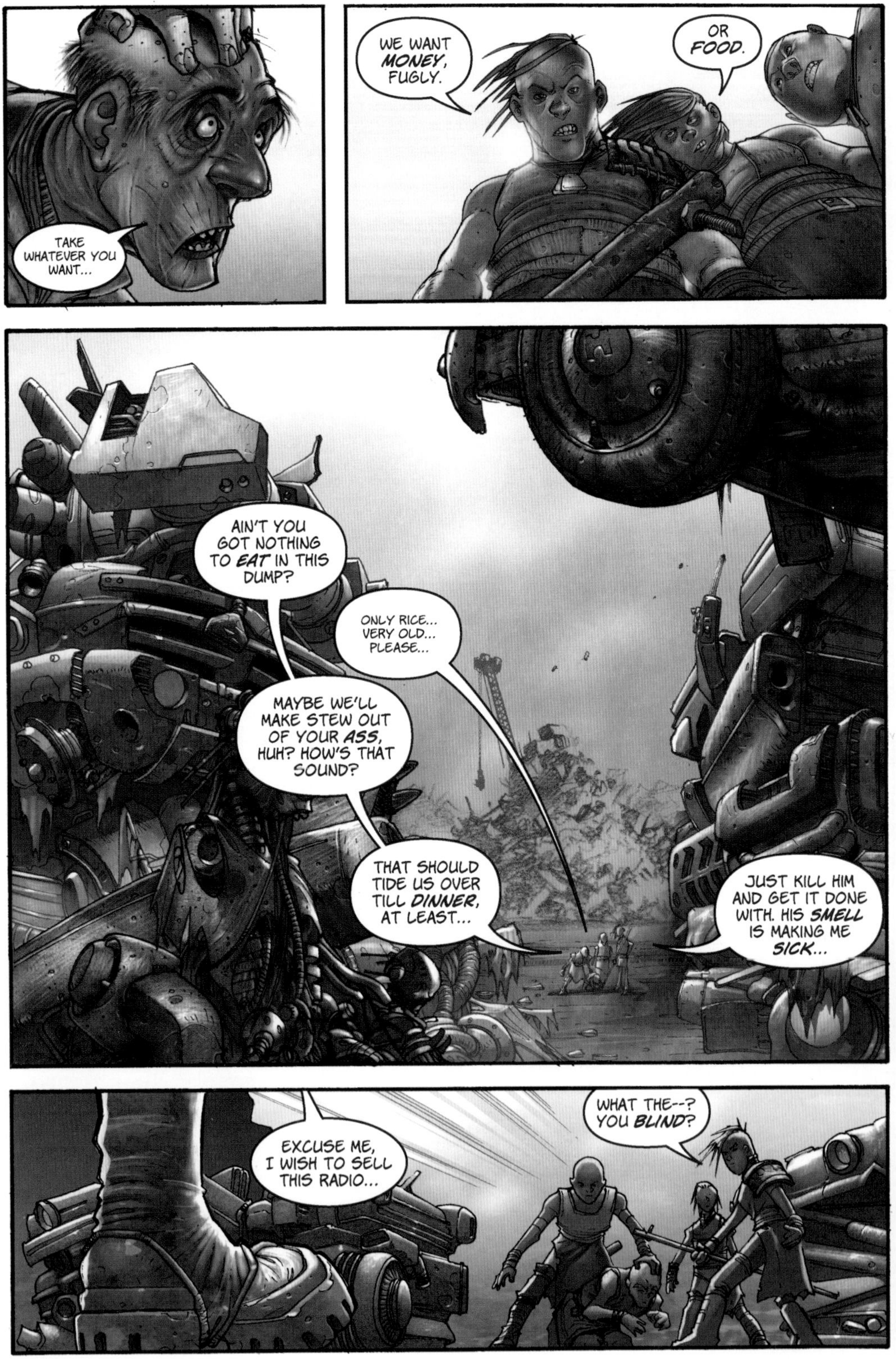
TAKE WHATEVER YOU WANT...
WE WANT *MONEY*, FUGLY.
OR *FOOD*.
AIN'T YOU GOT NOTHING TO *EAT* IN THIS DUMP?
ONLY RICE... VERY OLD... PLEASE...
MAYBE WE'LL MAKE STEW OUT OF YOUR *ASS*, HUH? HOW'S THAT SOUND?
THAT SHOULD TIDE US OVER TILL *DINNER*, AT LEAST...
JUST KILL HIM AND GET IT DONE WITH. HIS *SMELL* IS MAKING ME *SICK*...
EXCUSE ME, I WISH TO SELL THIS RADIO...
WHAT THE--? YOU *BLIND*?

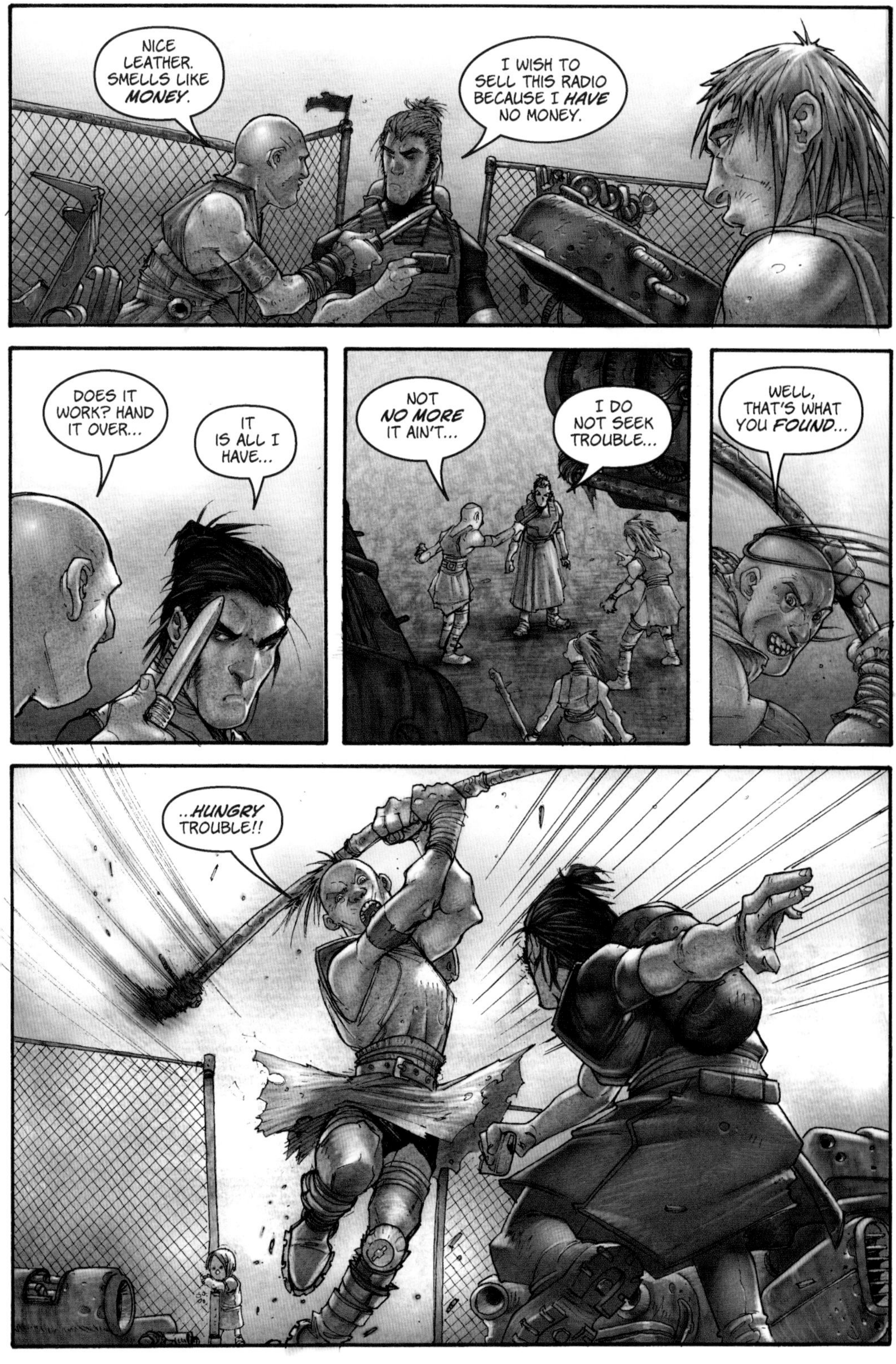
NICE LEATHER. SMELLS LIKE MONEY.
I WISH TO SELL THIS RADIO BECAUSE I HAVE NO MONEY.
DOES IT WORK? HAND IT OVER...
IT IS ALL I HAVE...
NOT NO MORE IT AIN'T...
I DO NOT SEEK TROUBLE...
WELL, THAT'S WHAT YOU FOUND...
...HUNGRY TROUBLE!!

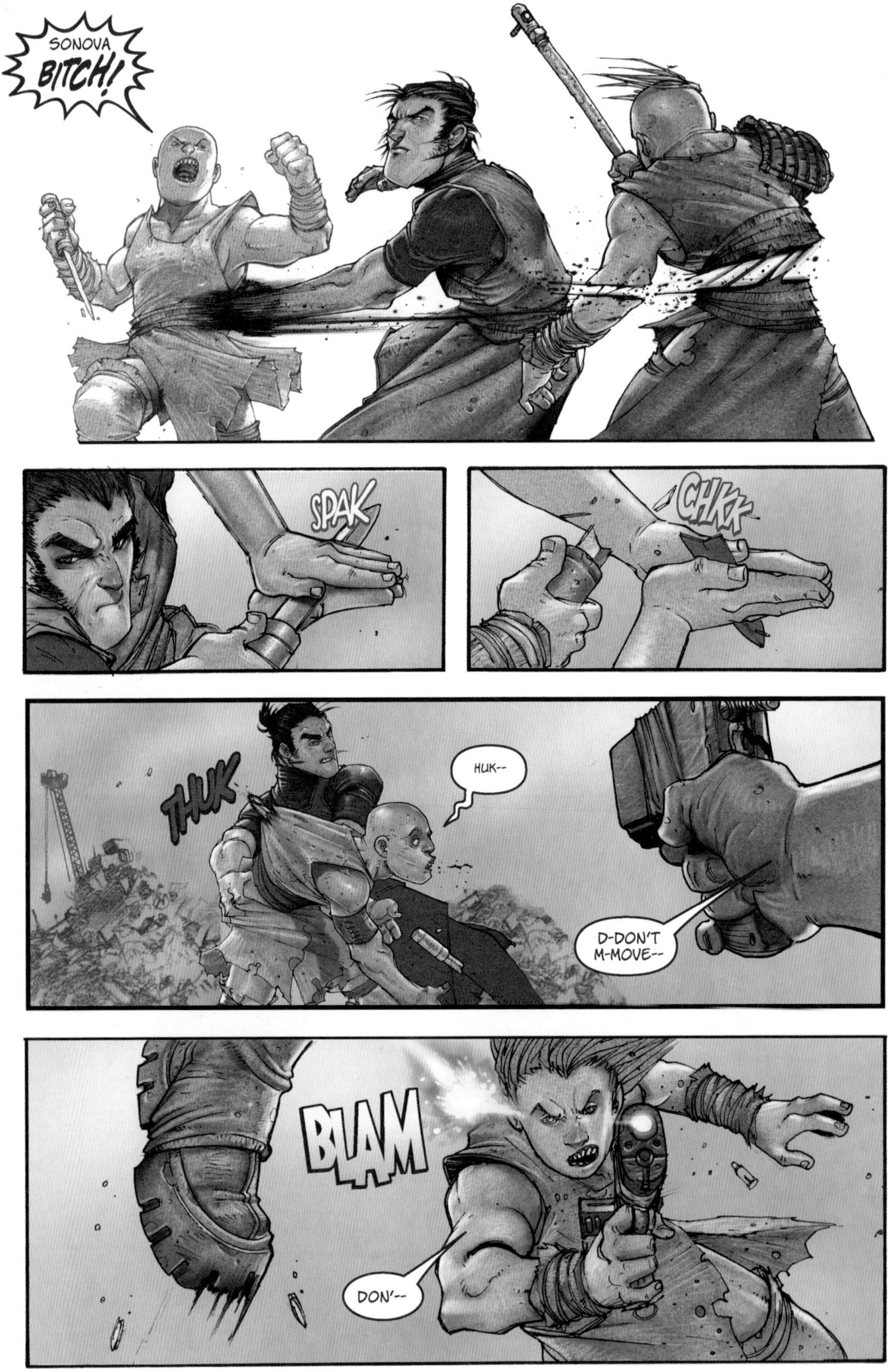
SONOVA BITCH!
SPAK
CHKK
THUK
HUK--
D-DON'T M-MOVE--
BLAM
DON'--

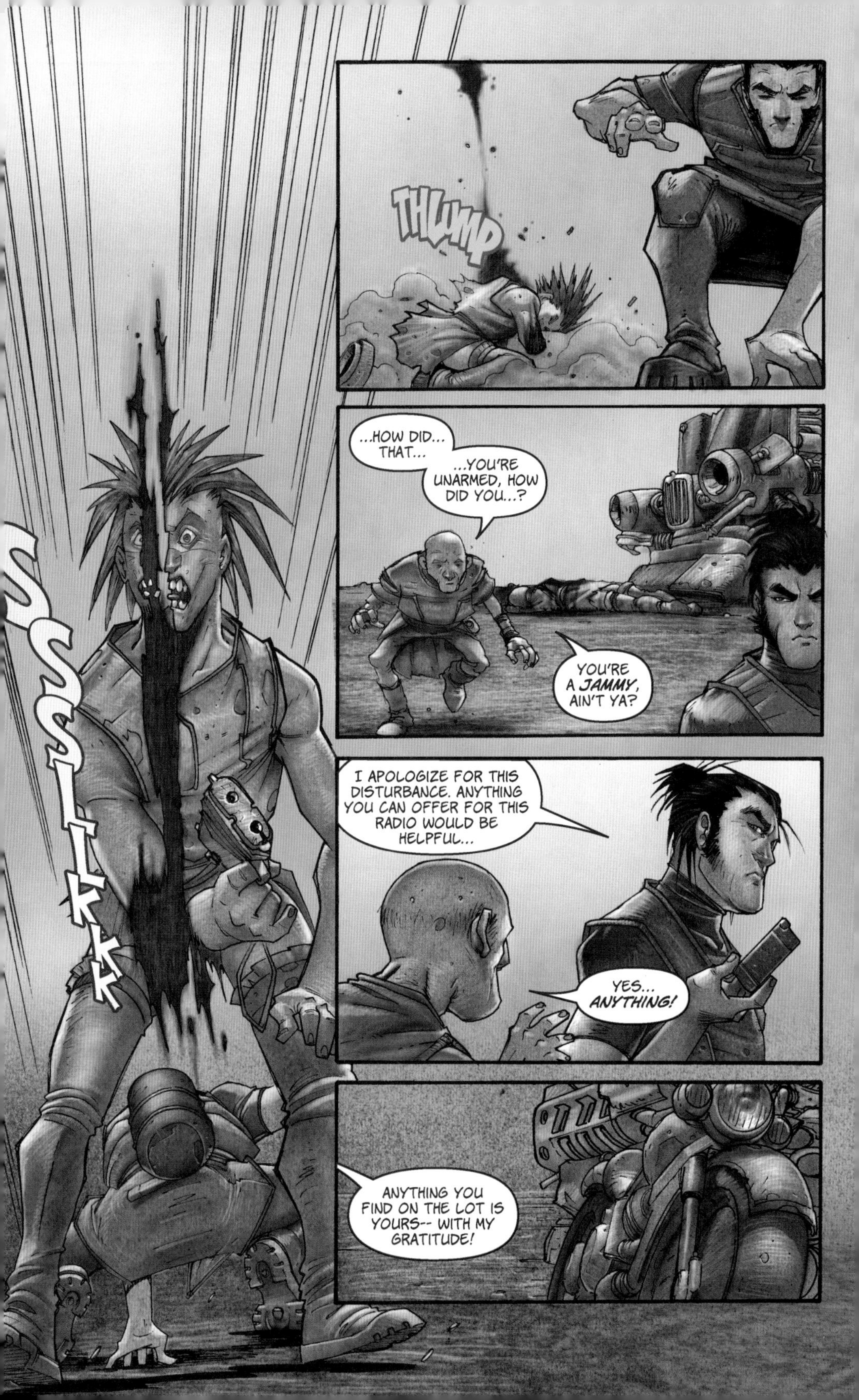
SSSLLKKKK
THUMP
...HOW DID... THAT...
...YOU'RE UNARMED, HOW DID YOU...?
YOU'RE A *JAMMY*, AIN'T YA?
I APOLOGIZE FOR THIS DISTURBANCE. ANYTHING YOU CAN OFFER FOR THIS RADIO WOULD BE HELPFUL...
YES... *ANYTHING!*
ANYTHING YOU FIND ON THE LOT IS YOURS-- WITH MY GRATITUDE!

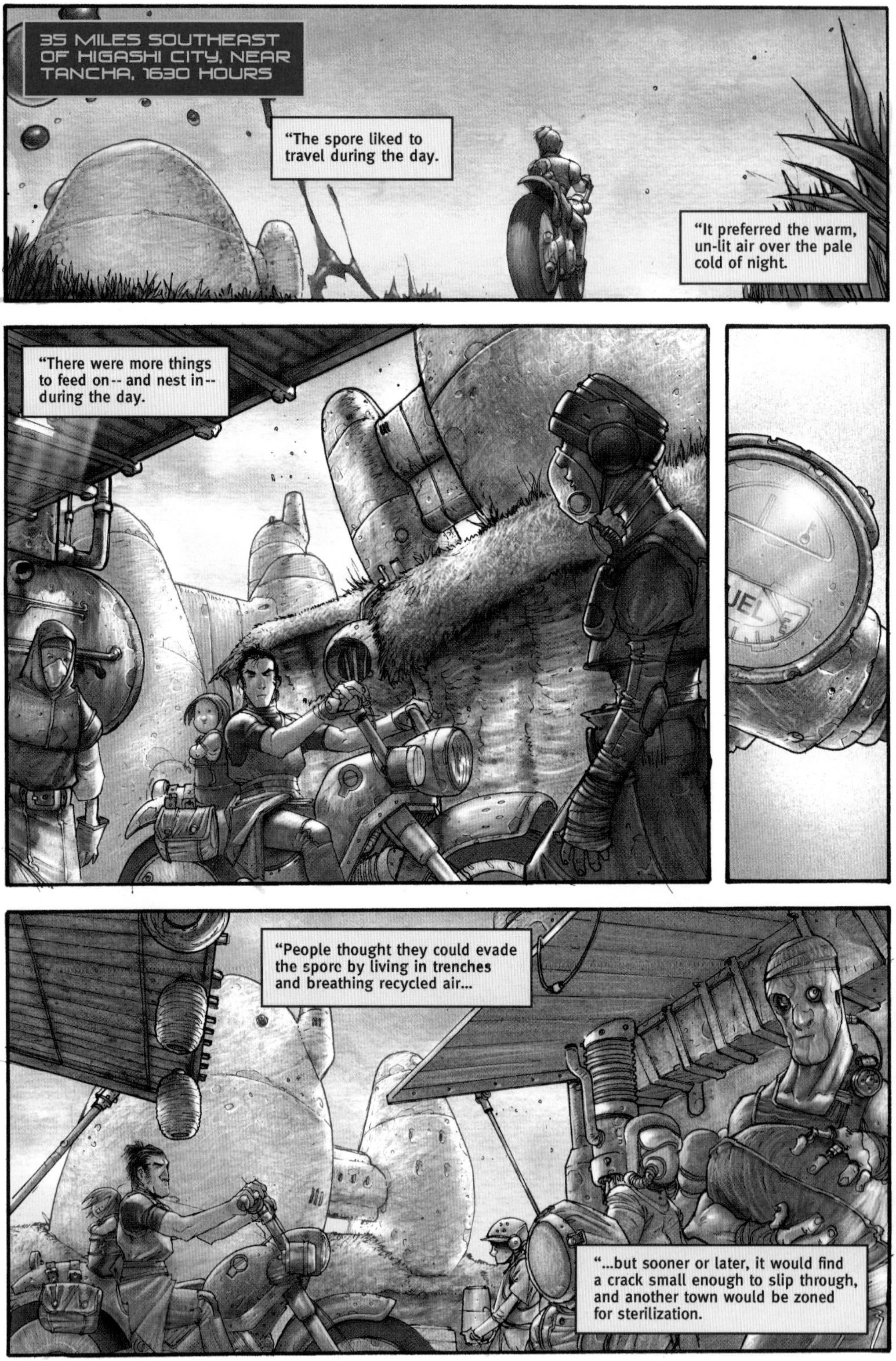
35 MILES SOUTHEAST OF HIGASHI CITY, NEAR TANCHA, 1630 HOURS
"The spore liked to travel during the day.
"It preferred the warm, un-lit air over the pale cold of night.
"There were more things to feed on-- and nest in-- during the day.
"People thought they could evade the spore by living in trenches and breathing recycled air...
"...but sooner or later, it would find a crack small enough to slip through, and another town would be zoned for sterilization.

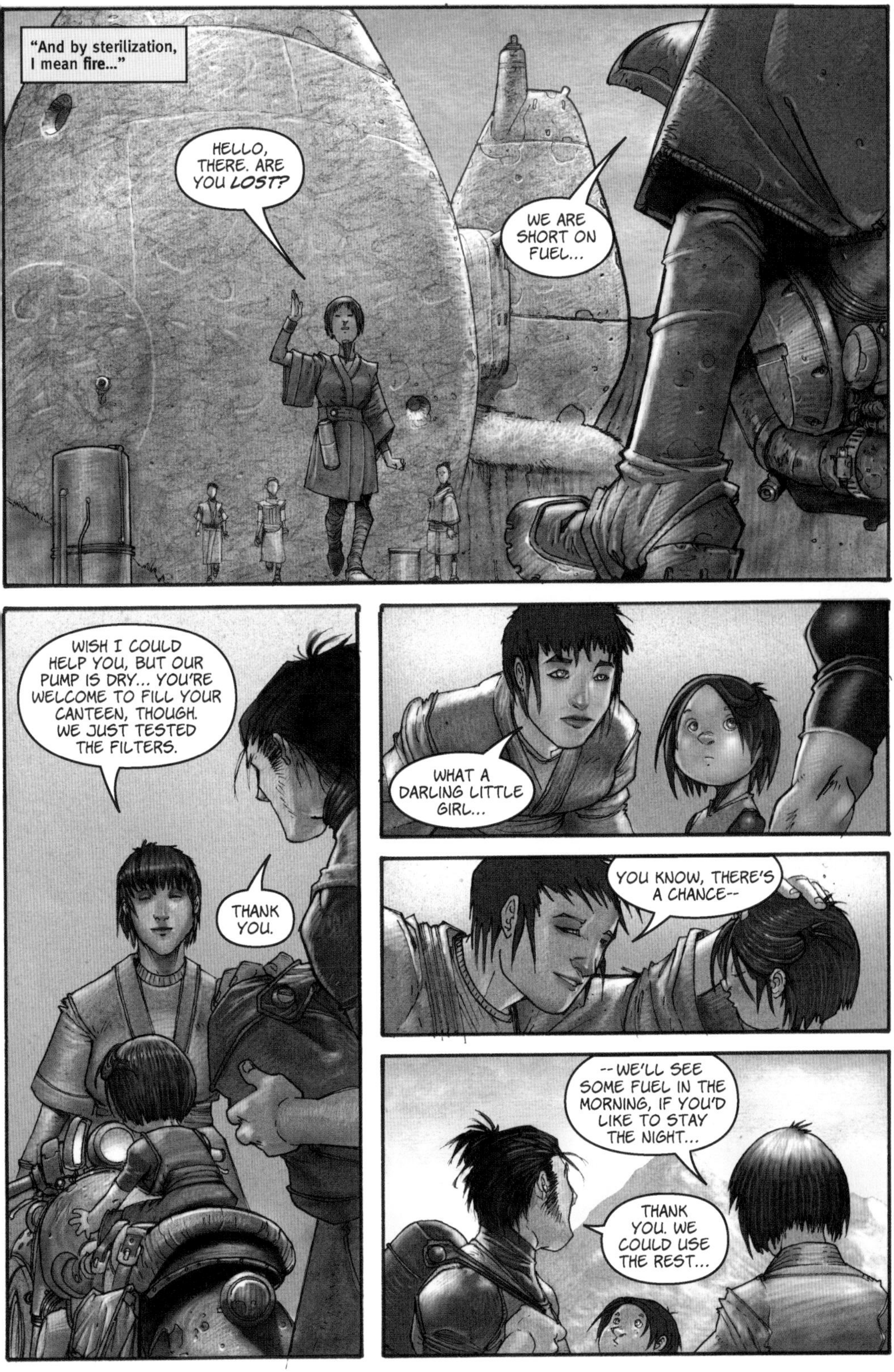
"And by sterilization, I mean fire..."
HELLO, THERE. ARE YOU LOST?
WE ARE SHORT ON FUEL...
WISH I COULD HELP YOU, BUT OUR PUMP IS DRY... YOU'RE WELCOME TO FILL YOUR CANTEEN, THOUGH. WE JUST TESTED THE FILTERS.
THANK YOU.
WHAT A DARLING LITTLE GIRL...
YOU KNOW, THERE'S A CHANCE--
--WE'LL SEE SOME FUEL IN THE MORNING, IF YOU'D LIKE TO STAY THE NIGHT...
THANK YOU. WE COULD USE THE REST...

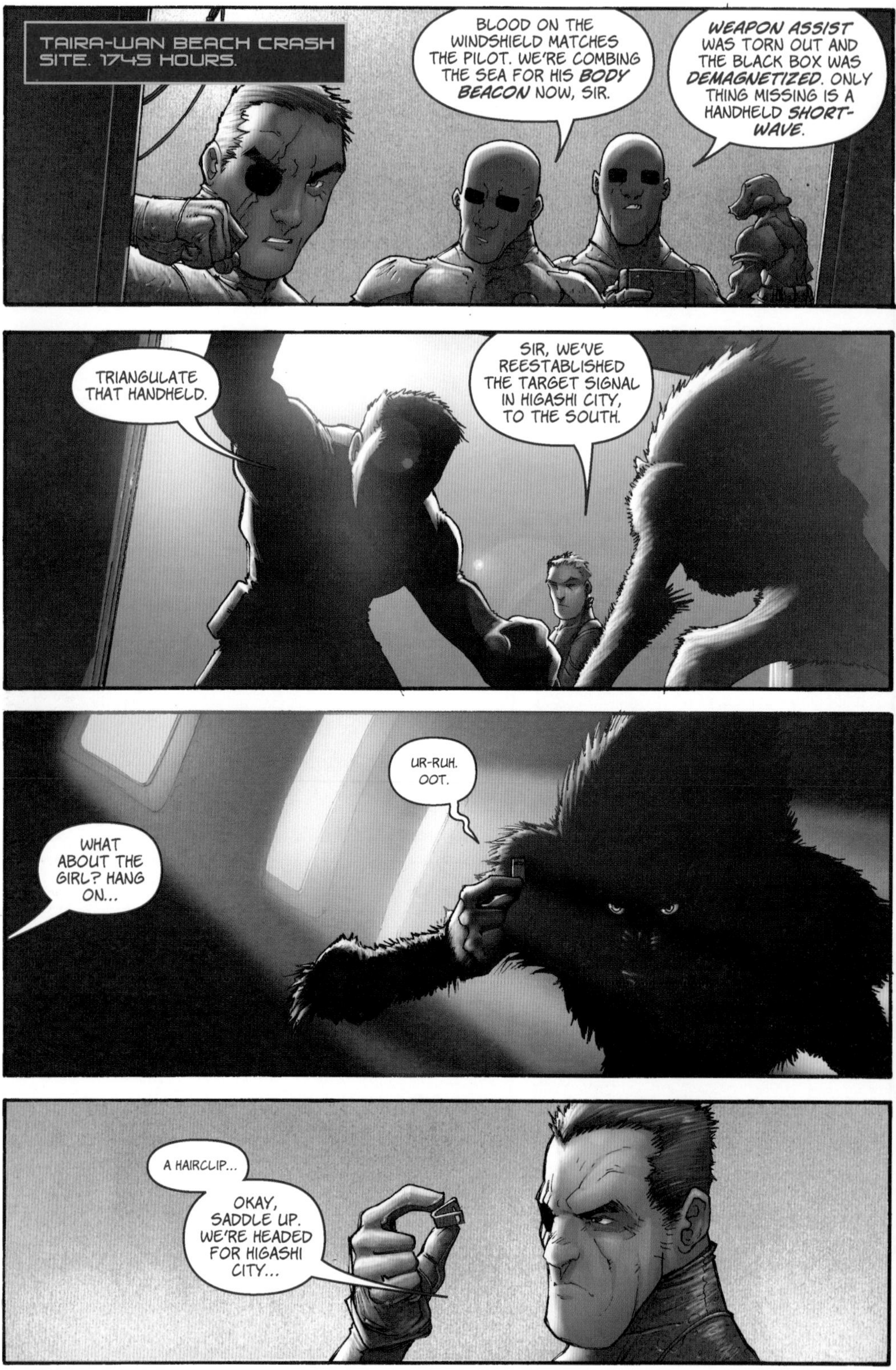
TAIRA-WAN BEACH CRASH SITE. 1745 HOURS.
BLOOD ON THE WINDSHIELD MATCHES THE PILOT. WE'RE COMBING THE SEA FOR HIS *BODY BEACON* NOW, SIR.
WEAPON ASSIST WAS TORN OUT AND THE BLACK BOX WAS *DEMAGNETIZED*. ONLY THING MISSING IS A HANDHELD *SHORT-WAVE*.
TRIANGULATE THAT HANDHELD.
SIR, WE'VE REESTABLISHED THE TARGET SIGNAL IN HIGASHI CITY, TO THE SOUTH.
WHAT ABOUT THE GIRL? HANG ON...
UR-RUH. OOT.
A HAIRCLIP...
OKAY, SADDLE UP. WE'RE HEADED FOR HIGASHI CITY...

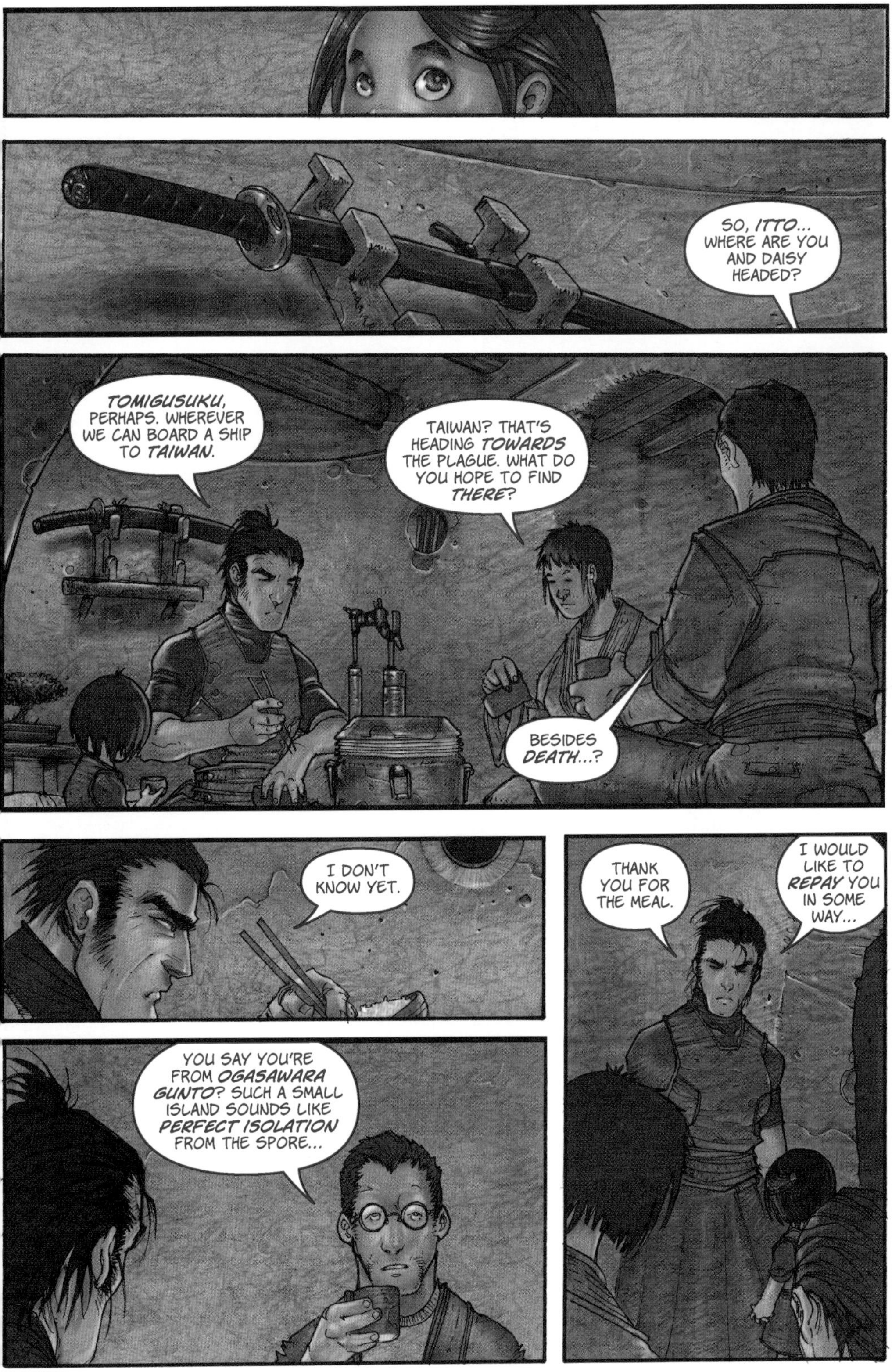
SO, ITTO... WHERE ARE YOU AND DAISY HEADED?
TOMIGUSUKU, PERHAPS. WHEREVER WE CAN BOARD A SHIP TO TAIWAN.
TAIWAN? THAT'S HEADING TOWARDS THE PLAGUE. WHAT DO YOU HOPE TO FIND THERE?
BESIDES DEATH...?
I DON'T KNOW YET.
YOU SAY YOU'RE FROM OGASAWARA GUNTO? SUCH A SMALL ISLAND SOUNDS LIKE PERFECT ISOLATION FROM THE SPORE...
THANK YOU FOR THE MEAL.
I WOULD LIKE TO REPAY YOU IN SOME WAY...

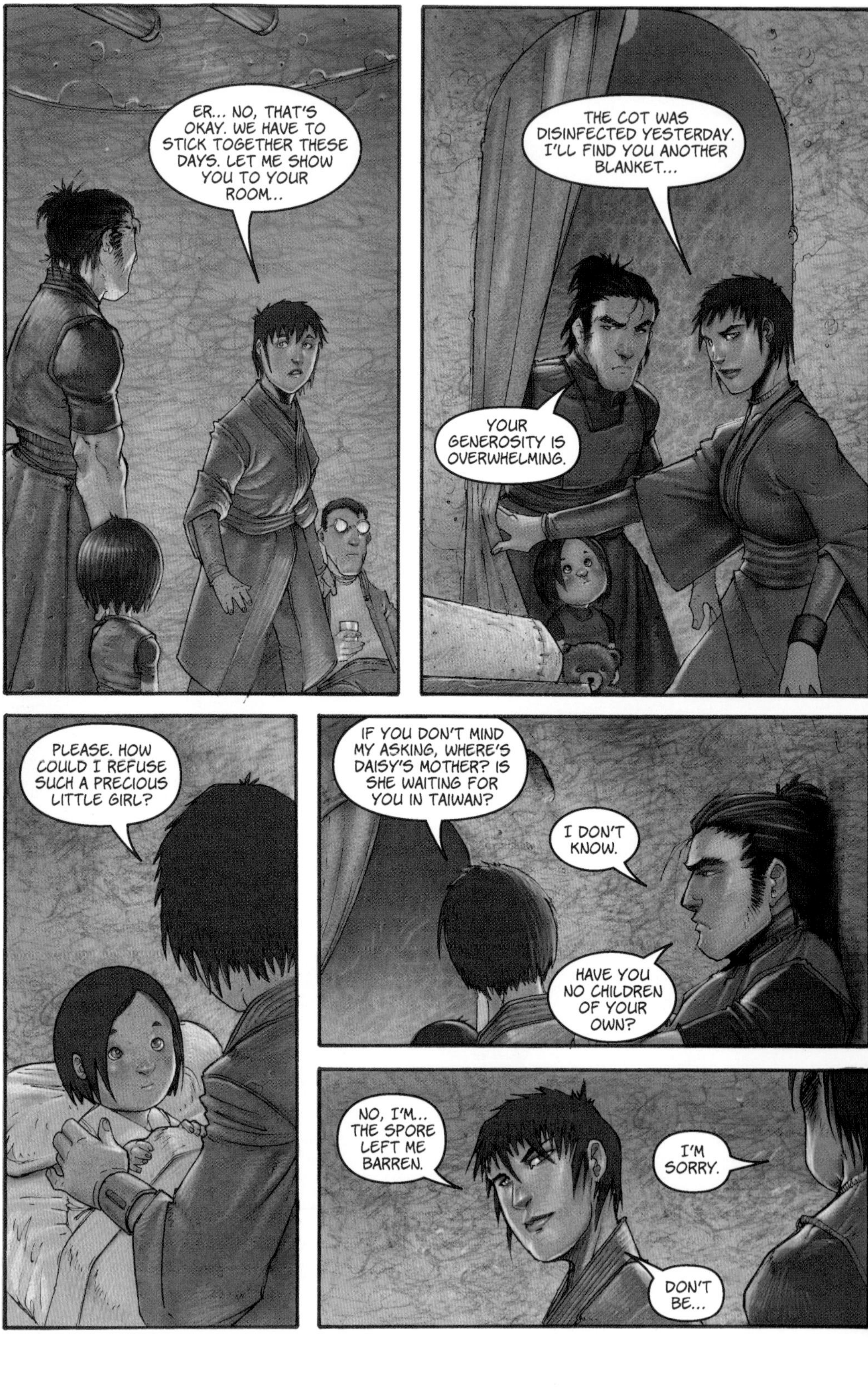
ER... NO, THAT'S OKAY. WE HAVE TO STICK TOGETHER THESE DAYS. LET ME SHOW YOU TO YOUR ROOM...
THE COT WAS DISINFECTED YESTERDAY. I'LL FIND YOU ANOTHER BLANKET...
YOUR GENEROSITY IS OVERWHELMING.
PLEASE. HOW COULD I REFUSE SUCH A PRECIOUS LITTLE GIRL?
IF YOU DON'T MIND MY ASKING, WHERE'S DAISY'S MOTHER? IS SHE WAITING FOR YOU IN TAIWAN?
I DON'T KNOW.
HAVE YOU NO CHILDREN OF YOUR OWN?
NO, I'M... THE SPORE LEFT ME BARREN.
I'M SORRY.
DON'T BE...

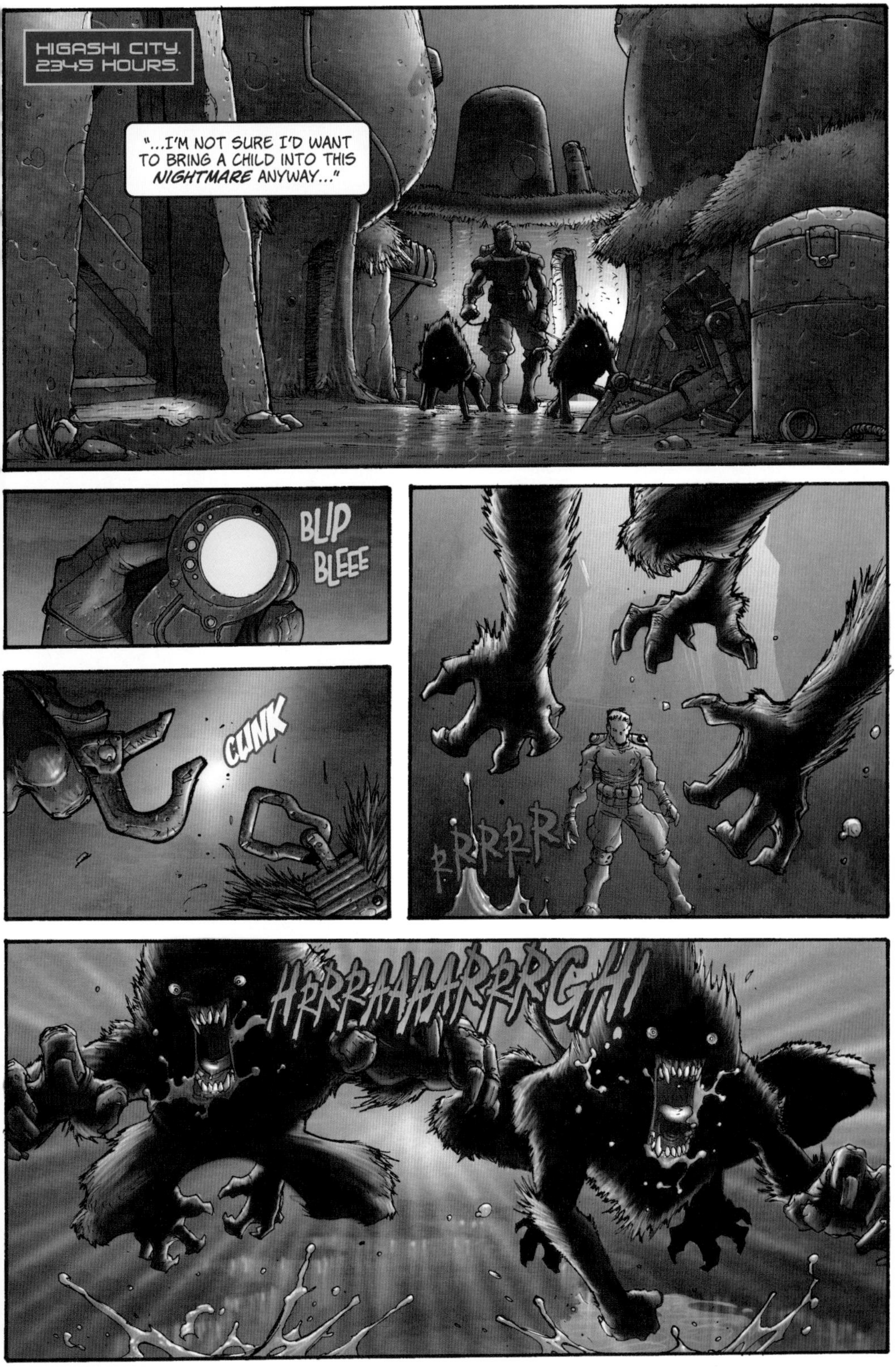
HIGASHI CITY.
2345 HOURS.
"...I'M NOT SURE I'D WANT TO BRING A CHILD INTO THIS NIGHTMARE ANYWAY..."
BLIP
BLEEE
CLINK
RRRRR
HRRRAAAARRRGH!

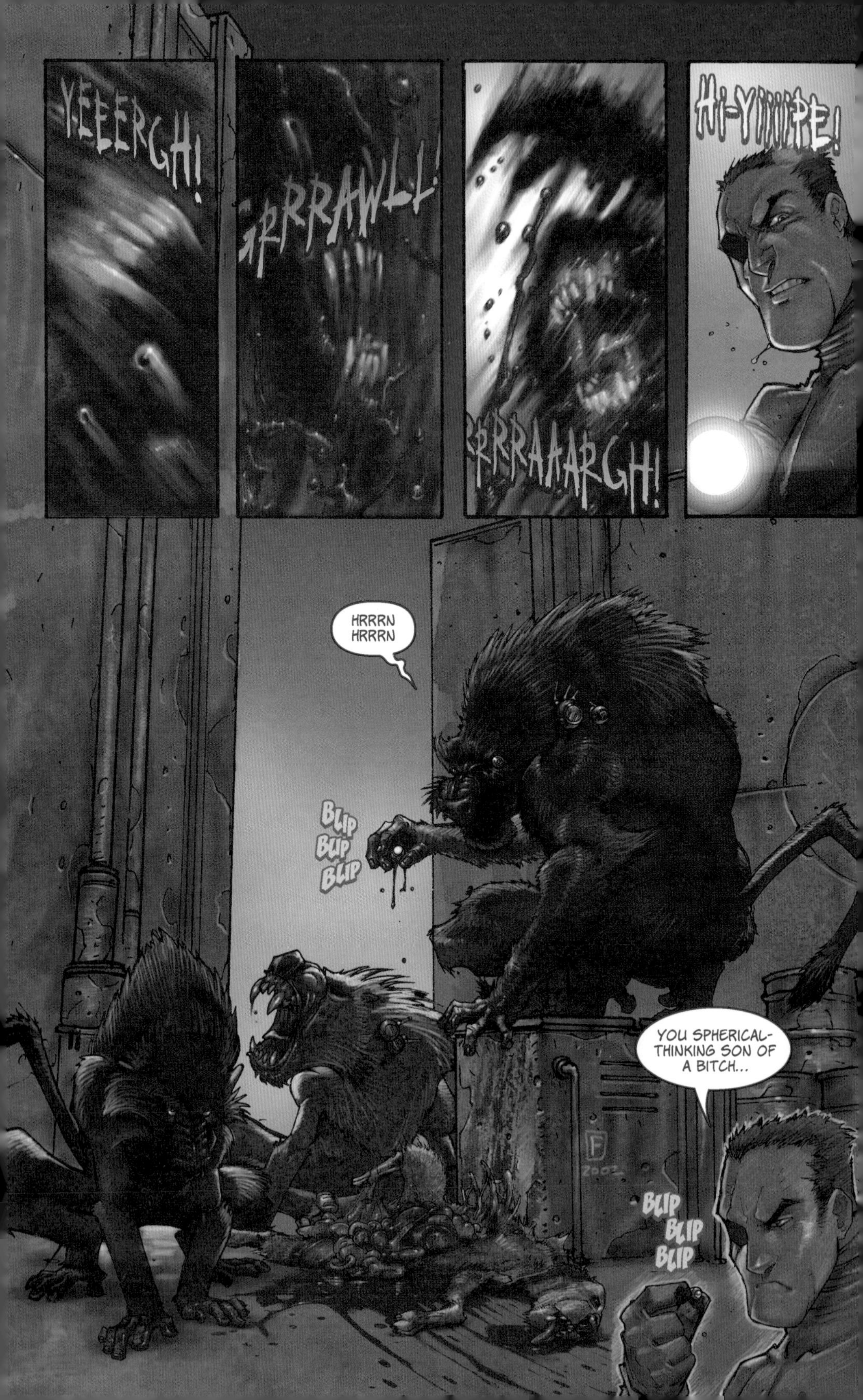
YEEERGH!
GRRRAWLL!
GRRRAAARGH!
Hi-YIIIIPE!
HRRRN HRRRN
BLIP BLIP BLIP
YOU SPHERICAL-THINKING SON OF A BITCH...
BLIP BLIP BLIP

CENTRAL OKINAWA, SOUTH OF TANCHA 1140 HOURS.

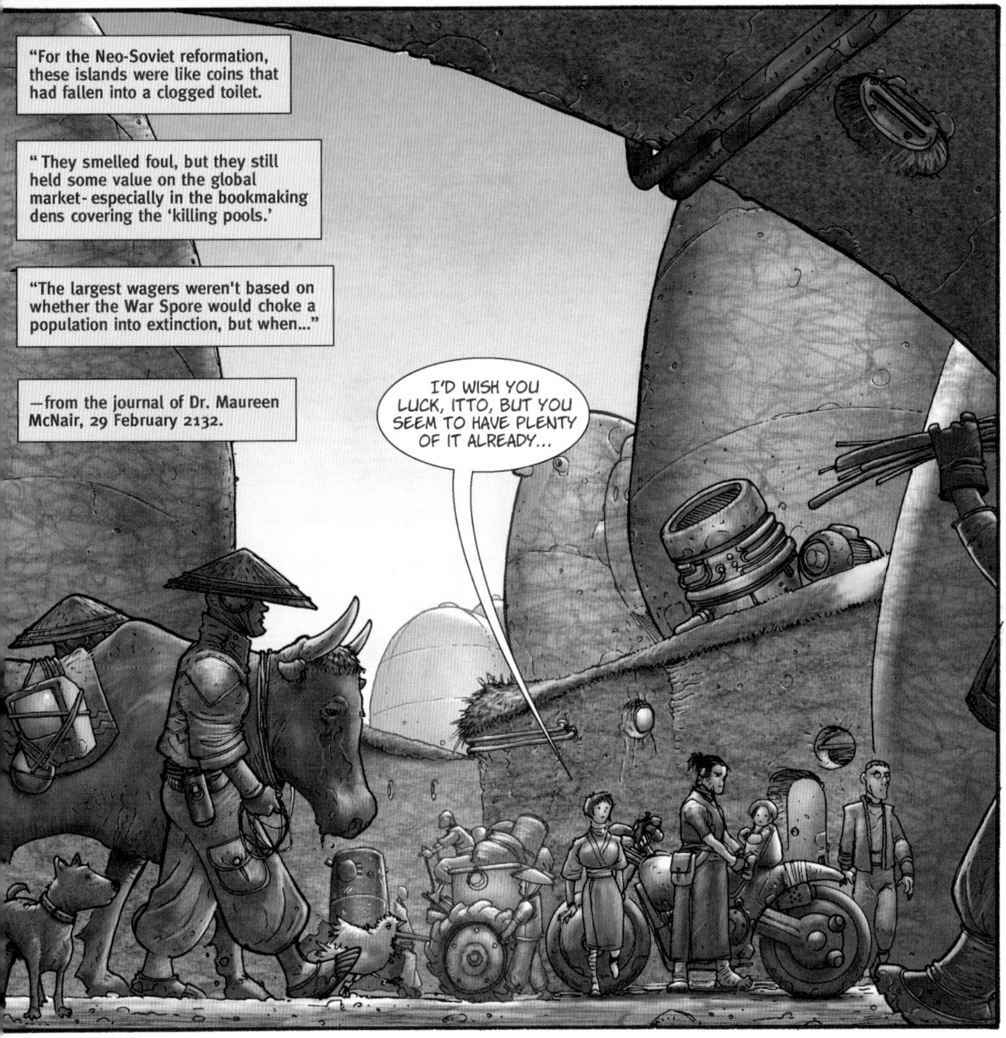
"For the Neo-Soviet reformation, these islands were like coins that had fallen into a clogged toilet.
" They smelled foul, but they still held some value on the global market- especially in the bookmaking dens covering the 'killing pools.'
"The largest wagers weren't based on whether the War Spore would choke a population into extinction, but when..."
—from the journal of Dr. Maureen McNair, 29 February 2132.
I'D WISH YOU LUCK, ITTO, BUT YOU SEEM TO HAVE PLENTY OF IT ALREADY...

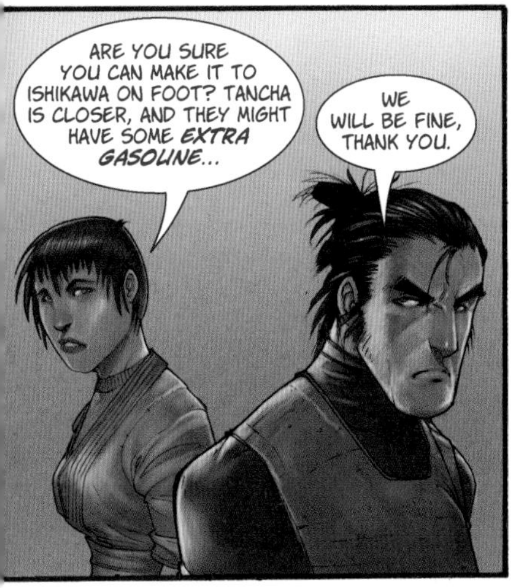
ARE YOU SURE YOU CAN MAKE IT TO ISHIKAWA ON FOOT? TANCHA IS CLOSER, AND THEY MIGHT HAVE SOME *EXTRA GASOLINE*...
WE WILL BE FINE, THANK YOU.

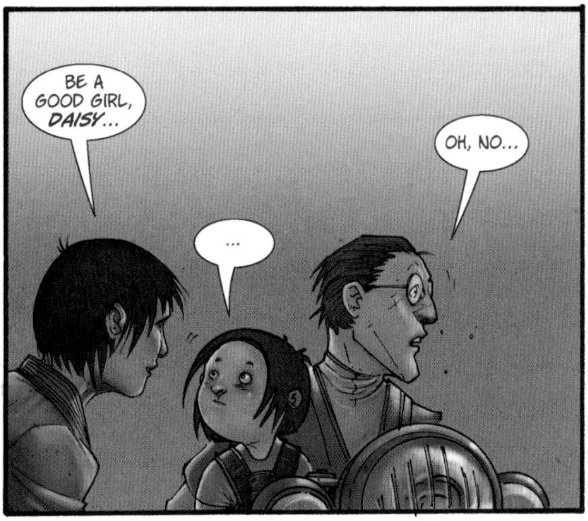
BE A GOOD GIRL, *DAISY*...
...
OH, NO...

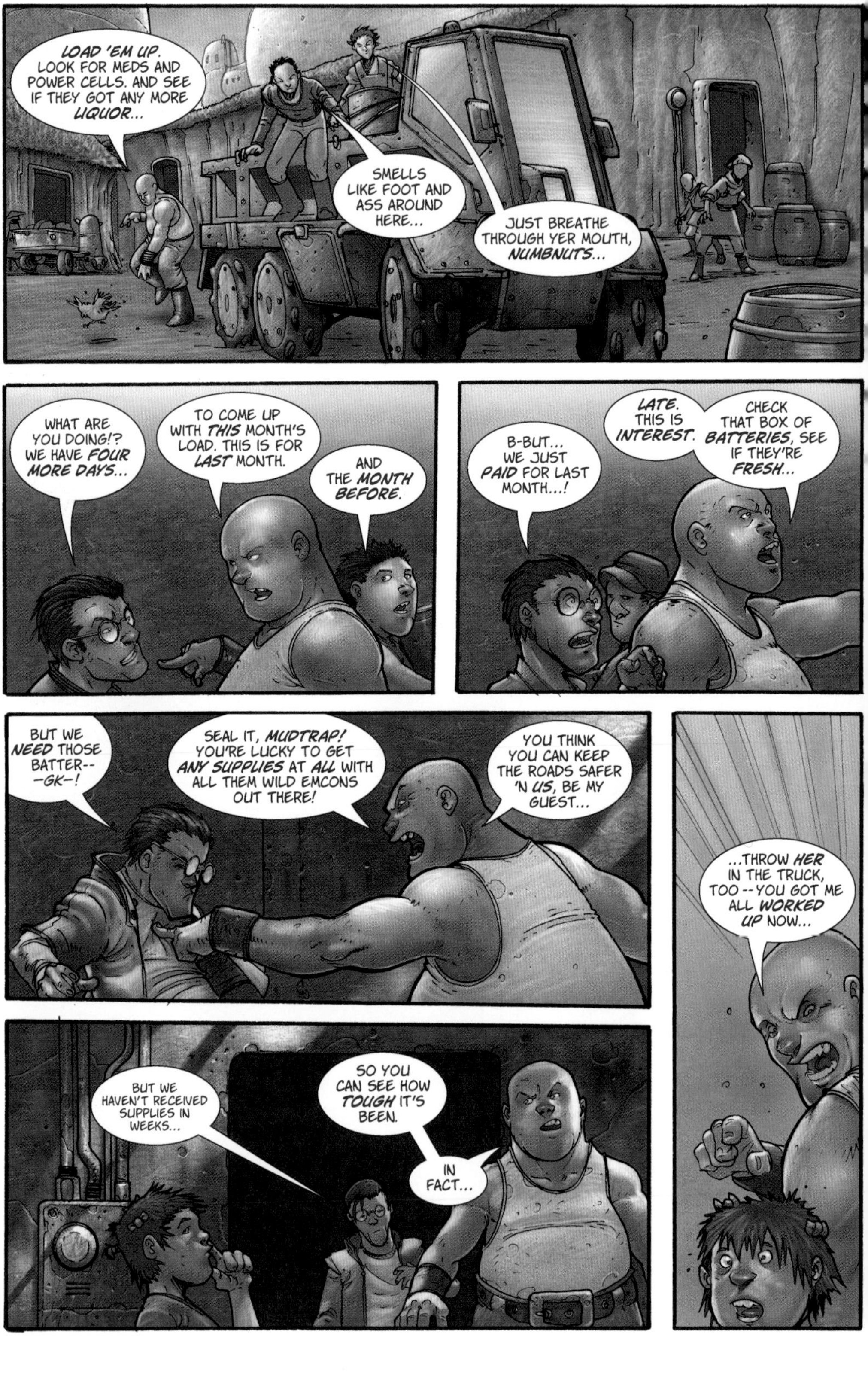
LOAD 'EM UP. LOOK FOR MEDS AND POWER CELLS. AND SEE IF THEY GOT ANY MORE LIQUOR...
SMELLS LIKE FOOT AND ASS AROUND HERE...
JUST BREATHE THROUGH YER MOUTH, NUMBNUTS...
WHAT ARE YOU DOING!? WE HAVE FOUR MORE DAYS...
TO COME UP WITH THIS MONTH'S LOAD. THIS IS FOR LAST MONTH.
AND THE MONTH BEFORE.
B-BUT... WE JUST PAID FOR LAST MONTH...!
LATE. THIS IS INTEREST.
CHECK THAT BOX OF BATTERIES, SEE IF THEY'RE FRESH...
BUT WE NEED THOSE BATTER-- --GK--!
SEAL IT, MUDTRAP! YOU'RE LUCKY TO GET ANY SUPPLIES AT ALL WITH ALL THEM WILD EMCONS OUT THERE!
YOU THINK YOU CAN KEEP THE ROADS SAFER 'N US, BE MY GUEST...
BUT WE HAVEN'T RECEIVED SUPPLIES IN WEEKS...
SO YOU CAN SEE HOW TOUGH IT'S BEEN.
IN FACT...
...THROW HER IN THE TRUCK, TOO--YOU GOT ME ALL WORKED UP NOW...

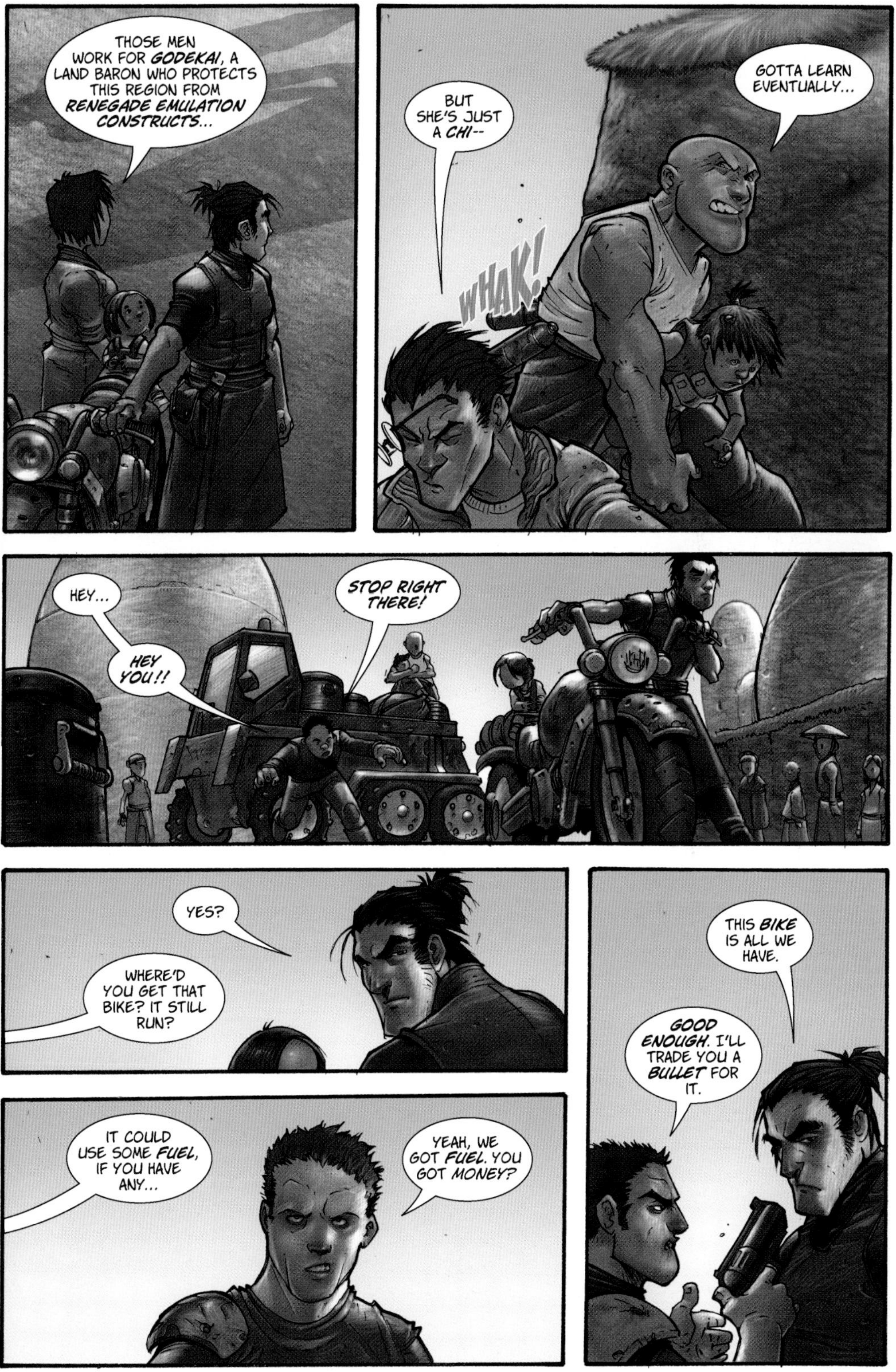
THOSE MEN WORK FOR GODEKAI, A LAND BARON WHO PROTECTS THIS REGION FROM RENEGADE EMULATION CONSTRUCTS...
BUT SHE'S JUST A CHI--
GOTTA LEARN EVENTUALLY...
WHAK!
HEY...
HEY YOU!!
STOP RIGHT THERE!
YES?
WHERE'D YOU GET THAT BIKE? IT STILL RUN?
IT COULD USE SOME FUEL, IF YOU HAVE ANY...
YEAH, WE GOT FUEL. YOU GOT MONEY?
THIS BIKE IS ALL WE HAVE.
GOOD ENOUGH. I'LL TRADE YOU A BULLET FOR IT.

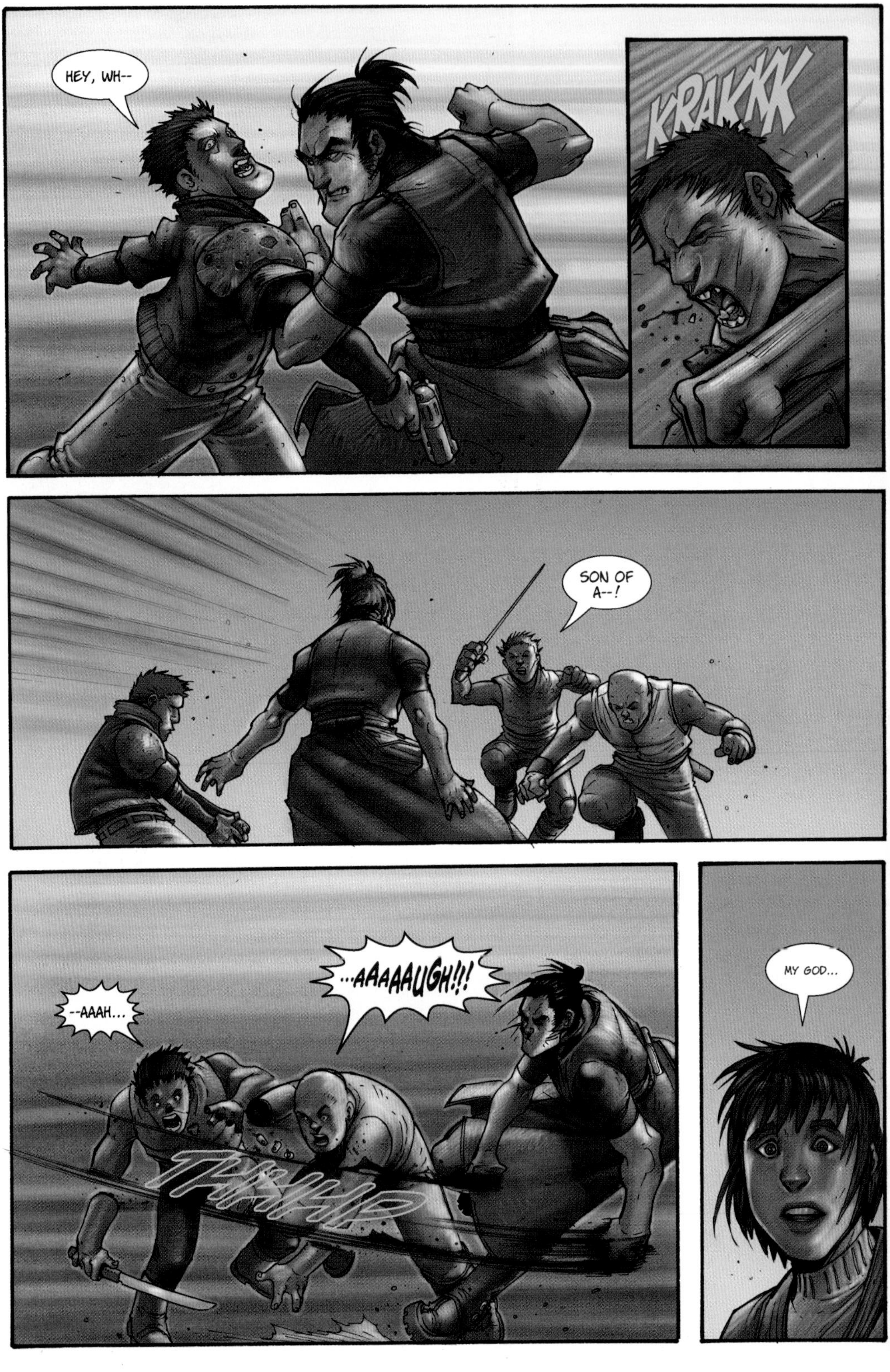
HEY, WH--
KRAKKK
SON OF A--!
--AAAH...
...AAAAAUGH!!!
THHHP
MY GOD...

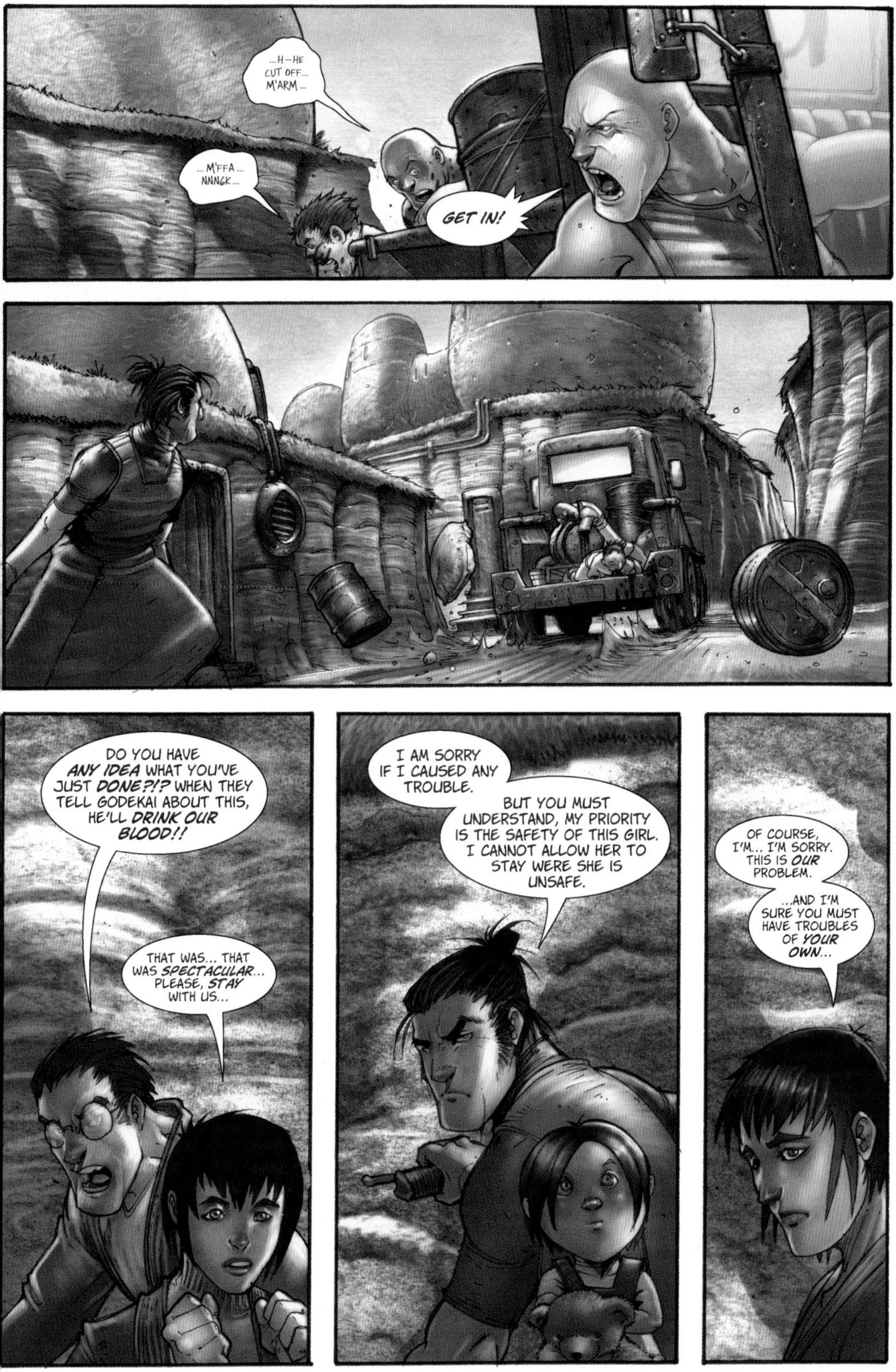
...H-HE CUT OFF... M'ARM...
... M'FFA... NNNGK...
GET IN!
DO YOU HAVE ANY IDEA WHAT YOU'VE JUST DONE?!? WHEN THEY TELL GODEKAI ABOUT THIS, HE'LL DRINK OUR BLOOD!!
THAT WAS... THAT WAS SPECTACULAR... PLEASE, STAY WITH US...
I AM SORRY IF I CAUSED ANY TROUBLE.
BUT YOU MUST UNDERSTAND, MY PRIORITY IS THE SAFETY OF THIS GIRL. I CANNOT ALLOW HER TO STAY WERE SHE IS UNSAFE.
OF COURSE, I'M... I'M SORRY. THIS IS OUR PROBLEM.
...AND I'M SURE YOU MUST HAVE TROUBLES OF YOUR OWN...

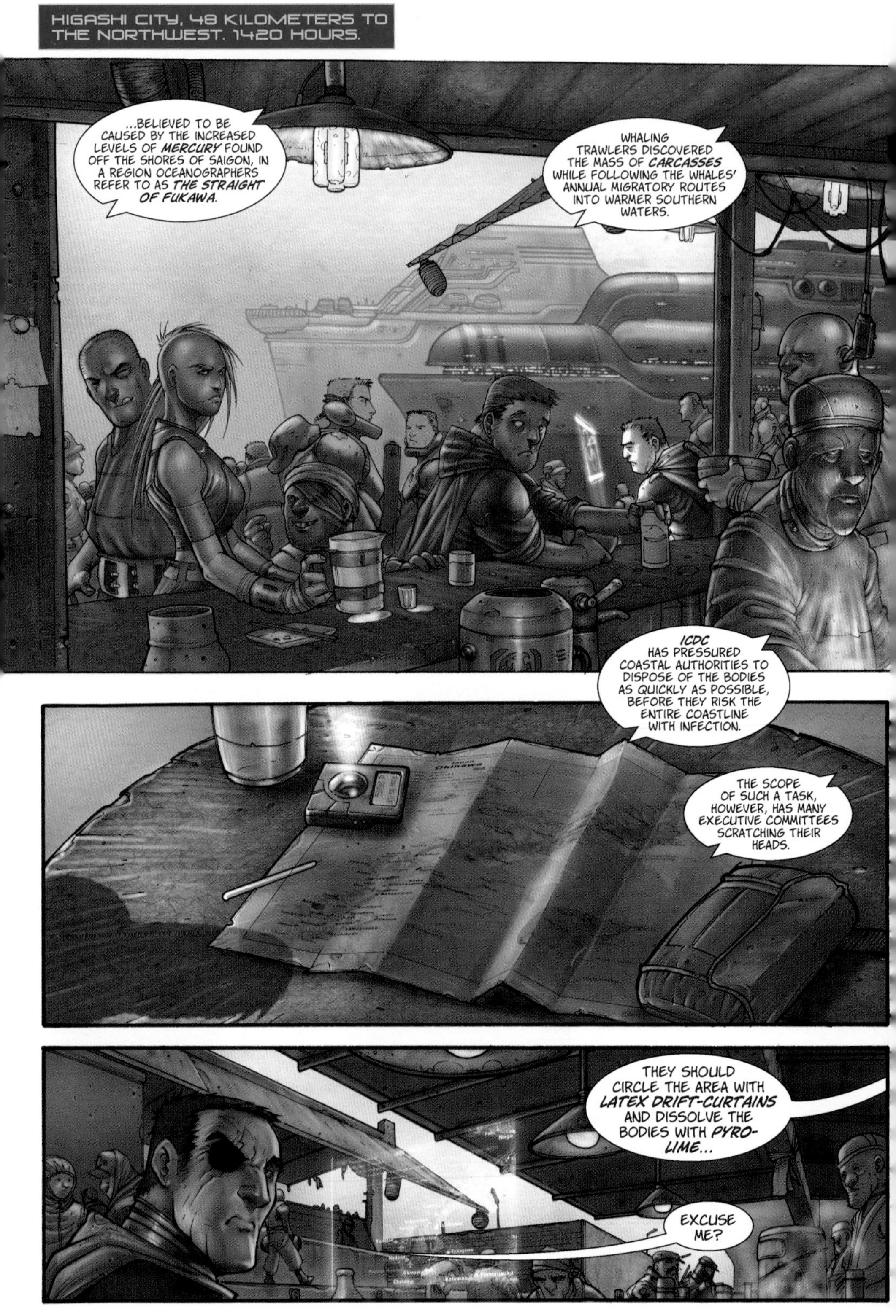
HIGASHI CITY, 48 KILOMETERS TO THE NORTHWEST. 1420 HOURS.
...BELIEVED TO BE CAUSED BY THE INCREASED LEVELS OF MERCURY FOUND OFF THE SHORES OF SAIGON, IN A REGION OCEANOGRAPHERS REFER TO AS THE STRAIGHT OF FUKAWA.
WHALING TRAWLERS DISCOVERED THE MASS OF CARCASSES WHILE FOLLOWING THE WHALES' ANNUAL MIGRATORY ROUTES INTO WARMER SOUTHERN WATERS.
ICDC HAS PRESSURED COASTAL AUTHORITIES TO DISPOSE OF THE BODIES AS QUICKLY AS POSSIBLE, BEFORE THEY RISK THE ENTIRE COASTLINE WITH INFECTION.
THE SCOPE OF SUCH A TASK, HOWEVER, HAS MANY EXECUTIVE COMMITTEES SCRATCHING THEIR HEADS.
THEY SHOULD CIRCLE THE AREA WITH LATEX DRIFT-CURTAINS AND DISSOLVE THE BODIES WITH PYRO-LIME...
EXCUSE ME?

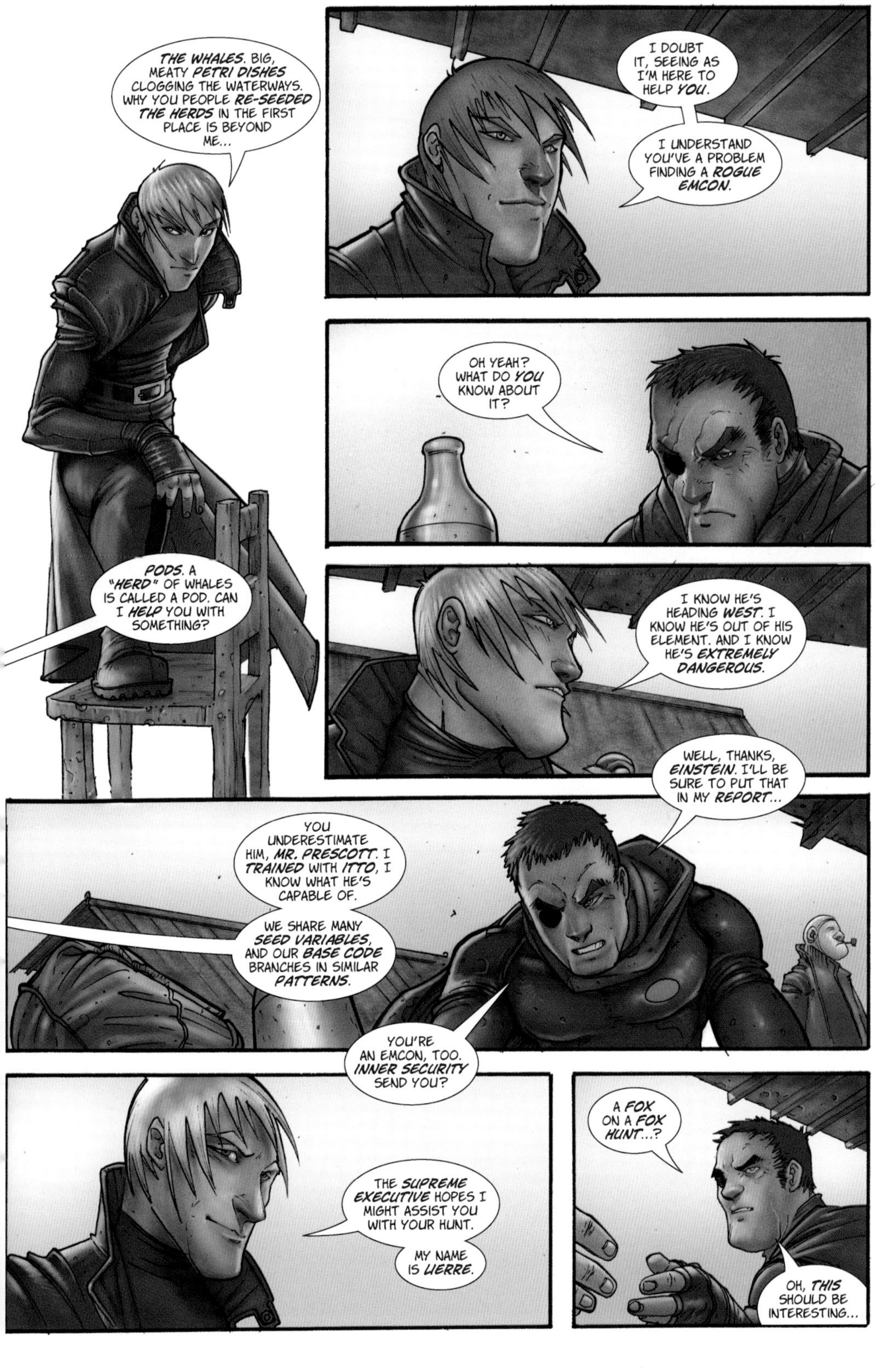
THE WHALES. BIG, MEATY PETRI DISHES CLOGGING THE WATERWAYS. WHY YOU PEOPLE RE-SEEDED THE HERDS IN THE FIRST PLACE IS BEYOND ME...
I DOUBT IT, SEEING AS I'M HERE TO HELP YOU.
I UNDERSTAND YOU'VE A PROBLEM FINDING A ROGUE EMCON.
OH YEAH? WHAT DO YOU KNOW ABOUT IT?
PODS. A "HERD" OF WHALES IS CALLED A POD. CAN I HELP YOU WITH SOMETHING?
I KNOW HE'S HEADING WEST. I KNOW HE'S OUT OF HIS ELEMENT. AND I KNOW HE'S EXTREMELY DANGEROUS.
WELL, THANKS, EINSTEIN. I'LL BE SURE TO PUT THAT IN MY REPORT...
YOU UNDERESTIMATE HIM, MR. PRESCOTT. I TRAINED WITH ITTO, I KNOW WHAT HE'S CAPABLE OF.
WE SHARE MANY SEED VARIABLES, AND OUR BASE CODE BRANCHES IN SIMILAR PATTERNS.
YOU'RE AN EMCON, TOO. INNER SECURITY SEND YOU?
THE SUPREME EXECUTIVE HOPES I MIGHT ASSIST YOU WITH YOUR HUNT.
MY NAME IS LIERRE.
A FOX ON A FOX HUNT...?
OH, THIS SHOULD BE INTERESTING...

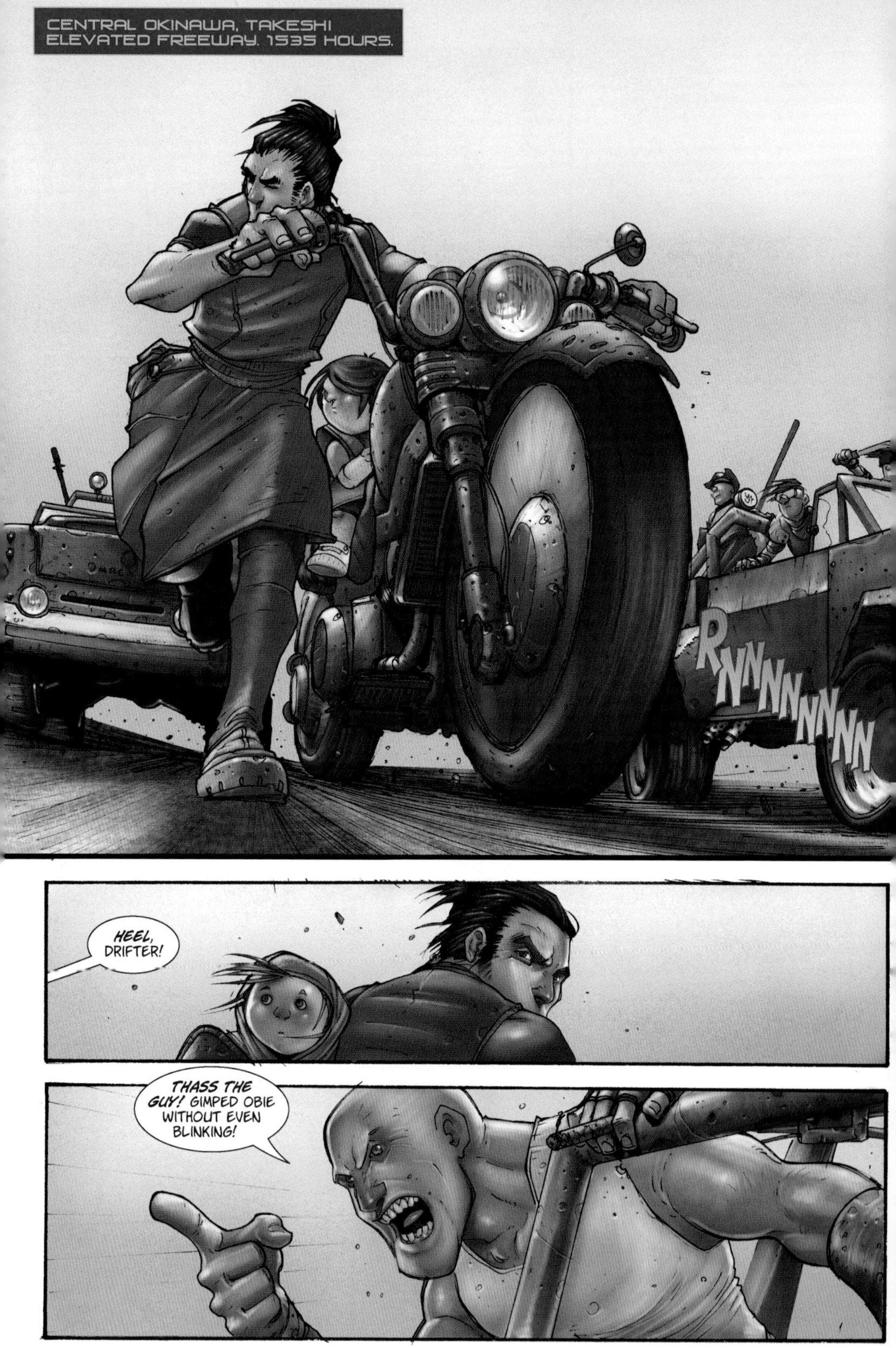
CENTRAL OKINAWA, TAKESHI ELEVATED FREEWAY. 1535 HOURS.
RNNNNNNNN
HEEL, DRIFTER!
THASS THE GUY! GIMPED OBIE WITHOUT EVEN BLINKING!

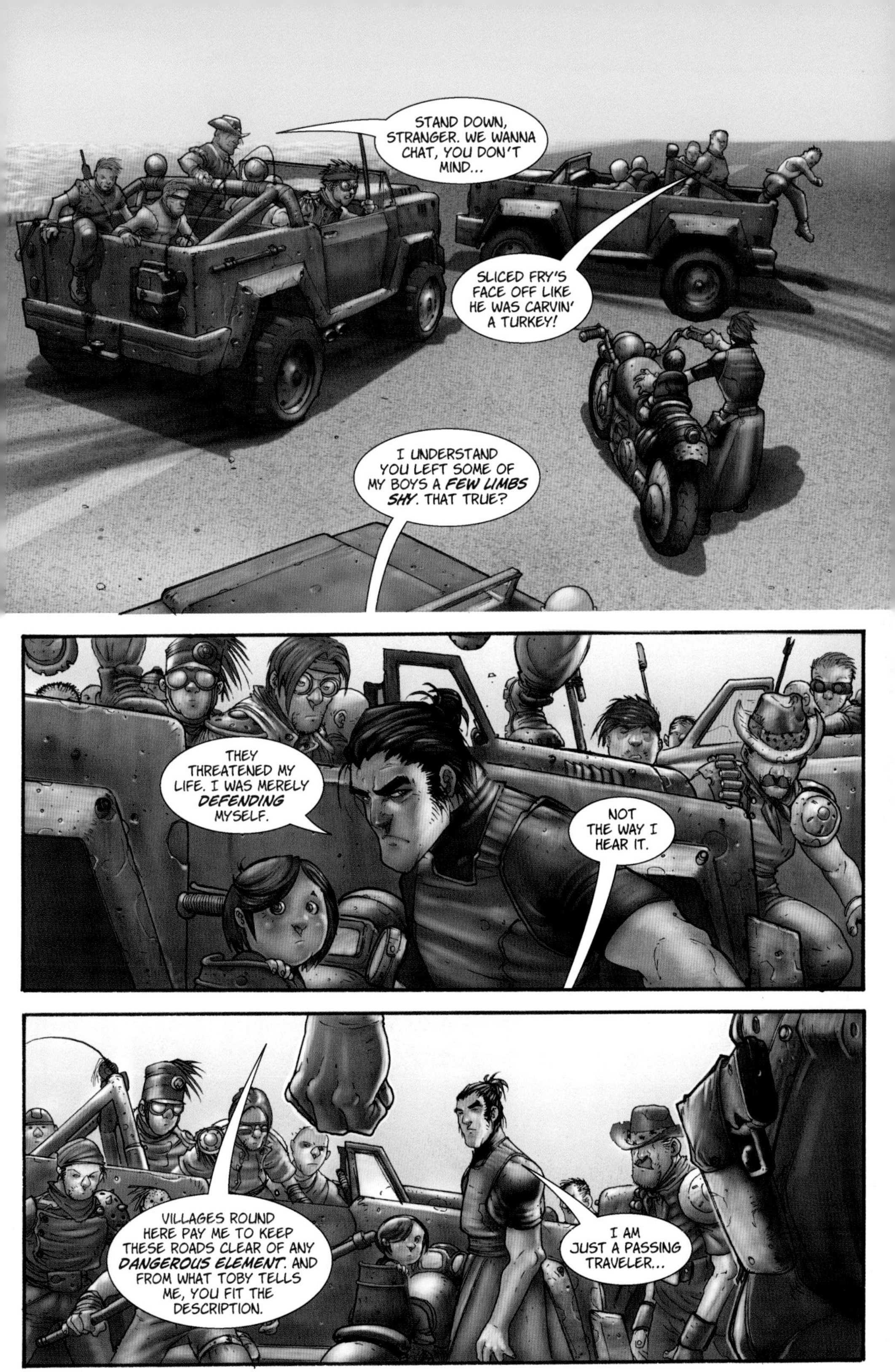
STAND DOWN, STRANGER. WE WANNA CHAT, YOU DON'T MIND...
SLICED FRY'S FACE OFF LIKE HE WAS CARVIN' A TURKEY!
I UNDERSTAND YOU LEFT SOME OF MY BOYS A FEW LIMBS SHY. THAT TRUE?
THEY THREATENED MY LIFE. I WAS MERELY DEFENDING MYSELF.
NOT THE WAY I HEAR IT.
VILLAGES ROUND HERE PAY ME TO KEEP THESE ROADS CLEAR OF ANY DANGEROUS ELEMENT. AND FROM WHAT TOBY TELLS ME, YOU FIT THE DESCRIPTION.
I AM JUST A PASSING TRAVELER...

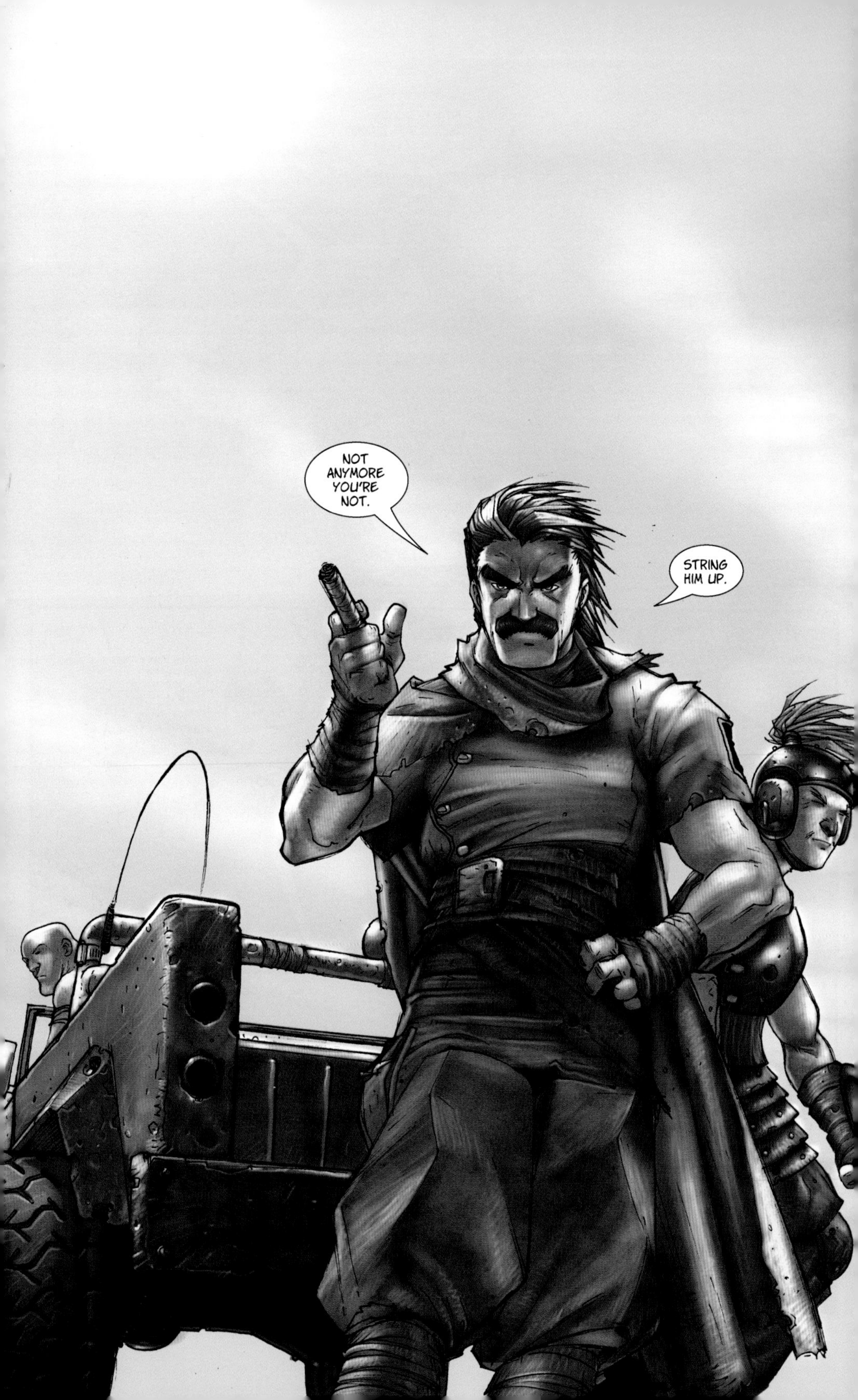
NOT ANYMORE YOU'RE NOT.
STRING HIM UP.

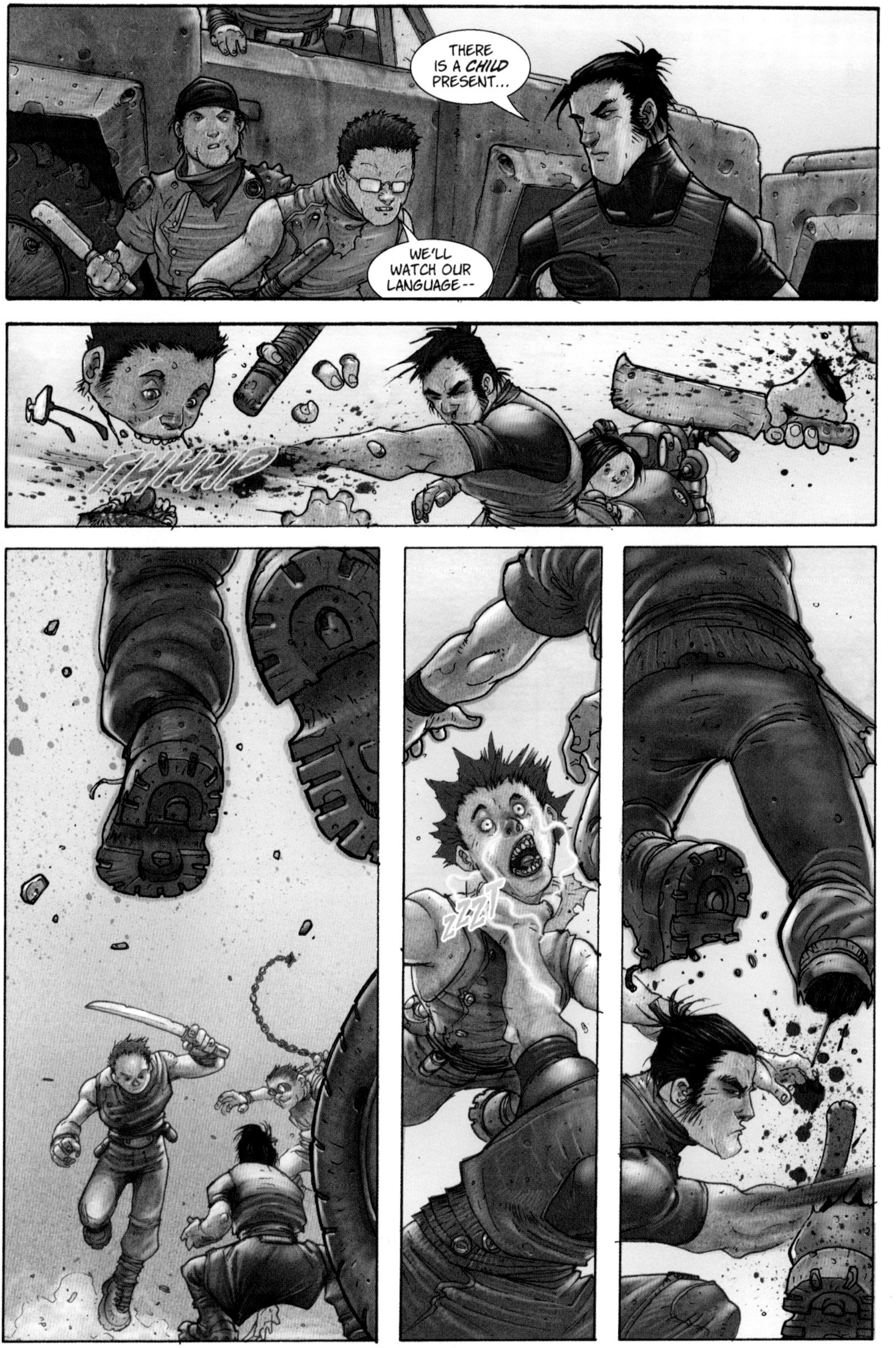
THERE IS A CHILD PRESENT...
WE'LL WATCH OUR LANGUAGE--
THHHP
ZZZT

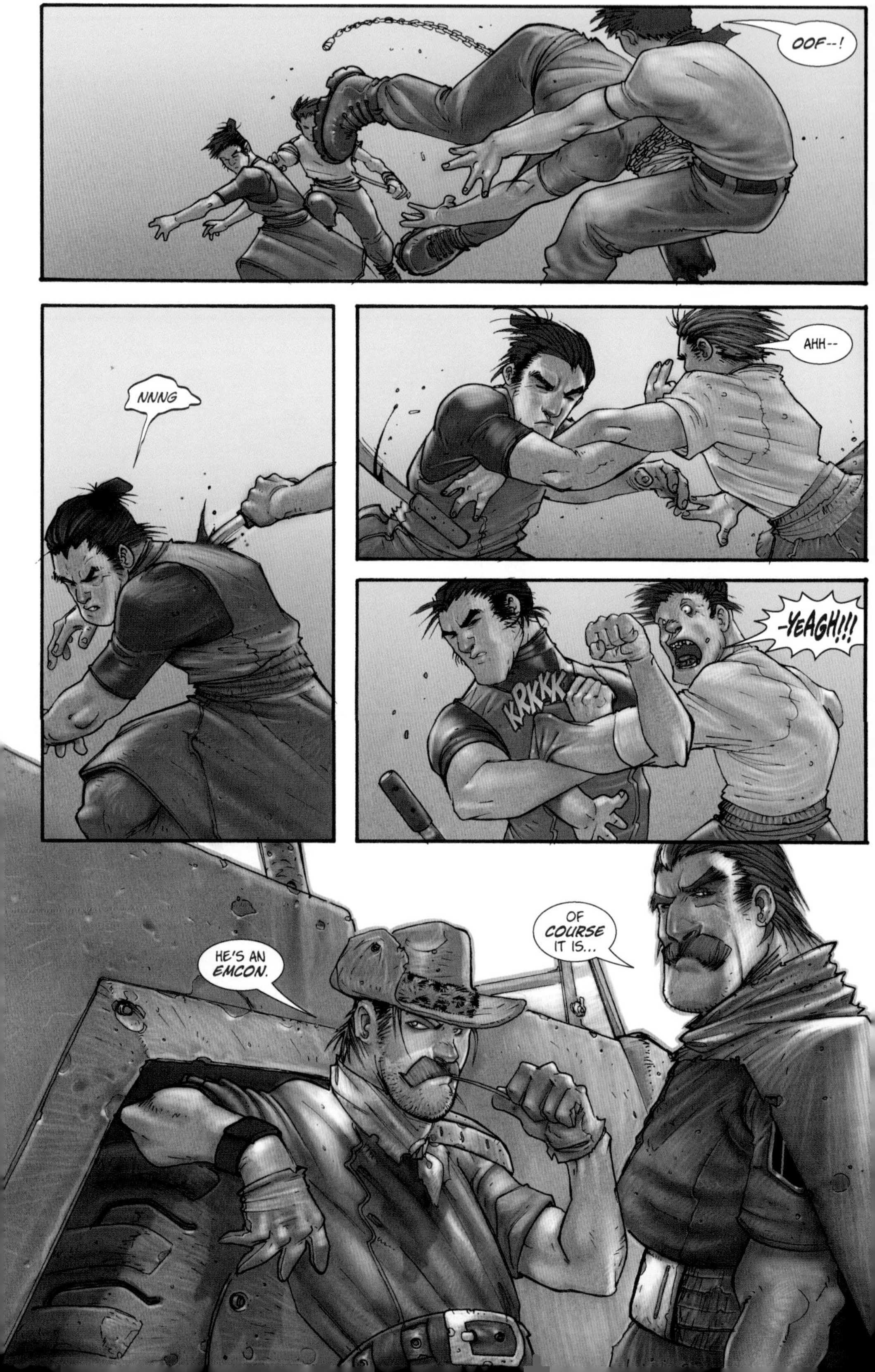
OOF--!
NNNG
AHH--
KRKKK
-YEAGH!!!
HE'S AN EMCON.
OF COURSE IT IS...

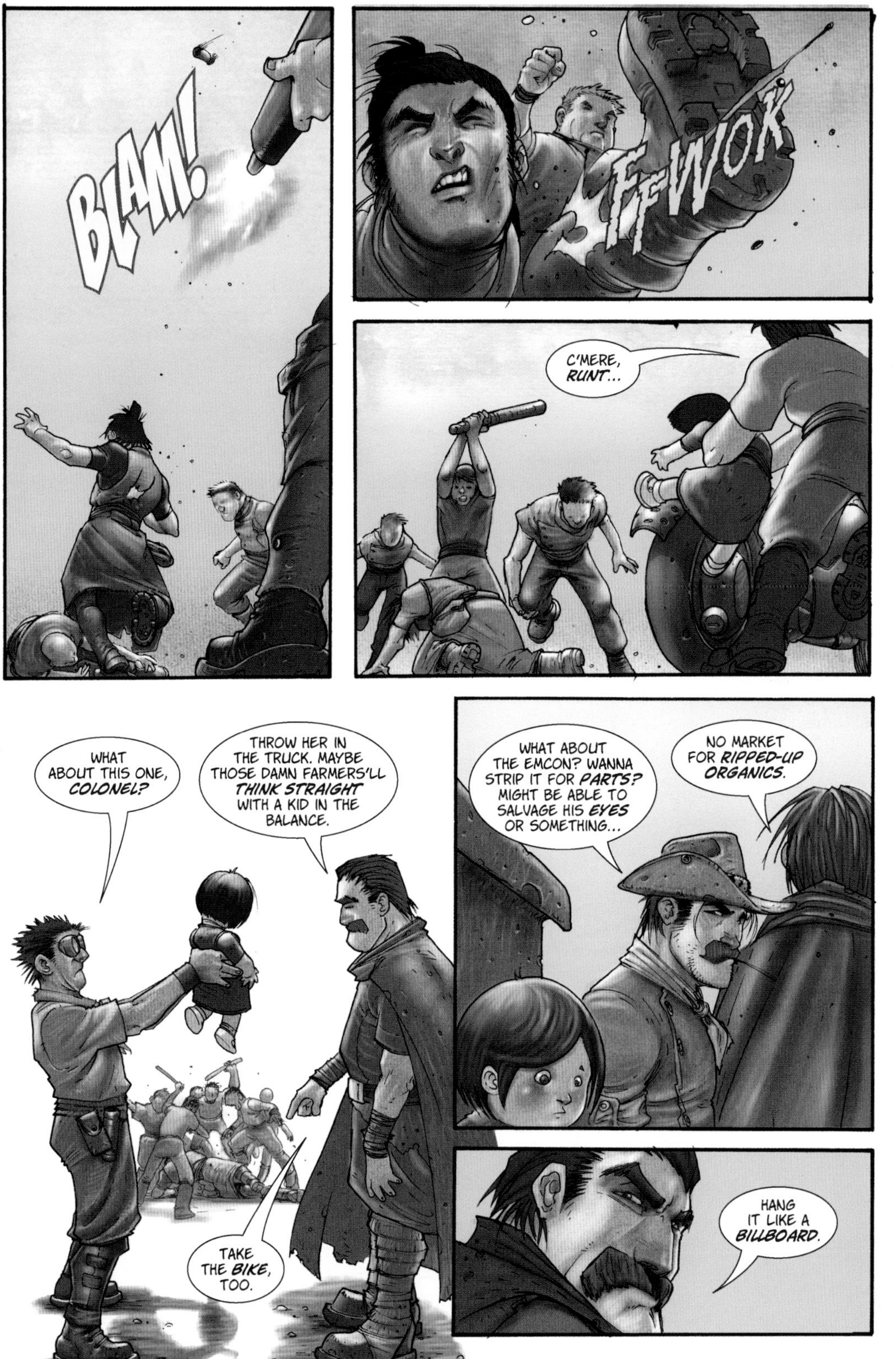
BLAM!
FF-WOK
C'MERE, *RUNT*...
WHAT ABOUT THIS ONE, *COLONEL?*
THROW HER IN THE TRUCK. MAYBE THOSE DAMN FARMERS'LL *THINK STRAIGHT* WITH A KID IN THE BALANCE.
TAKE THE *BIKE*, TOO.
WHAT ABOUT THE EMCON? WANNA STRIP IT FOR *PARTS?* MIGHT BE ABLE TO SALVAGE HIS *EYES* OR SOMETHING...
NO MARKET FOR *RIPPED-UP ORGANICS*.
HANG IT LIKE A *BILLBOARD*.

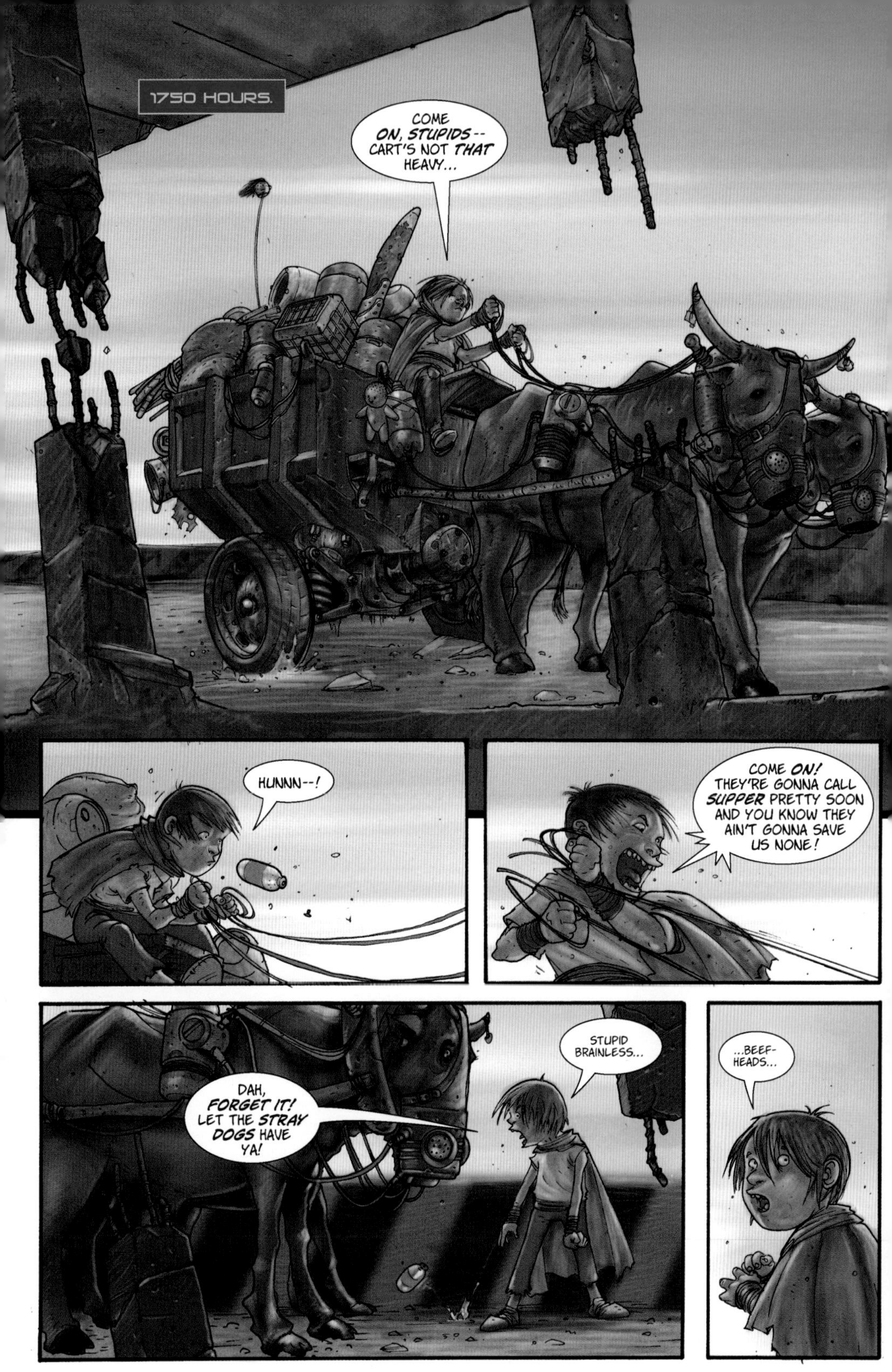
1750 HOURS.
COME ON, STUPIDS-- CART'S NOT THAT HEAVY...
HUNNN--!
COME ON! THEY'RE GONNA CALL SUPPER PRETTY SOON AND YOU KNOW THEY AIN'T GONNA SAVE US NONE!
DAH, FORGET IT! LET THE STRAY DOGS HAVE YA!
STUPID BRAINLESS...
...BEEF-HEADS...

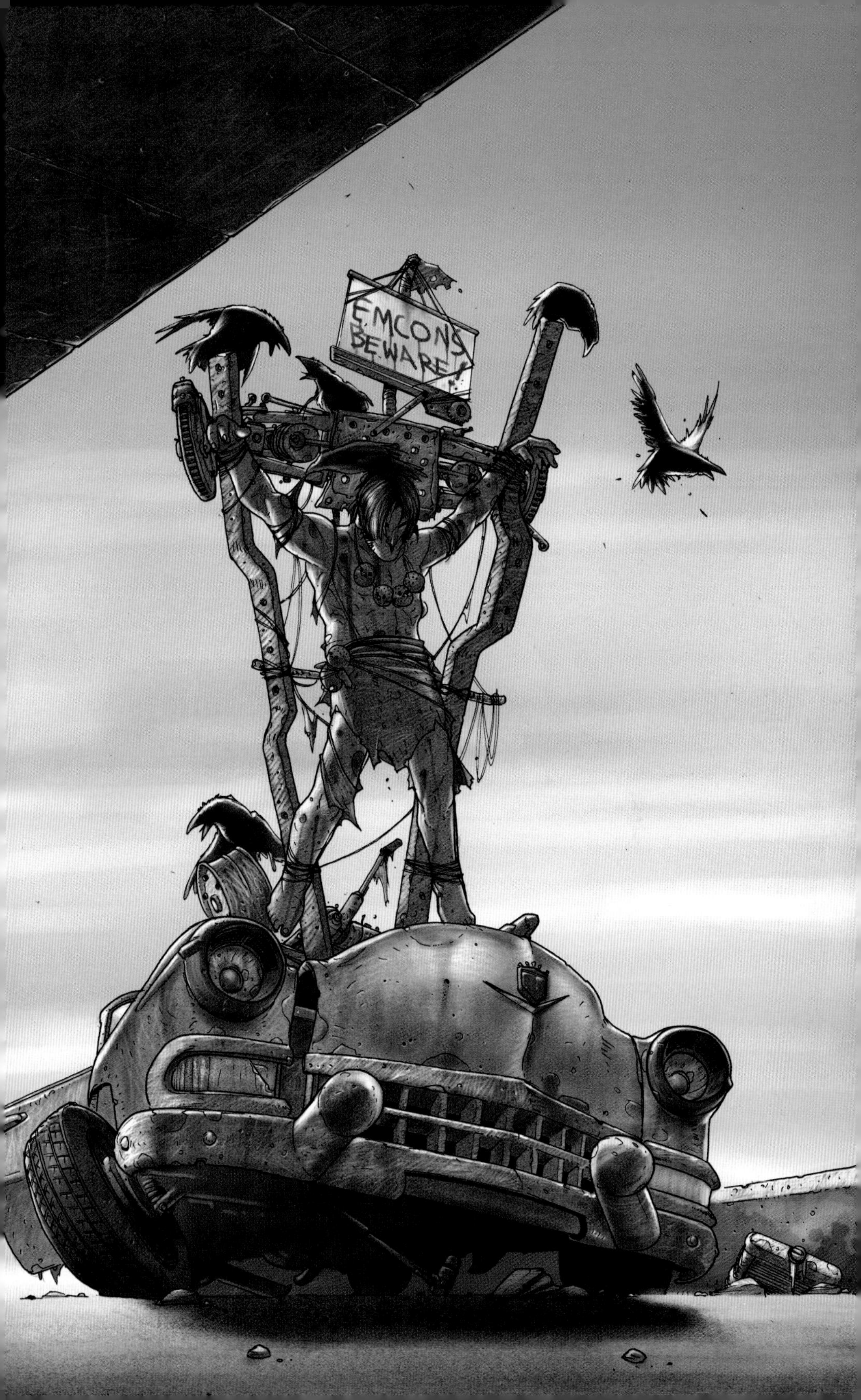
EMCONS BEWARE!

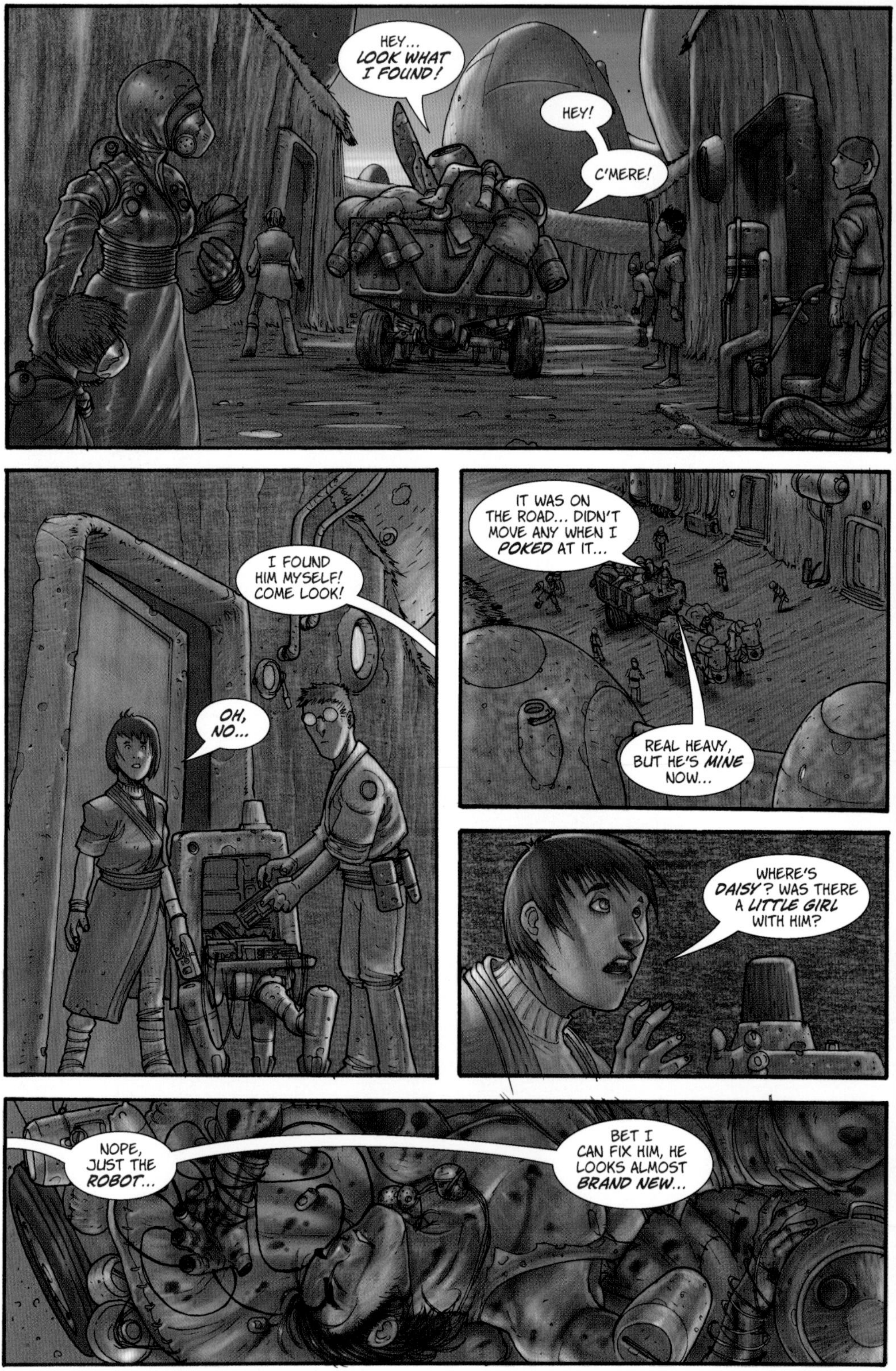
HEY... LOOK WHAT I FOUND!
HEY!
C'MERE!
I FOUND HIM MYSELF! COME LOOK!
OH, NO...
IT WAS ON THE ROAD... DIDN'T MOVE ANY WHEN I POKED AT IT...
REAL HEAVY, BUT HE'S MINE NOW...
WHERE'S DAISY? WAS THERE A LITTLE GIRL WITH HIM?
NOPE, JUST THE ROBOT...
BET I CAN FIX HIM, HE LOOKS ALMOST BRAND NEW...

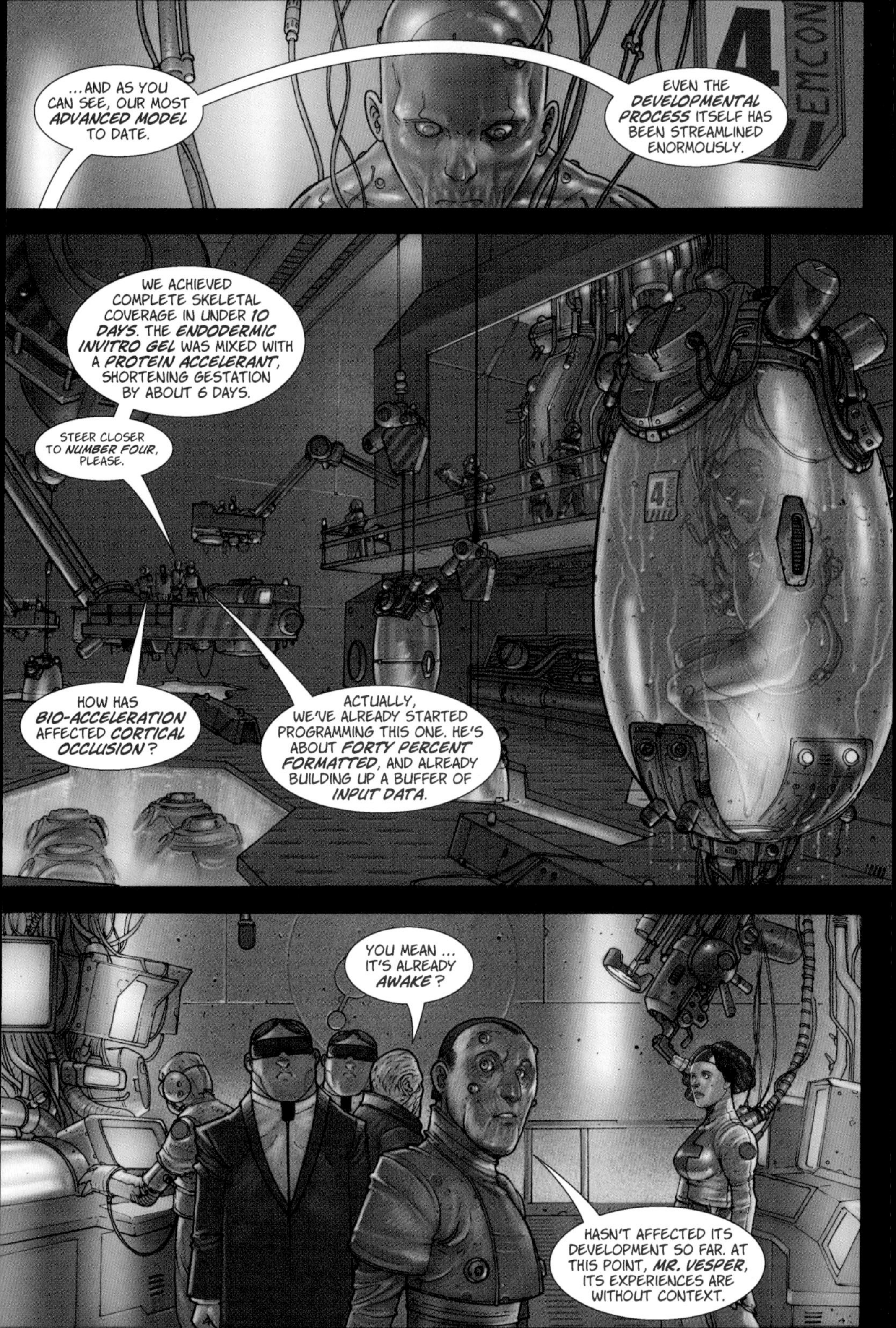
...AND AS YOU CAN SEE, OUR MOST ADVANCED MODEL TO DATE.
EVEN THE DEVELOPMENTAL PROCESS ITSELF HAS BEEN STREAMLINED ENORMOUSLY.
WE ACHIEVED COMPLETE SKELETAL COVERAGE IN UNDER 10 DAYS. THE ENDODERMIC INVITRO GEL WAS MIXED WITH A PROTEIN ACCELERANT, SHORTENING GESTATION BY ABOUT 6 DAYS.
STEER CLOSER TO NUMBER FOUR, PLEASE.
HOW HAS BIO-ACCELERATION AFFECTED CORTICAL OCCLUSION?
ACTUALLY, WE'VE ALREADY STARTED PROGRAMMING THIS ONE. HE'S ABOUT FORTY PERCENT FORMATTED, AND ALREADY BUILDING UP A BUFFER OF INPUT DATA.
YOU MEAN ... IT'S ALREADY AWAKE?
HASN'T AFFECTED ITS DEVELOPMENT SO FAR. AT THIS POINT, MR. VESPER, ITS EXPERIENCES ARE WITHOUT CONTEXT.

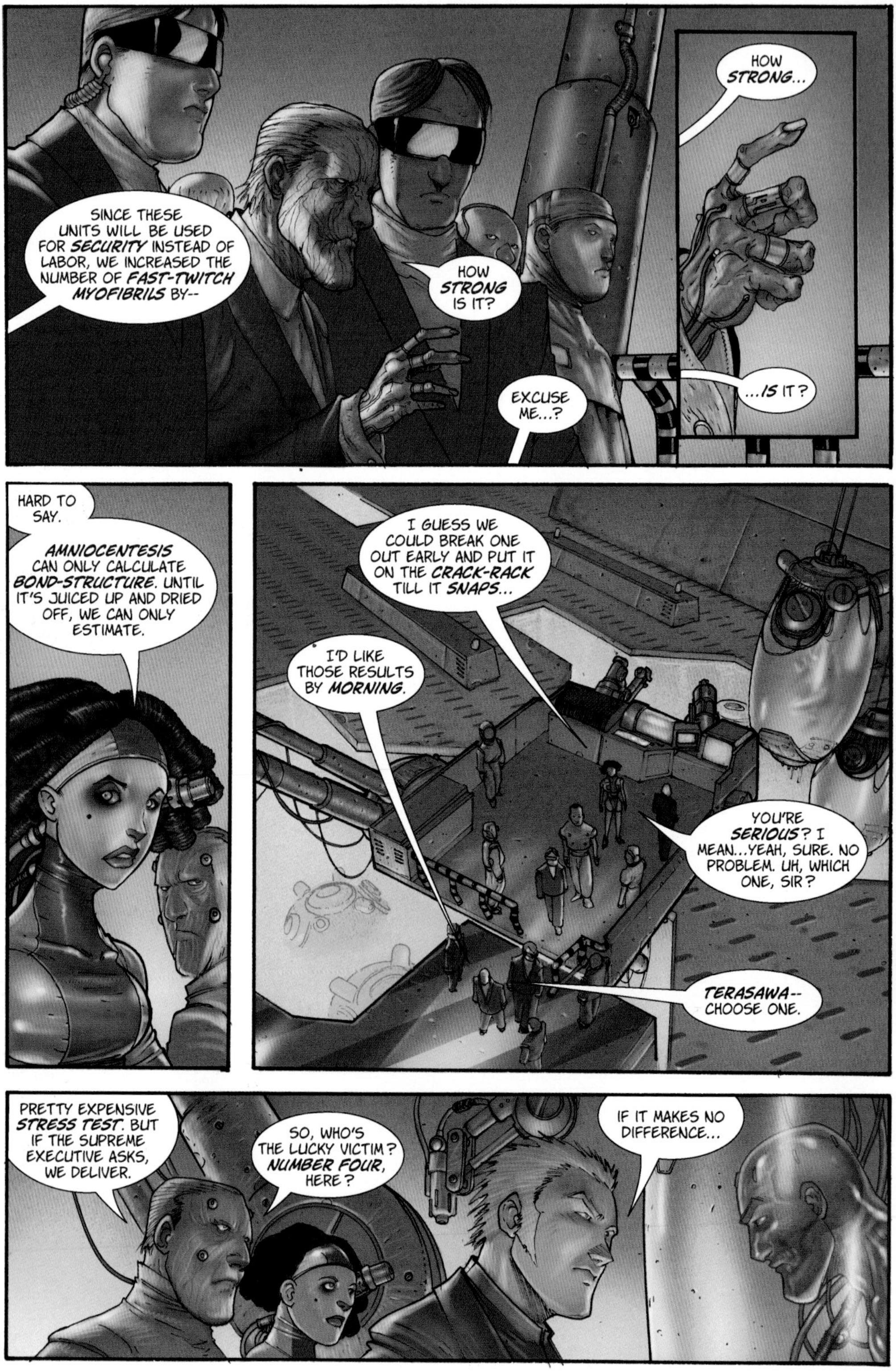
SINCE THESE UNITS WILL BE USED FOR SECURITY INSTEAD OF LABOR, WE INCREASED THE NUMBER OF FAST-TWITCH MYOFIBRILS BY--
HOW STRONG IS IT?
EXCUSE ME...?
HOW STRONG...
...IS IT?
HARD TO SAY.
AMNIOCENTESIS CAN ONLY CALCULATE BOND-STRUCTURE. UNTIL IT'S JUICED UP AND DRIED OFF, WE CAN ONLY ESTIMATE.
I GUESS WE COULD BREAK ONE OUT EARLY AND PUT IT ON THE CRACK-RACK TILL IT SNAPS...
I'D LIKE THOSE RESULTS BY MORNING.
YOU'RE SERIOUS? I MEAN...YEAH, SURE. NO PROBLEM. UH, WHICH ONE, SIR?
TERASAWA-- CHOOSE ONE.
PRETTY EXPENSIVE STRESS TEST. BUT IF THE SUPREME EXECUTIVE ASKS, WE DELIVER.
SO, WHO'S THE LUCKY VICTIM? NUMBER FOUR, HERE?
IF IT MAKES NO DIFFERENCE...

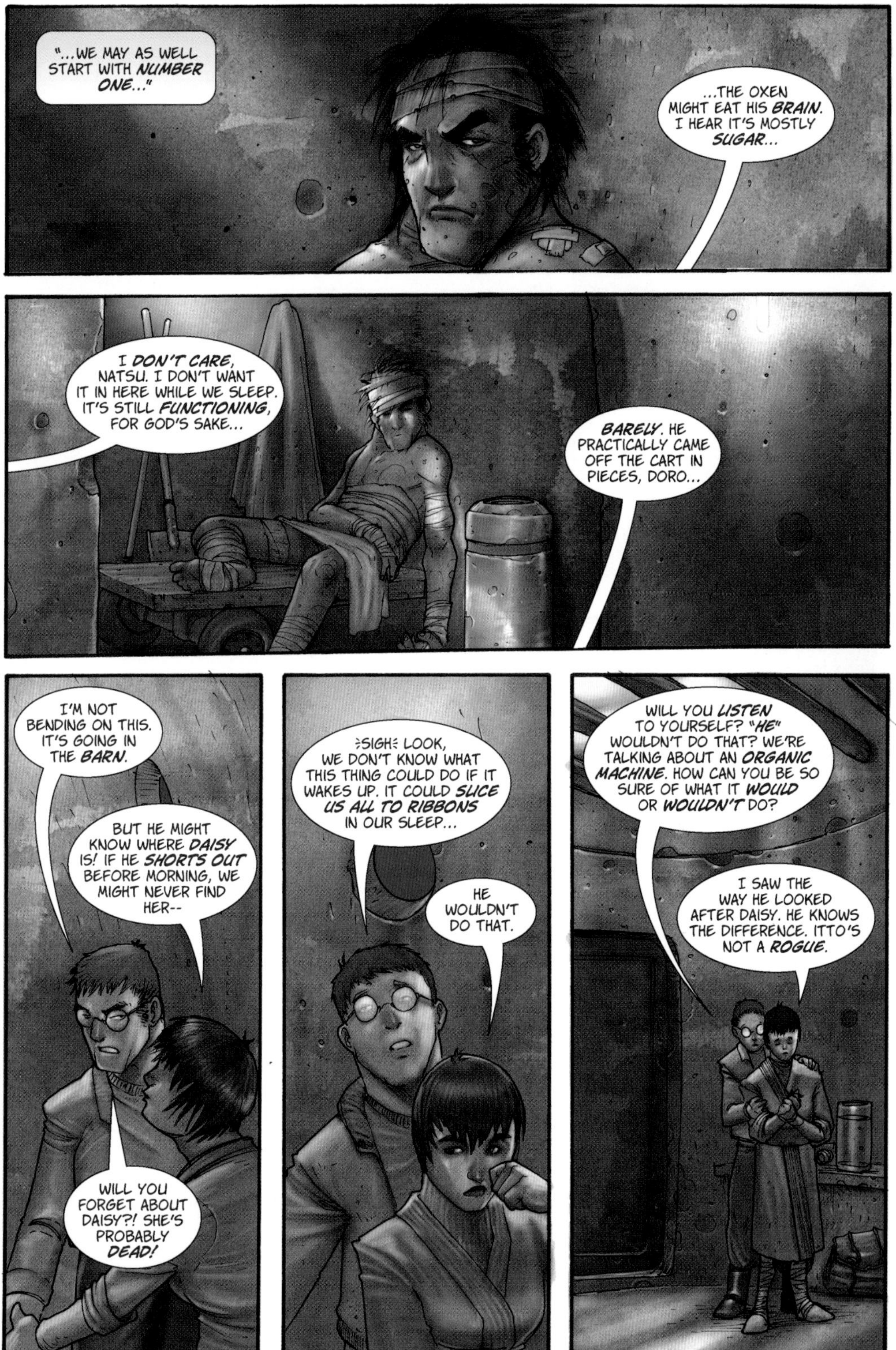
"...WE MAY AS WELL START WITH NUMBER ONE..."
...THE OXEN MIGHT EAT HIS BRAIN. I HEAR IT'S MOSTLY SUGAR...
I DON'T CARE, NATSU. I DON'T WANT IT IN HERE WHILE WE SLEEP. IT'S STILL FUNCTIONING, FOR GOD'S SAKE...
BARELY. HE PRACTICALLY CAME OFF THE CART IN PIECES, DORO...
I'M NOT BENDING ON THIS. IT'S GOING IN THE BARN.
BUT HE MIGHT KNOW WHERE DAISY IS! IF HE SHORTS OUT BEFORE MORNING, WE MIGHT NEVER FIND HER--
WILL YOU FORGET ABOUT DAISY?! SHE'S PROBABLY DEAD!
⁝SIGH⁝ LOOK, WE DON'T KNOW WHAT THIS THING COULD DO IF IT WAKES UP. IT COULD SLICE US ALL TO RIBBONS IN OUR SLEEP...
HE WOULDN'T DO THAT.
WILL YOU LISTEN TO YOURSELF? "HE" WOULDN'T DO THAT? WE'RE TALKING ABOUT AN ORGANIC MACHINE. HOW CAN YOU BE SO SURE OF WHAT IT WOULD OR WOULDN'T DO?
I SAW THE WAY HE LOOKED AFTER DAISY. HE KNOWS THE DIFFERENCE. ITTO'S NOT A ROGUE.

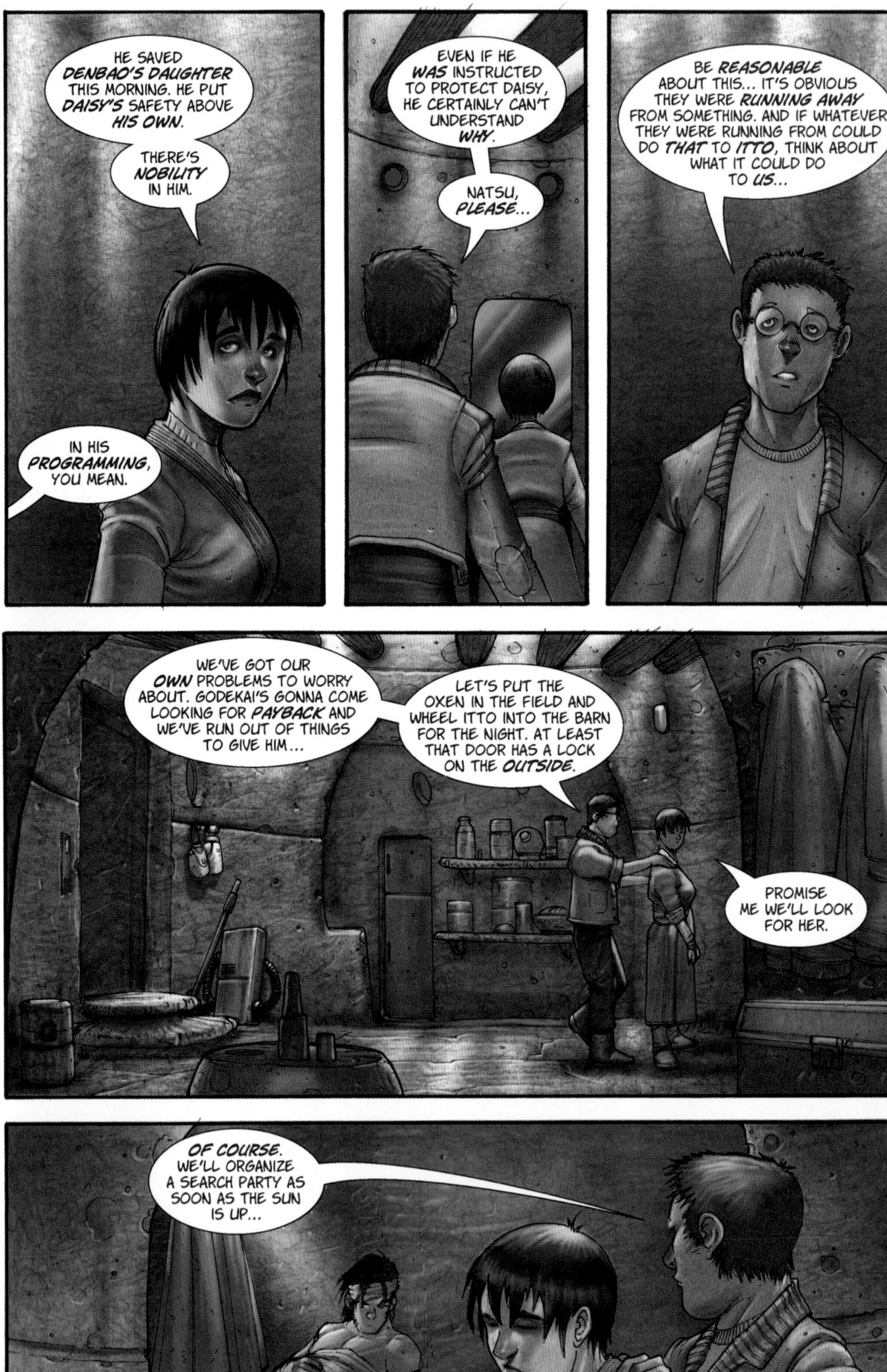
HE SAVED DENBAO'S DAUGHTER THIS MORNING. HE PUT DAISY'S SAFETY ABOVE HIS OWN.
THERE'S NOBILITY IN HIM.
IN HIS PROGRAMMING, YOU MEAN.
EVEN IF HE WAS INSTRUCTED TO PROTECT DAISY, HE CERTAINLY CAN'T UNDERSTAND WHY.
NATSU, PLEASE...
BE REASONABLE ABOUT THIS... IT'S OBVIOUS THEY WERE RUNNING AWAY FROM SOMETHING. AND IF WHATEVER THEY WERE RUNNING FROM COULD DO THAT TO ITTO, THINK ABOUT WHAT IT COULD DO TO US...
WE'VE GOT OUR OWN PROBLEMS TO WORRY ABOUT. GODEKAI'S GONNA COME LOOKING FOR PAYBACK AND WE'VE RUN OUT OF THINGS TO GIVE HIM...
LET'S PUT THE OXEN IN THE FIELD AND WHEEL ITTO INTO THE BARN FOR THE NIGHT. AT LEAST THAT DOOR HAS A LOCK ON THE OUTSIDE.
PROMISE ME WE'LL LOOK FOR HER.
OF COURSE. WE'LL ORGANIZE A SEARCH PARTY AS SOON AS THE SUN IS UP...

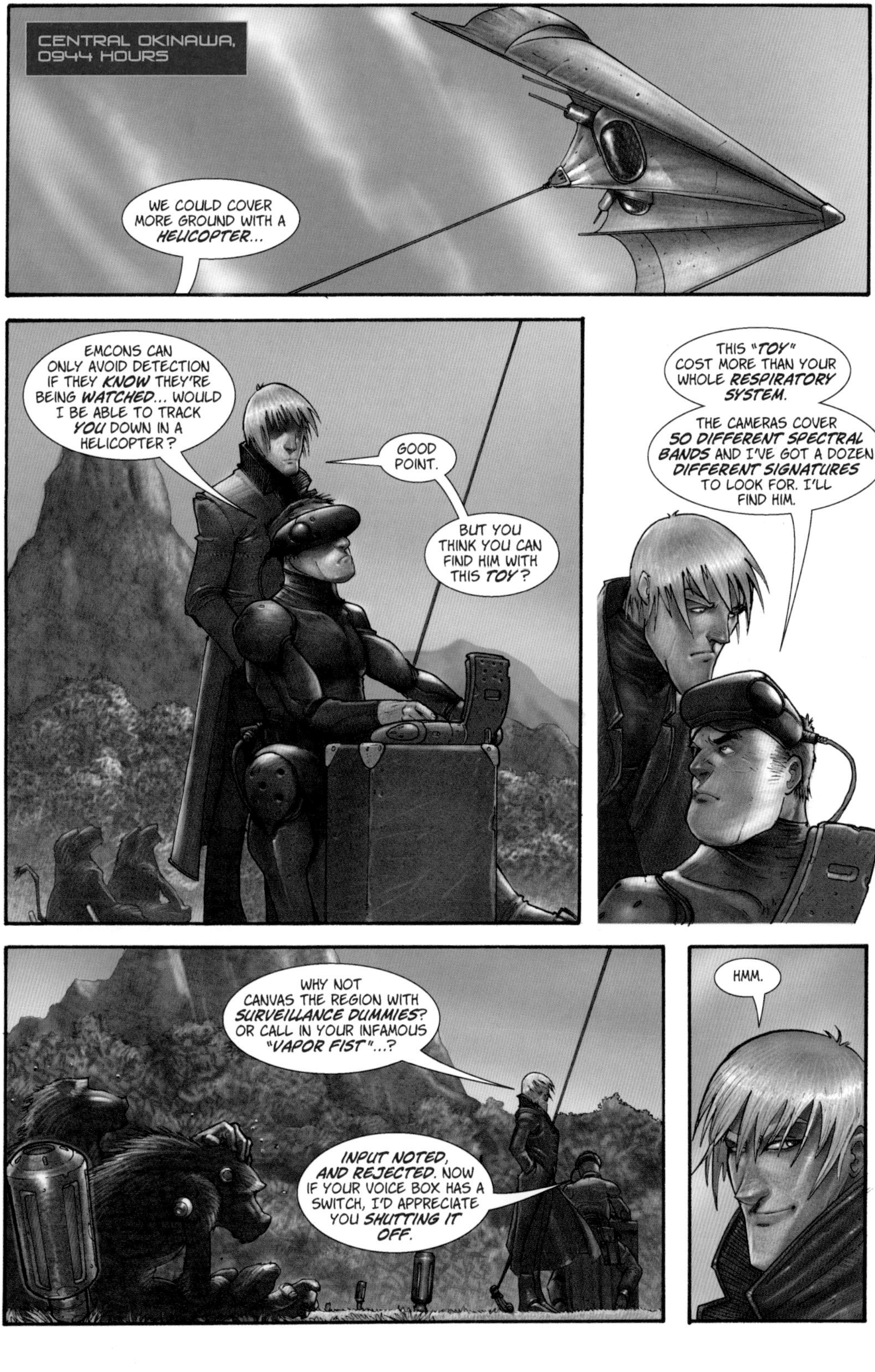
CENTRAL OKINAWA, 0944 HOURS
WE COULD COVER MORE GROUND WITH A *HELICOPTER*...
EMCONS CAN ONLY AVOID DETECTION IF THEY *KNOW* THEY'RE BEING *WATCHED*... WOULD I BE ABLE TO TRACK *YOU* DOWN IN A HELICOPTER?
GOOD POINT.
BUT YOU THINK YOU CAN FIND HIM WITH THIS *TOY*?
THIS *"TOY"* COST MORE THAN YOUR WHOLE *RESPIRATORY SYSTEM*.
THE CAMERAS COVER *50 DIFFERENT SPECTRAL BANDS* AND I'VE GOT A DOZEN *DIFFERENT SIGNATURES* TO LOOK FOR. I'LL FIND HIM.
WHY NOT CANVAS THE REGION WITH *SURVEILLANCE DUMMIES*? OR CALL IN YOUR INFAMOUS *"VAPOR FIST"*...?
INPUT NOTED, AND REJECTED. NOW IF YOUR VOICE BOX HAS A SWITCH, I'D APPRECIATE YOU *SHUTTING IT OFF*.
HMM.

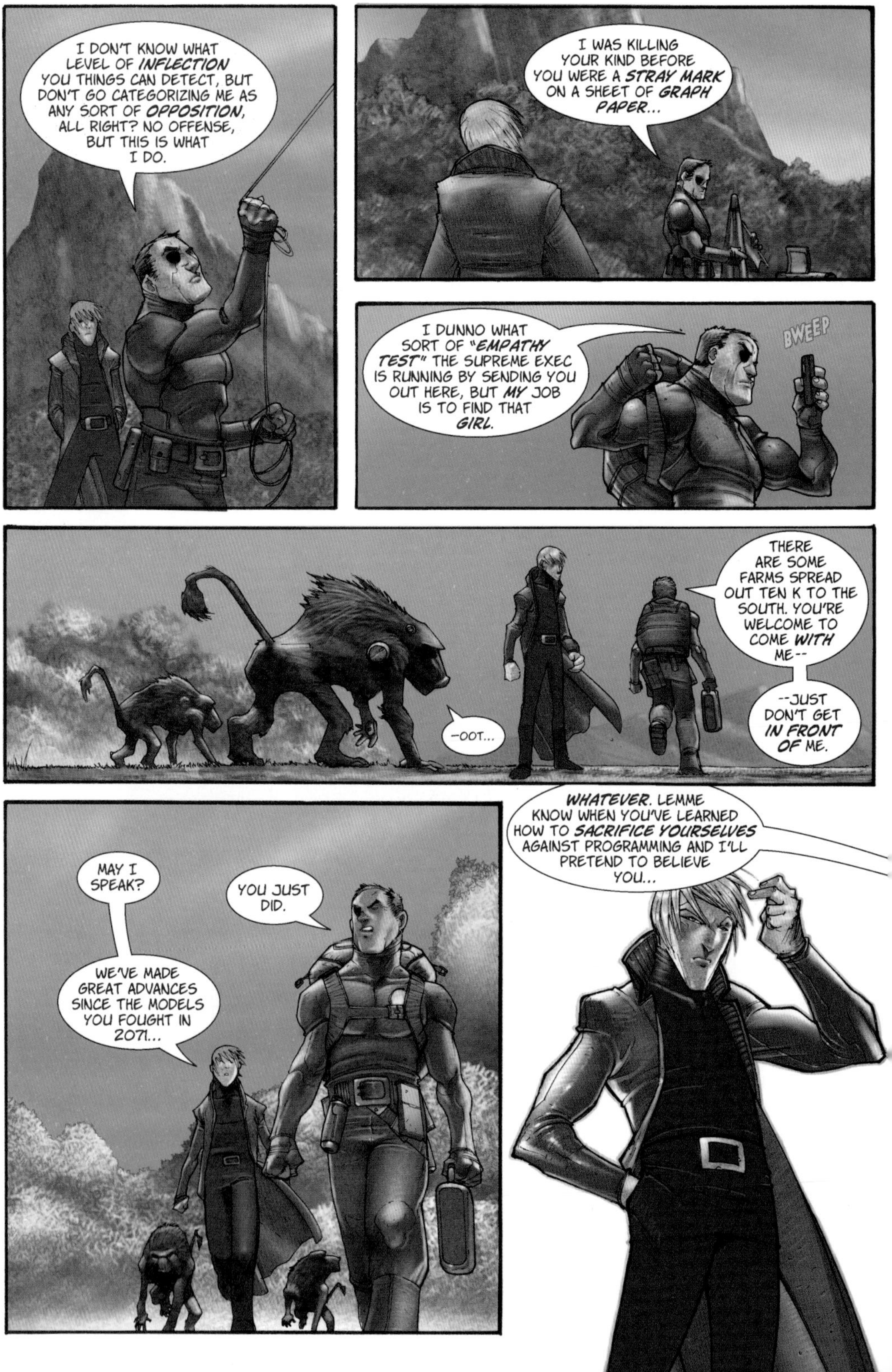
I DON'T KNOW WHAT LEVEL OF *INFLECTION* YOU THINGS CAN DETECT, BUT DON'T GO CATEGORIZING ME AS ANY SORT OF *OPPOSITION*, ALL RIGHT? NO OFFENSE, BUT THIS IS WHAT I DO.
I WAS KILLING YOUR KIND BEFORE YOU WERE A *STRAY MARK* ON A SHEET OF *GRAPH PAPER*...
I DUNNO WHAT SORT OF *"EMPATHY TEST"* THE SUPREME EXEC IS RUNNING BY SENDING YOU OUT HERE, BUT *MY* JOB IS TO FIND THAT *GIRL*.
BWEEP
--OOT...
THERE ARE SOME FARMS SPREAD OUT TEN K TO THE SOUTH. YOU'RE WELCOME TO COME *WITH* ME--
--JUST DON'T GET *IN FRONT OF* ME.
MAY I SPEAK?
YOU JUST DID.
WE'VE MADE GREAT ADVANCES SINCE THE MODELS YOU FOUGHT IN 2071...
WHATEVER. LEMME KNOW WHEN YOU'VE LEARNED HOW TO *SACRIFICE YOURSELVES* AGAINST PROGRAMMING AND I'LL PRETEND TO BELIEVE YOU...

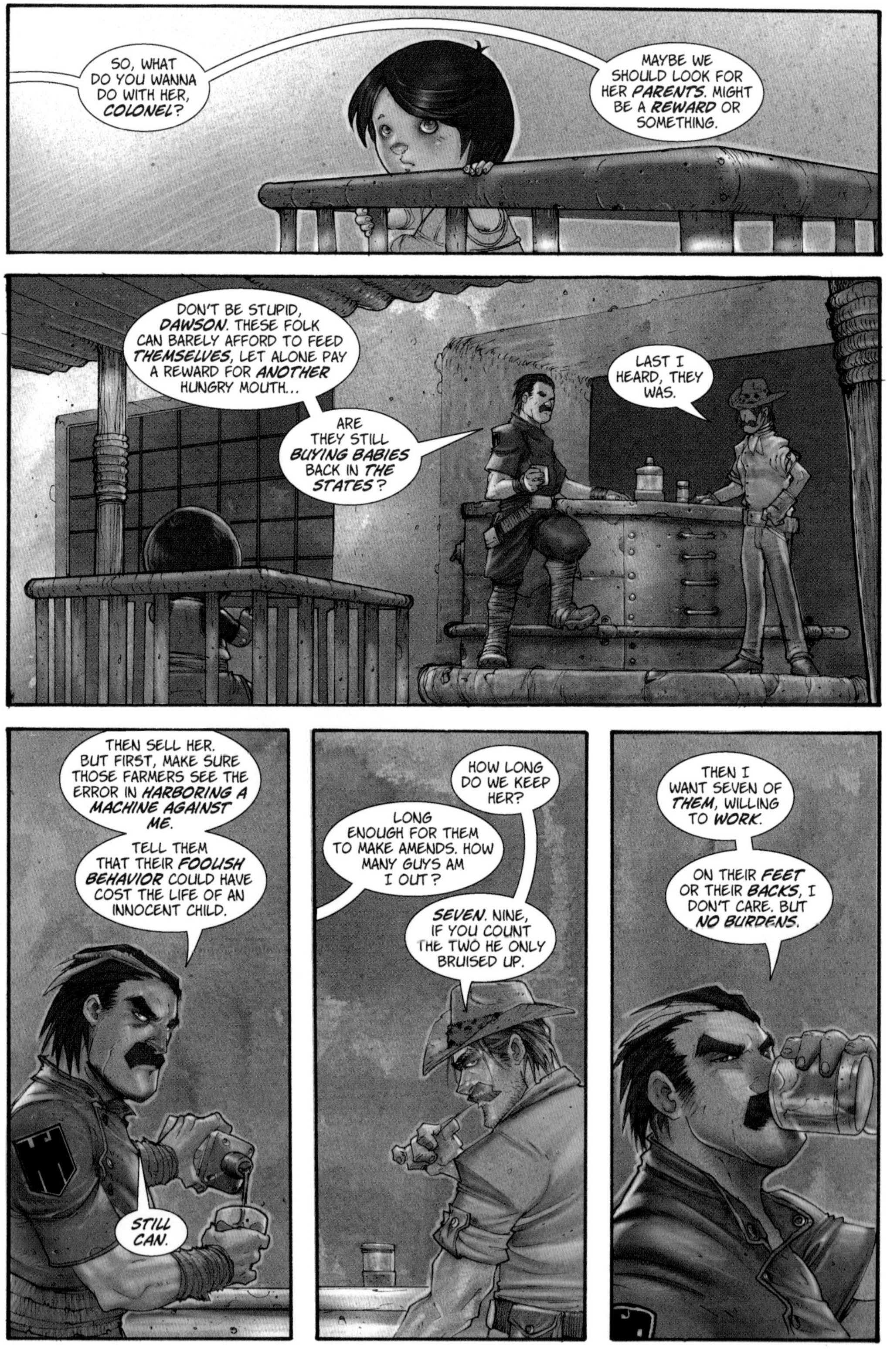
SO, WHAT DO YOU WANNA DO WITH HER, COLONEL?
MAYBE WE SHOULD LOOK FOR HER PARENTS. MIGHT BE A REWARD OR SOMETHING.
DON'T BE STUPID, DAWSON. THESE FOLK CAN BARELY AFFORD TO FEED THEMSELVES, LET ALONE PAY A REWARD FOR ANOTHER HUNGRY MOUTH...
ARE THEY STILL BUYING BABIES BACK IN THE STATES?
LAST I HEARD, THEY WAS.
THEN SELL HER. BUT FIRST, MAKE SURE THOSE FARMERS SEE THE ERROR IN HARBORING A MACHINE AGAINST ME.
TELL THEM THAT THEIR FOOLISH BEHAVIOR COULD HAVE COST THE LIFE OF AN INNOCENT CHILD.
STILL CAN.
HOW LONG DO WE KEEP HER?
LONG ENOUGH FOR THEM TO MAKE AMENDS. HOW MANY GUYS AM I OUT?
SEVEN. NINE, IF YOU COUNT THE TWO HE ONLY BRUISED UP.
THEN I WANT SEVEN OF THEM, WILLING TO WORK.
ON THEIR FEET OR THEIR BACKS, I DON'T CARE. BUT NO BURDENS.

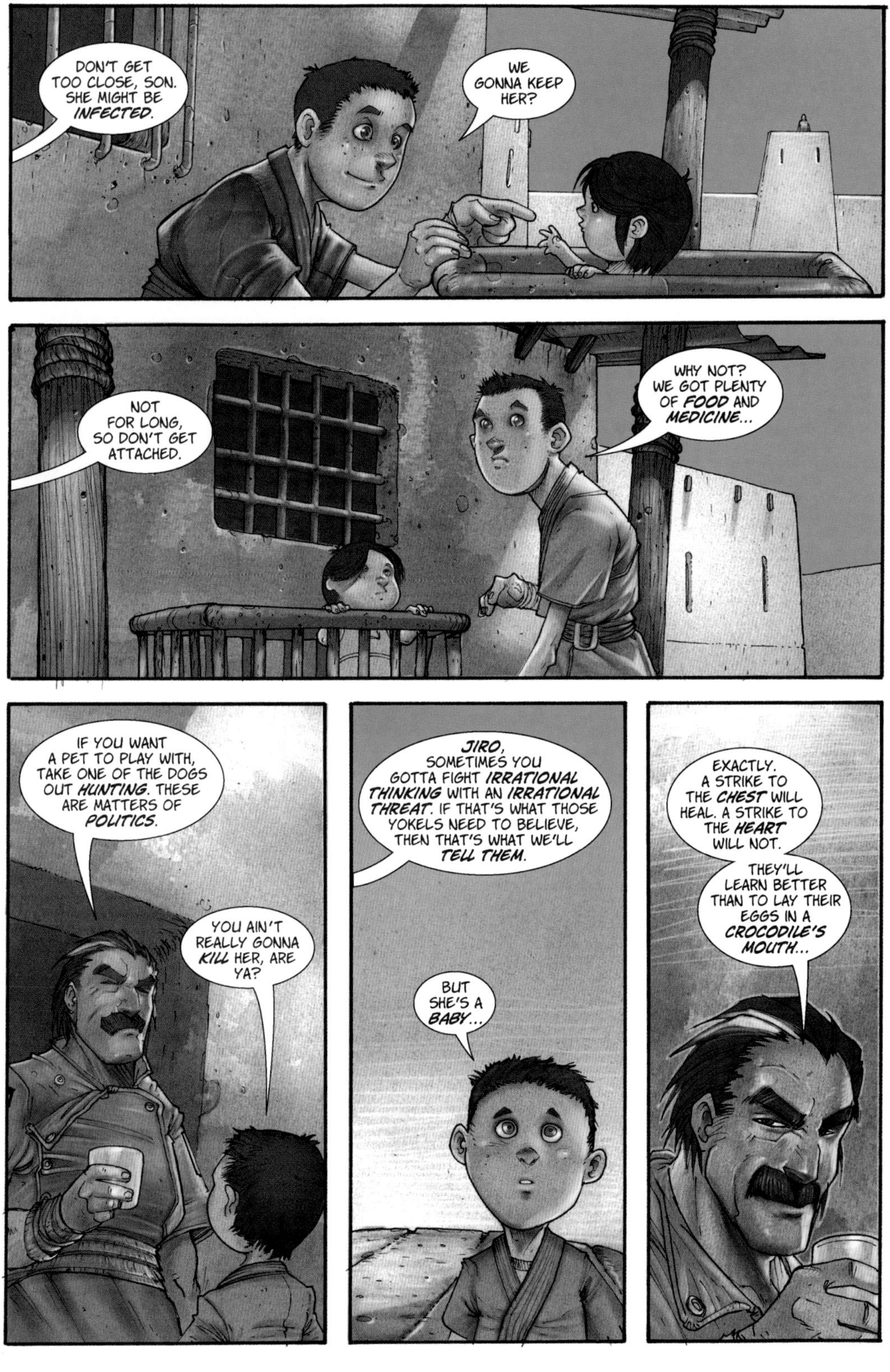
DON'T GET TOO CLOSE, SON. SHE MIGHT BE INFECTED.
WE GONNA KEEP HER?
NOT FOR LONG, SO DON'T GET ATTACHED.
WHY NOT? WE GOT PLENTY OF FOOD AND MEDICINE...
IF YOU WANT A PET TO PLAY WITH, TAKE ONE OF THE DOGS OUT HUNTING. THESE ARE MATTERS OF POLITICS.
YOU AIN'T REALLY GONNA KILL HER, ARE YA?
JIRO, SOMETIMES YOU GOTTA FIGHT IRRATIONAL THINKING WITH AN IRRATIONAL THREAT. IF THAT'S WHAT THOSE YOKELS NEED TO BELIEVE, THEN THAT'S WHAT WE'LL TELL THEM.
BUT SHE'S A BABY...
EXACTLY. A STRIKE TO THE CHEST WILL HEAL. A STRIKE TO THE HEART WILL NOT.
THEY'LL LEARN BETTER THAN TO LAY THEIR EGGS IN A CROCODILE'S MOUTH...

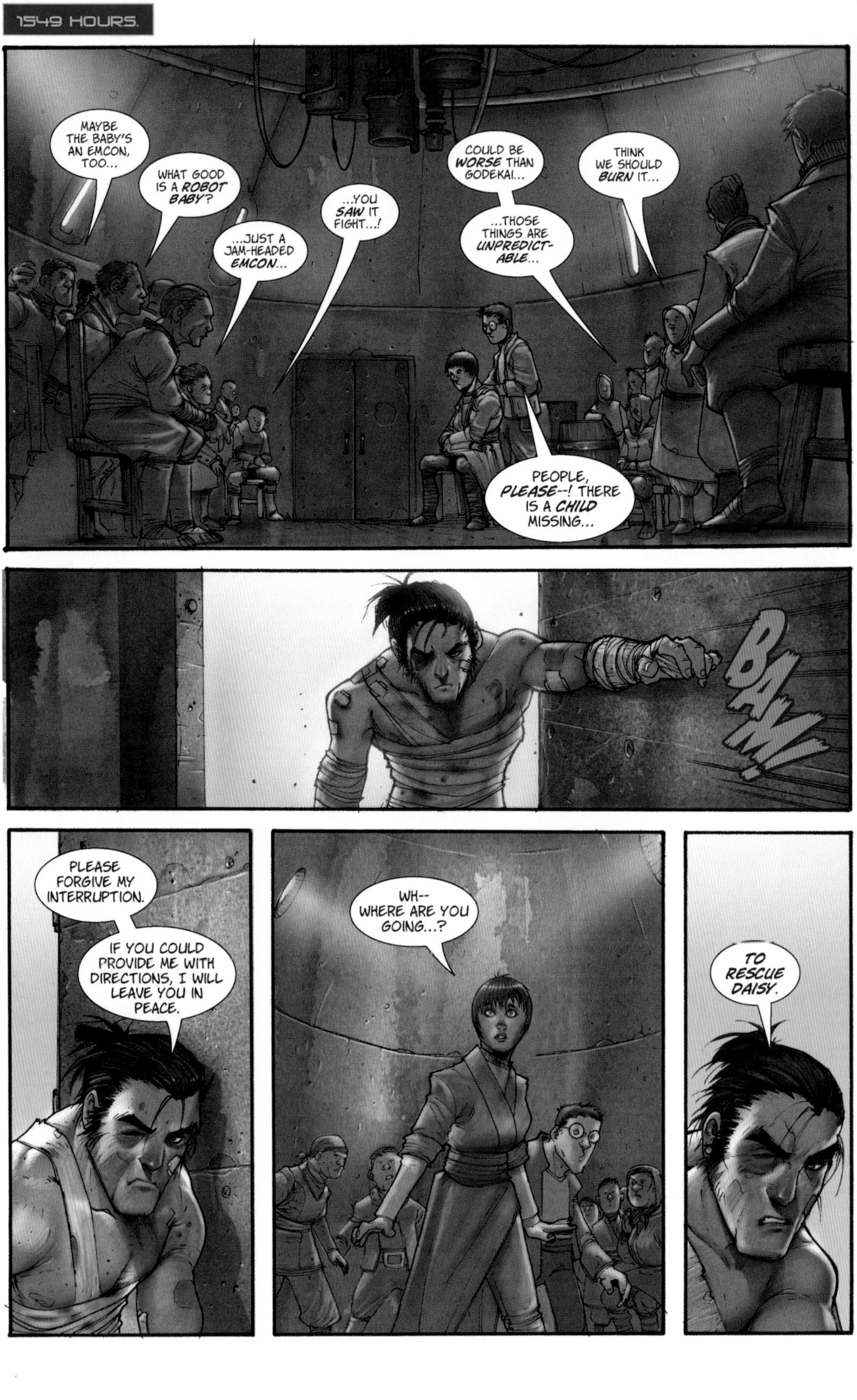
1549 HOURS.
MAYBE THE BABY'S AN EMCON, TOO...
WHAT GOOD IS A ROBOT BABY?
...JUST A JAM-HEADED EMCON...
...YOU SAW IT FIGHT...!
COULD BE WORSE THAN GODEKAI...
...THOSE THINGS ARE UNPREDICT-ABLE...
THINK WE SHOULD BURN IT...
PEOPLE, PLEASE--! THERE IS A CHILD MISSING...
BAM!
PLEASE FORGIVE MY INTERRUPTION.
IF YOU COULD PROVIDE ME WITH DIRECTIONS, I WILL LEAVE YOU IN PEACE.
WH-- WHERE ARE YOU GOING...?
TO RESCUE DAISY.

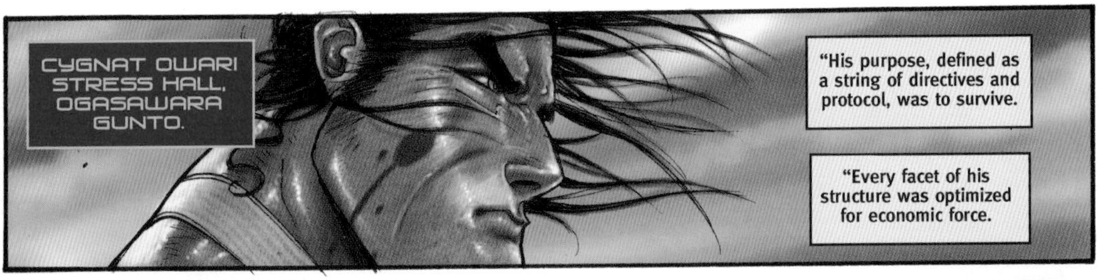
CYGNAT OWARI STRESS HALL, OGASAWARA GUNTO.
"His purpose, defined as a string of directives and protocol, was to survive.
"Every facet of his structure was optimized for economic force.

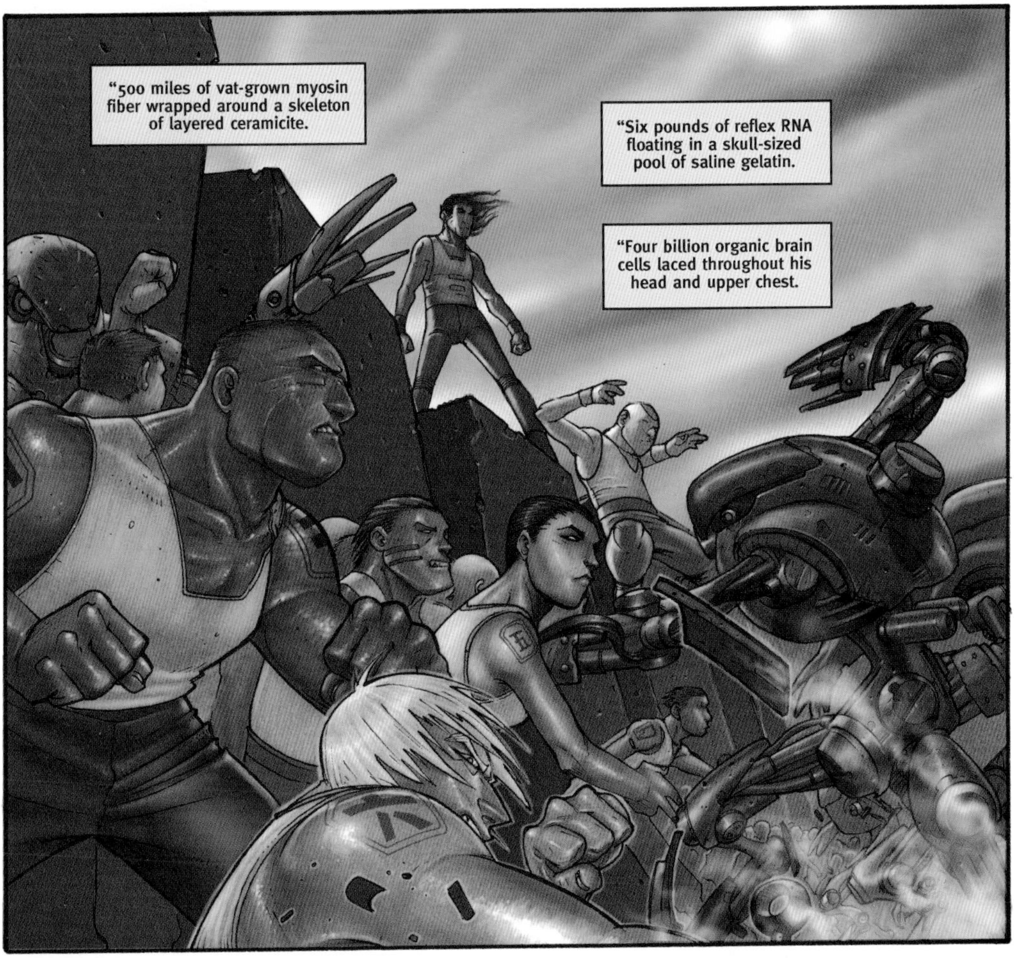
"500 miles of vat-grown myosin fiber wrapped around a skeleton of layered ceramicite.
"Six pounds of reflex RNA floating in a skull-sized pool of saline gelatin.
"Four billion organic brain cells laced throughout his head and upper chest.

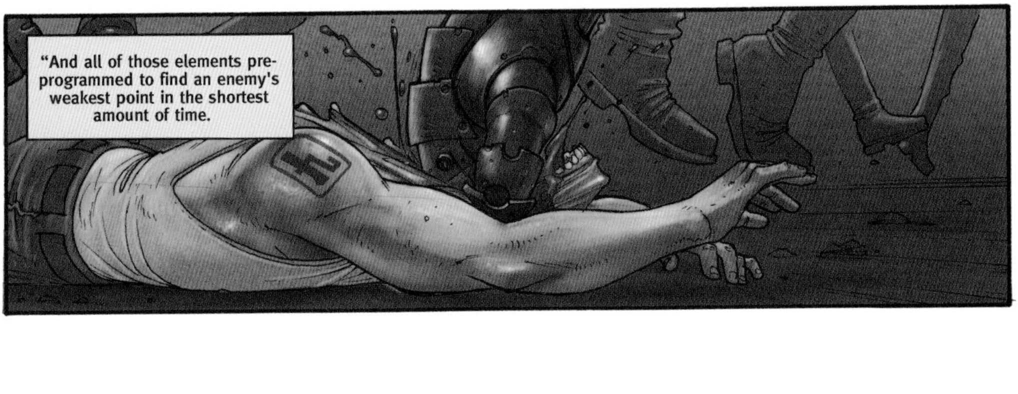
"And all of those elements pre-programmed to find an enemy's weakest point in the shortest amount of time.

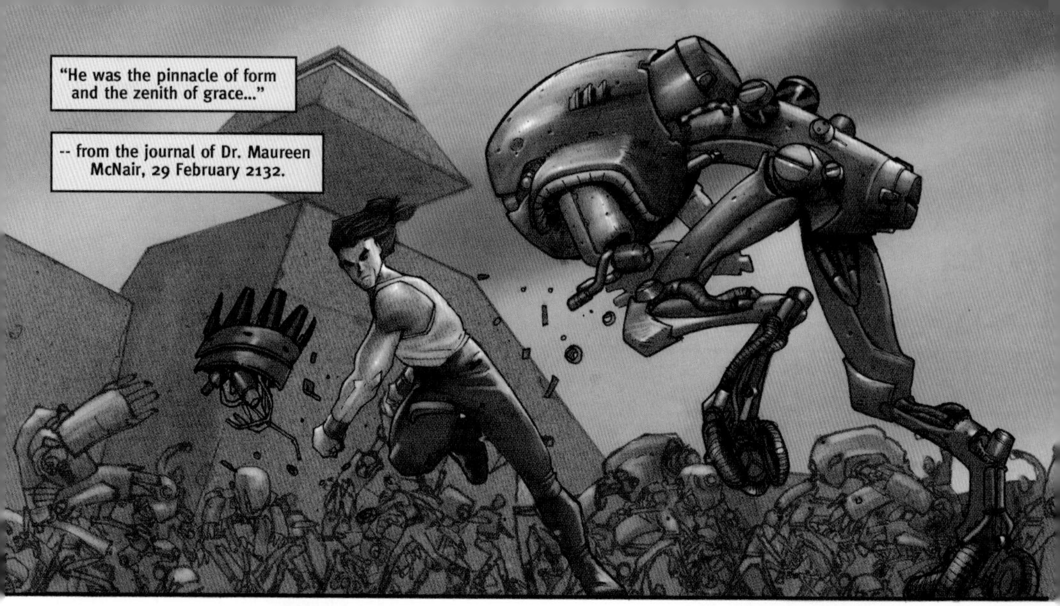
"He was the pinnacle of form and the zenith of grace..."
-- from the journal of Dr. Maureen McNair, 29 February 2132.

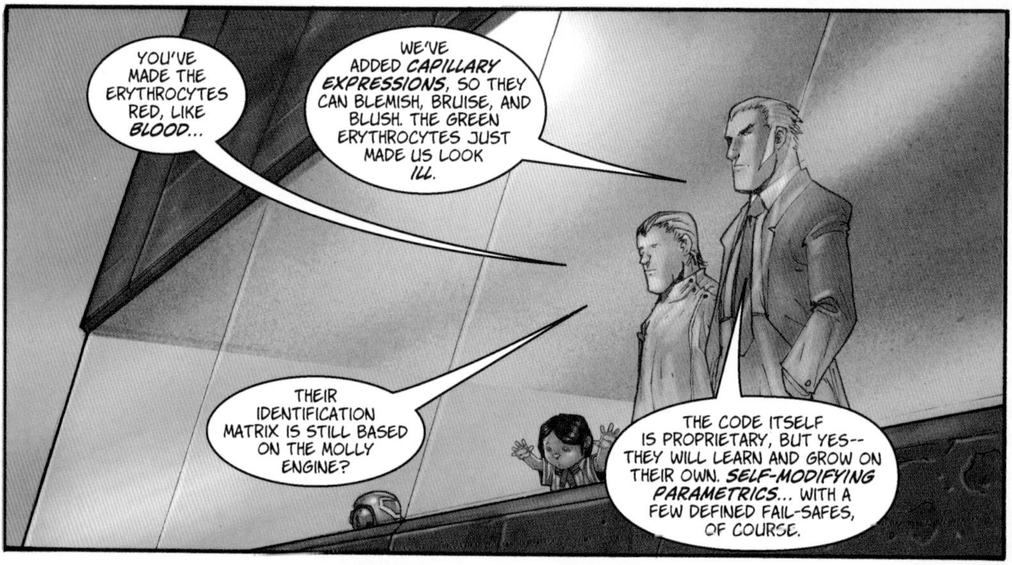
YOU'VE MADE THE ERYTHROCYTES RED, LIKE BLOOD...
WE'VE ADDED CAPILLARY EXPRESSIONS, SO THEY CAN BLEMISH, BRUISE, AND BLUSH. THE GREEN ERYTHROCYTES JUST MADE US LOOK ILL.
THEIR IDENTIFICATION MATRIX IS STILL BASED ON THE MOLLY ENGINE?
THE CODE ITSELF IS PROPRIETARY, BUT YES-- THEY WILL LEARN AND GROW ON THEIR OWN. SELF-MODIFYING PARAMETRICS... WITH A FEW DEFINED FAIL-SAFES, OF COURSE.

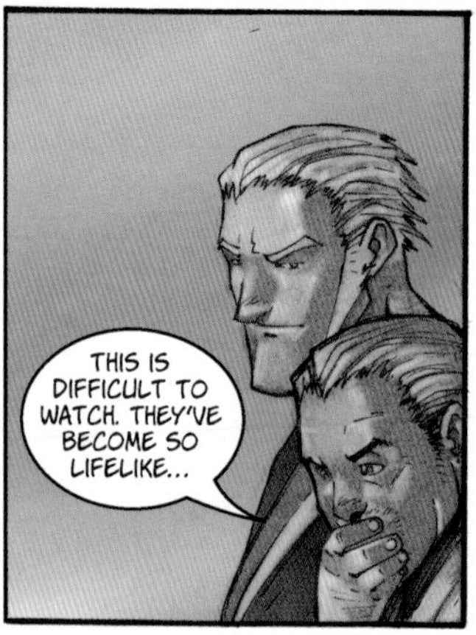
THIS IS DIFFICULT TO WATCH. THEY'VE BECOME SO LIFELIKE...

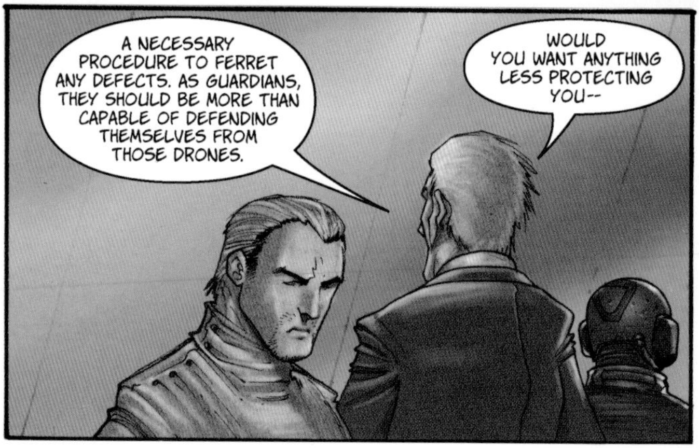
A NECESSARY PROCEDURE TO FERRET ANY DEFECTS. AS GUARDIANS, THEY SHOULD BE MORE THAN CAPABLE OF DEFENDING THEMSELVES FROM THOSE DRONES.
WOULD YOU WANT ANYTHING LESS PROTECTING YOU--

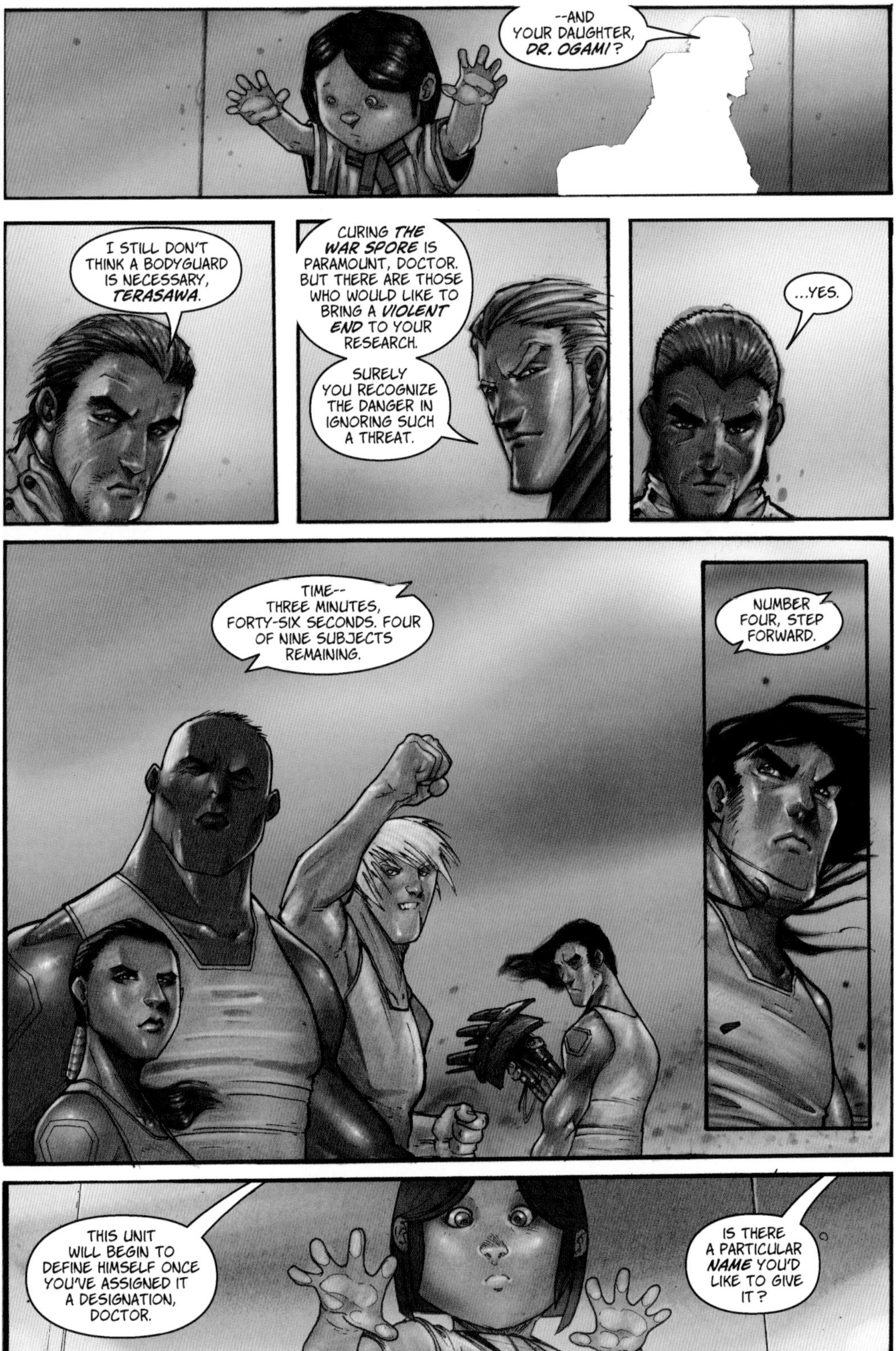
--AND YOUR DAUGHTER, *DR. OGAMI*?
I STILL DON'T THINK A BODYGUARD IS NECESSARY, *TERASAWA*.
CURING *THE WAR SPORE* IS PARAMOUNT, DOCTOR. BUT THERE ARE THOSE WHO WOULD LIKE TO BRING A *VIOLENT END* TO YOUR RESEARCH.
SURELY YOU RECOGNIZE THE DANGER IN IGNORING SUCH A THREAT.
...YES.
TIME-- THREE MINUTES, FORTY-SIX SECONDS. FOUR OF NINE SUBJECTS REMAINING.
NUMBER FOUR, STEP FORWARD.
THIS UNIT WILL BEGIN TO DEFINE HIMSELF ONCE YOU'VE ASSIGNED IT A DESIGNATION, DOCTOR.
IS THERE A PARTICULAR *NAME* YOU'D LIKE TO GIVE IT?

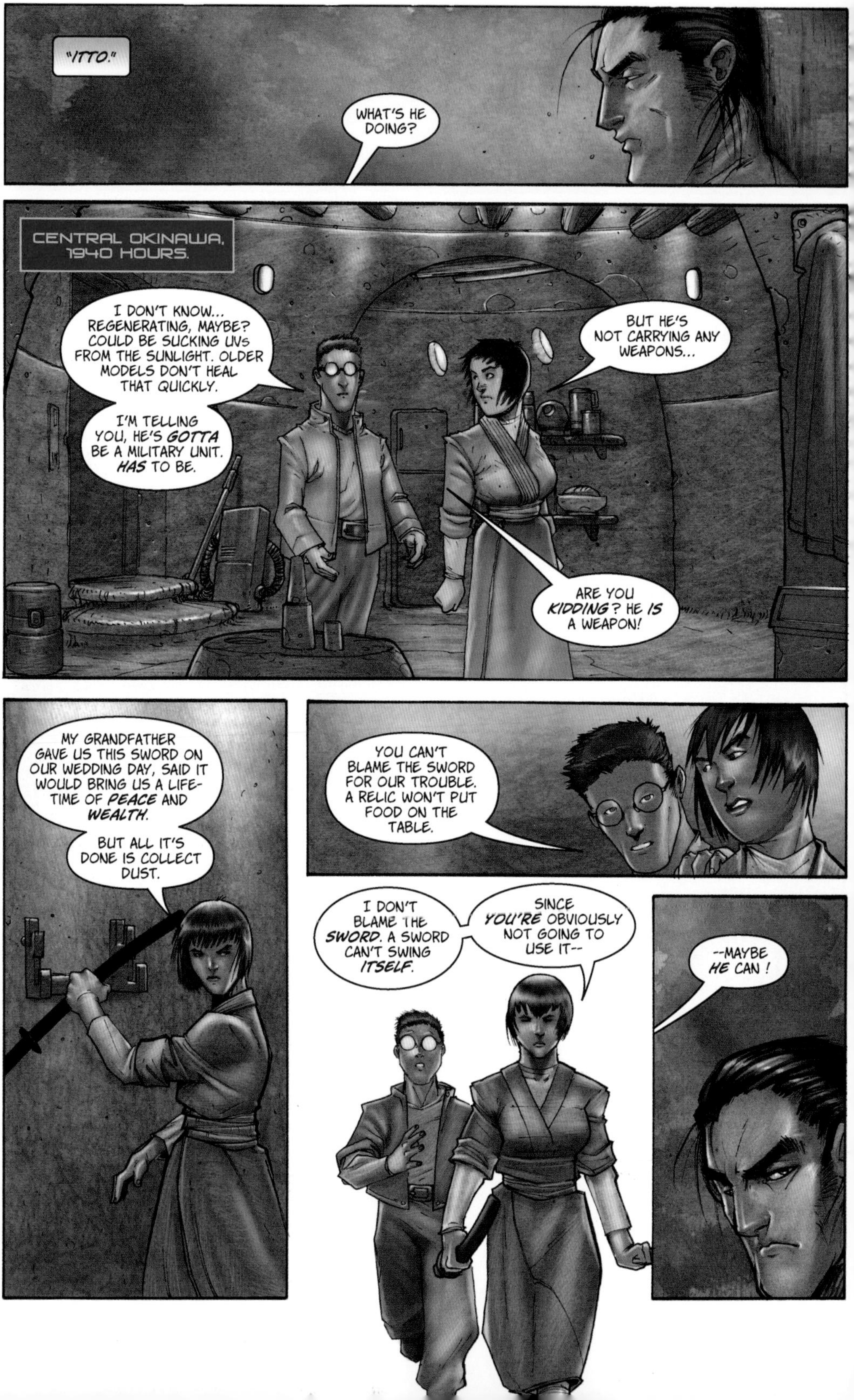
"ITTO."
WHAT'S HE DOING?
CENTRAL OKINAWA, 1940 HOURS.
I DON'T KNOW... REGENERATING, MAYBE? COULD BE SUCKING UVs FROM THE SUNLIGHT. OLDER MODELS DON'T HEAL THAT QUICKLY.
I'M TELLING YOU, HE'S GOTTA BE A MILITARY UNIT. HAS TO BE.
BUT HE'S NOT CARRYING ANY WEAPONS...
ARE YOU KIDDING? HE IS A WEAPON!
MY GRANDFATHER GAVE US THIS SWORD ON OUR WEDDING DAY, SAID IT WOULD BRING US A LIFE-TIME OF PEACE AND WEALTH.
BUT ALL IT'S DONE IS COLLECT DUST.
YOU CAN'T BLAME THE SWORD FOR OUR TROUBLE. A RELIC WON'T PUT FOOD ON THE TABLE.
I DON'T BLAME THE SWORD. A SWORD CAN'T SWING ITSELF.
SINCE YOU'RE OBVIOUSLY NOT GOING TO USE IT--
--MAYBE HE CAN!

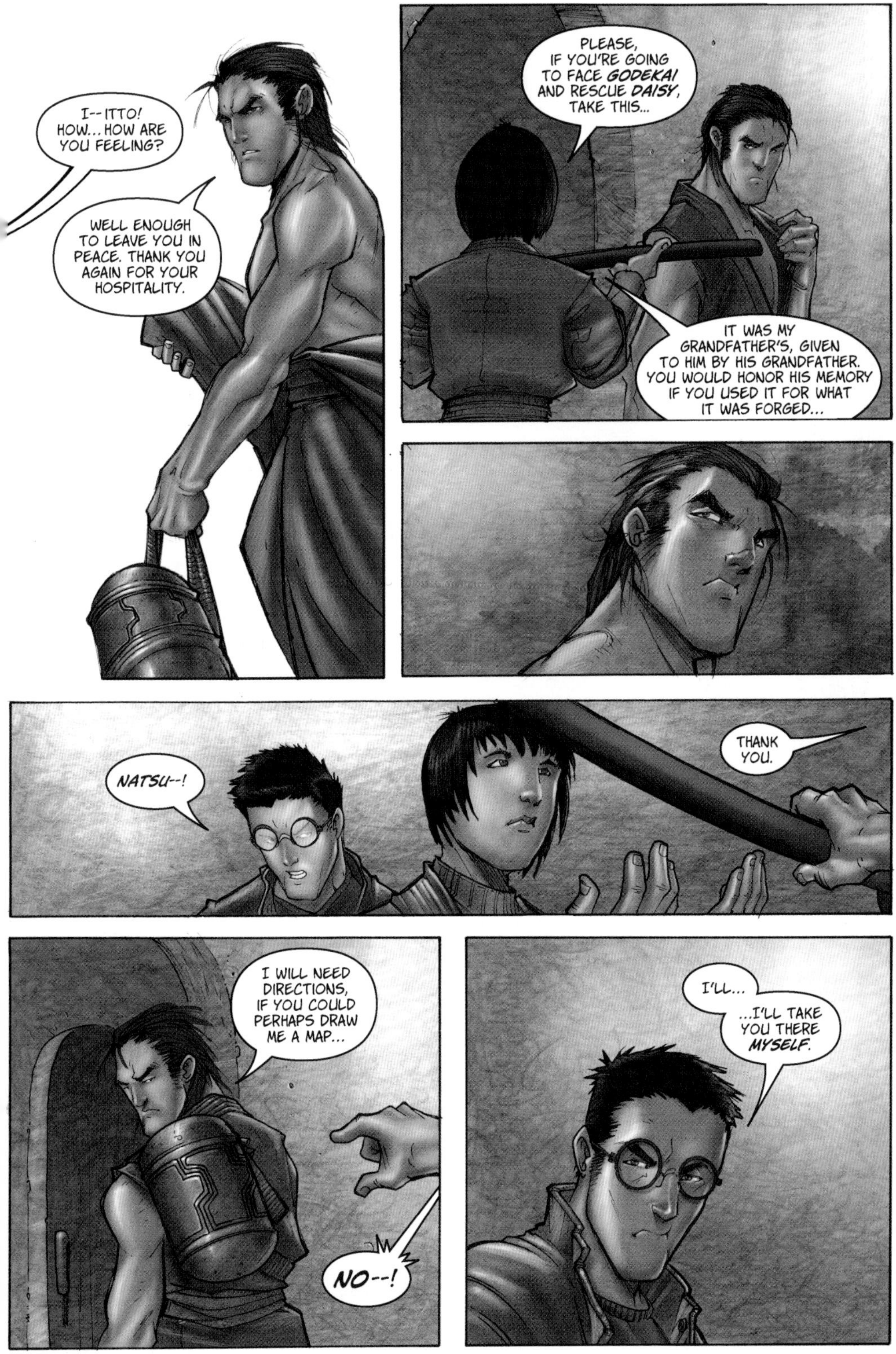
I--ITTO! HOW... HOW ARE YOU FEELING?
WELL ENOUGH TO LEAVE YOU IN PEACE. THANK YOU AGAIN FOR YOUR HOSPITALITY.
PLEASE, IF YOU'RE GOING TO FACE GODEKAI AND RESCUE DAISY, TAKE THIS...
IT WAS MY GRANDFATHER'S, GIVEN TO HIM BY HIS GRANDFATHER. YOU WOULD HONOR HIS MEMORY IF YOU USED IT FOR WHAT IT WAS FORGED...
NATSU--!
THANK YOU.
I WILL NEED DIRECTIONS, IF YOU COULD PERHAPS DRAW ME A MAP...
NO--!
I'LL...
...I'LL TAKE YOU THERE MYSELF.

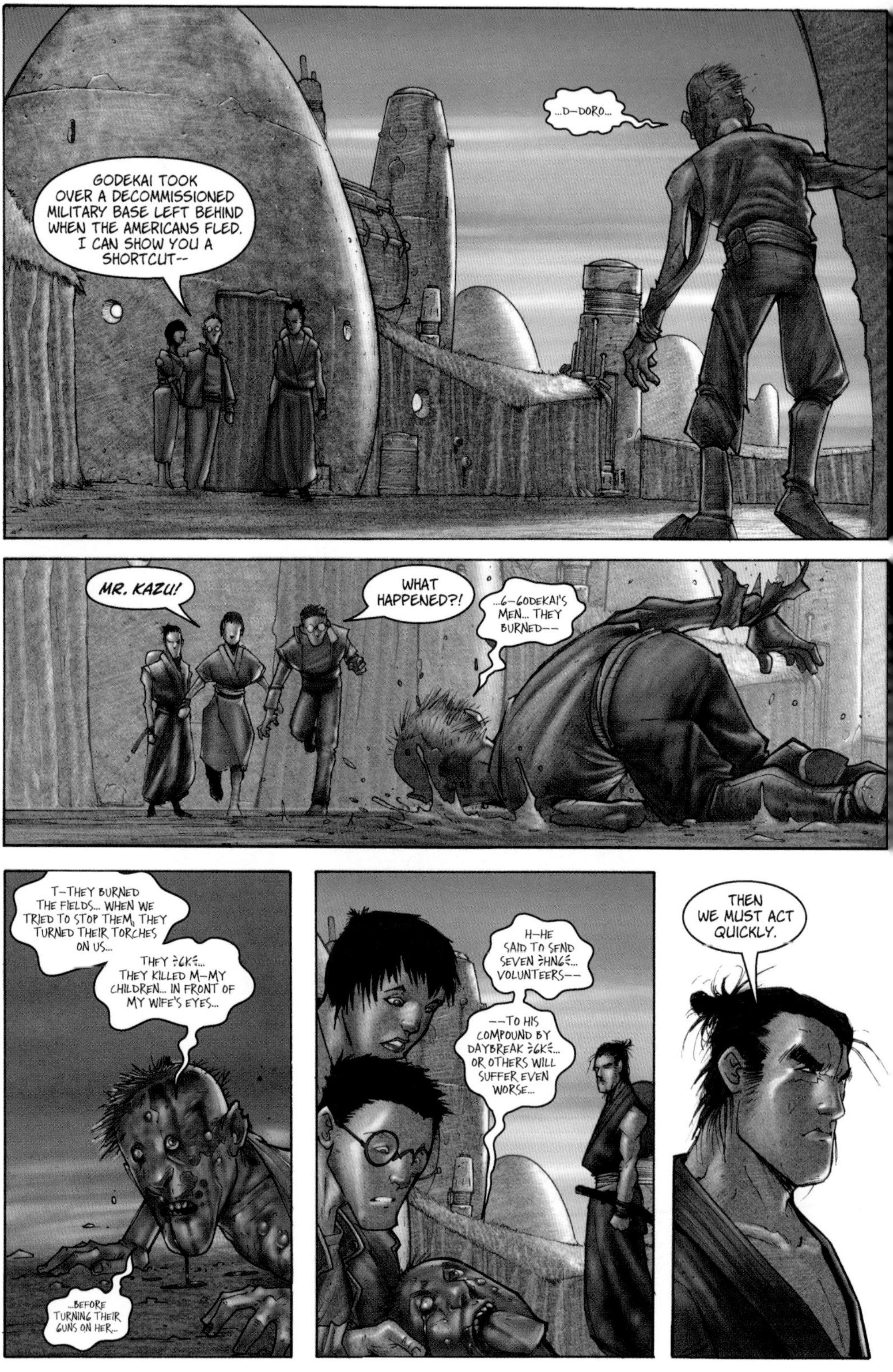
GODEKAI TOOK OVER A DECOMMISSIONED MILITARY BASE LEFT BEHIND WHEN THE AMERICANS FLED. I CAN SHOW YOU A SHORTCUT--
...D-DORO...
MR. KAZU!
WHAT HAPPENED?!
...G-GODEKAI'S MEN... THEY BURNED--
T-THEY BURNED THE FIELDS... WHEN WE TRIED TO STOP THEM, THEY TURNED THEIR TORCHES ON US...
THEY GK... THEY KILLED M-MY CHILDREN... IN FRONT OF MY WIFE'S EYES...
...BEFORE TURNING THEIR GUNS ON HER...
H-HE SAID TO SEND SEVEN HNG... VOLUNTEERS--
--TO HIS COMPOUND BY DAYBREAK GK... OR OTHERS WILL SUFFER EVEN WORSE...
THEN WE MUST ACT QUICKLY.

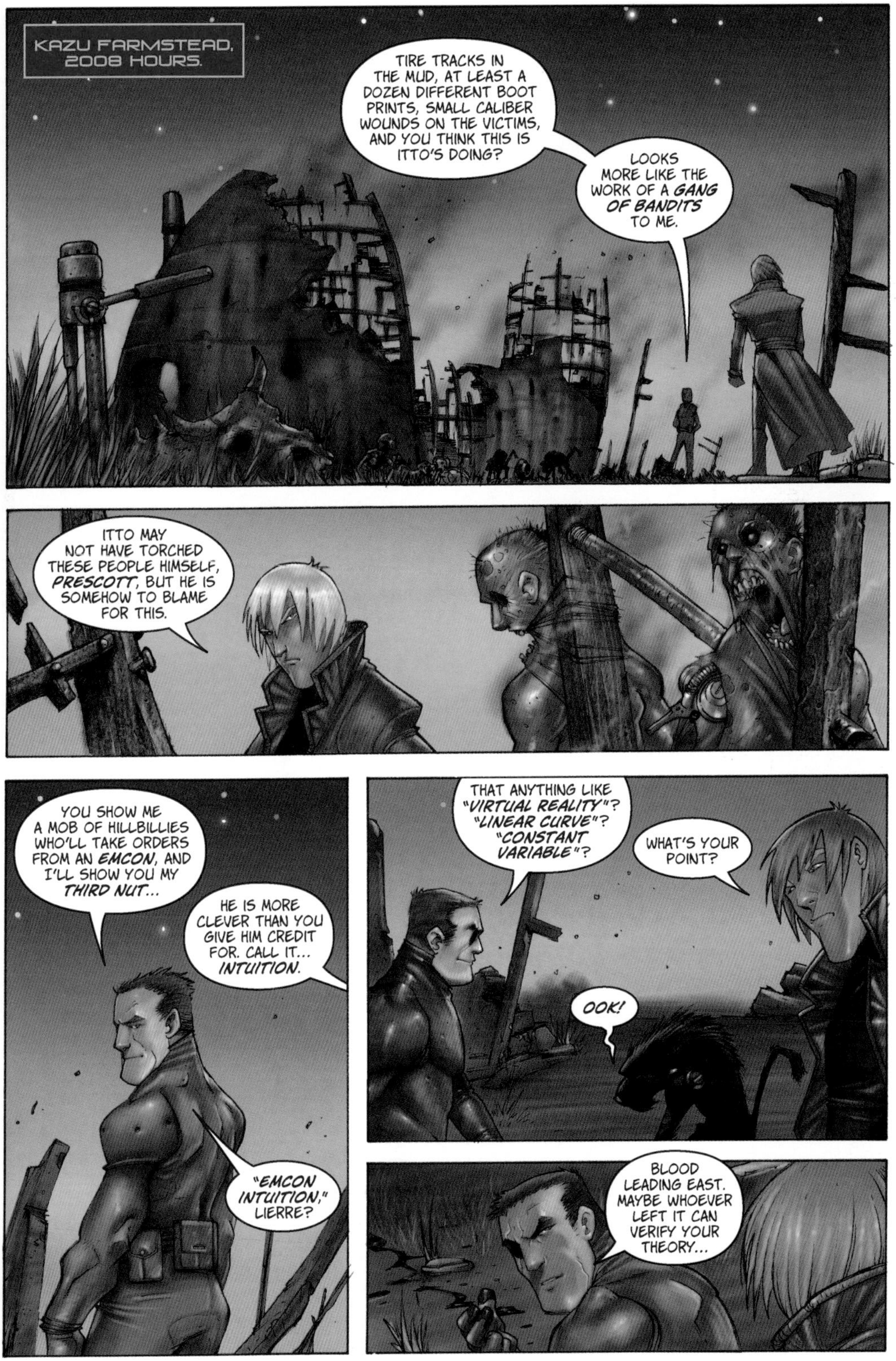
KAZU FARMSTEAD, 2008 HOURS.
TIRE TRACKS IN THE MUD, AT LEAST A DOZEN DIFFERENT BOOT PRINTS, SMALL CALIBER WOUNDS ON THE VICTIMS, AND YOU THINK THIS IS ITTO'S DOING?
LOOKS MORE LIKE THE WORK OF A GANG OF BANDITS TO ME.
ITTO MAY NOT HAVE TORCHED THESE PEOPLE HIMSELF, PRESCOTT, BUT HE IS SOMEHOW TO BLAME FOR THIS.
YOU SHOW ME A MOB OF HILLBILLIES WHO'LL TAKE ORDERS FROM AN EMCON, AND I'LL SHOW YOU MY THIRD NUT...
HE IS MORE CLEVER THAN YOU GIVE HIM CREDIT FOR. CALL IT... INTUITION.
"EMCON INTUITION," LIERRE?
THAT ANYTHING LIKE "VIRTUAL REALITY"? "LINEAR CURVE"? "CONSTANT VARIABLE"?
WHAT'S YOUR POINT?
OOK!
BLOOD LEADING EAST. MAYBE WHOEVER LEFT IT CAN VERIFY YOUR THEORY...

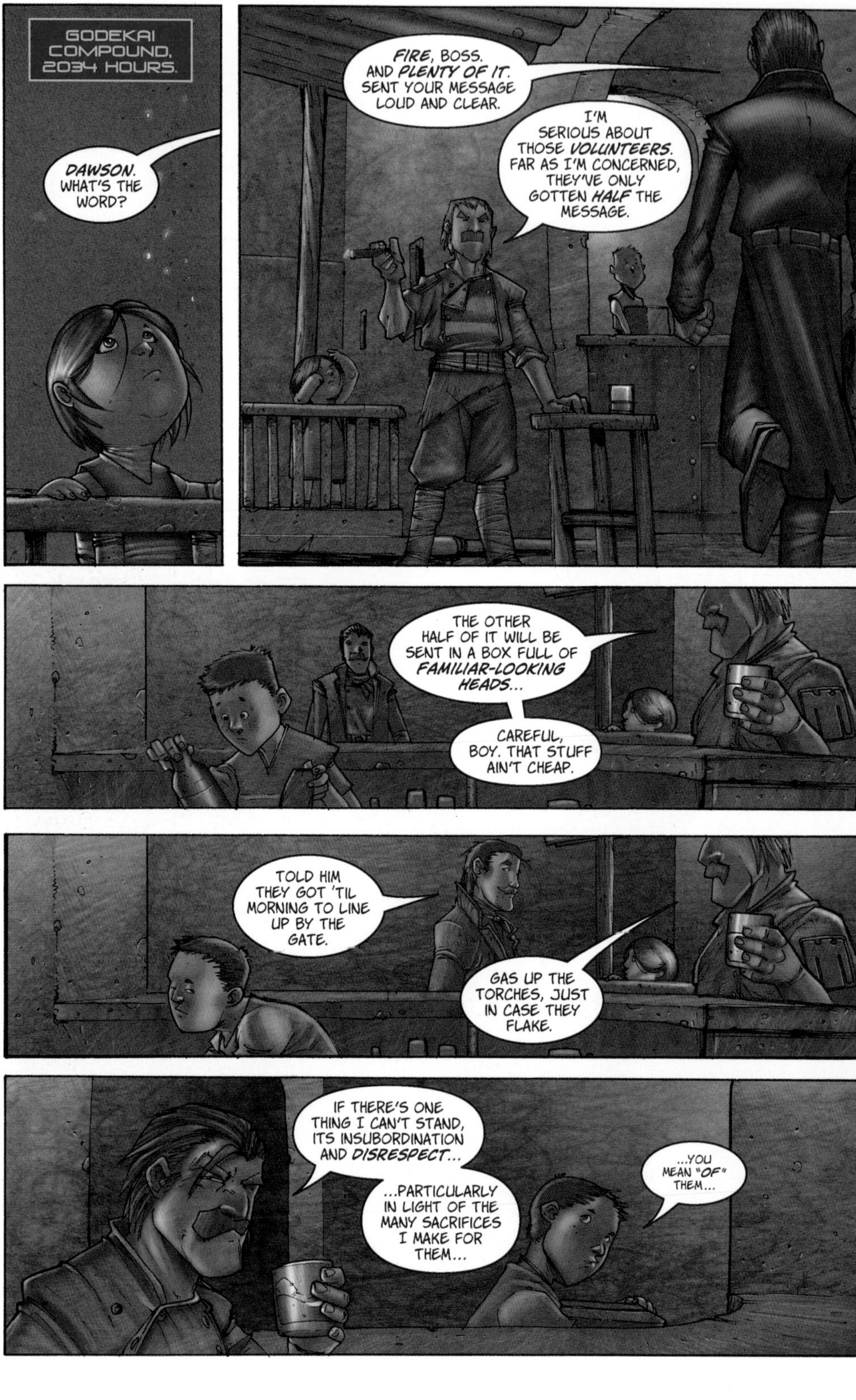
GODEKAI COMPOUND, 2034 HOURS.
DAWSON. WHAT'S THE WORD?
FIRE, BOSS. AND PLENTY OF IT. SENT YOUR MESSAGE LOUD AND CLEAR.
I'M SERIOUS ABOUT THOSE VOLUNTEERS. FAR AS I'M CONCERNED, THEY'VE ONLY GOTTEN HALF THE MESSAGE.
THE OTHER HALF OF IT WILL BE SENT IN A BOX FULL OF FAMILIAR-LOOKING HEADS...
CAREFUL, BOY. THAT STUFF AIN'T CHEAP.
TOLD HIM THEY GOT 'TIL MORNING TO LINE UP BY THE GATE.
GAS UP THE TORCHES, JUST IN CASE THEY FLAKE.
IF THERE'S ONE THING I CAN'T STAND, ITS INSUBORDINATION AND DISRESPECT...
...PARTICULARLY IN LIGHT OF THE MANY SACRIFICES I MAKE FOR THEM...
...YOU MEAN "OF" THEM...

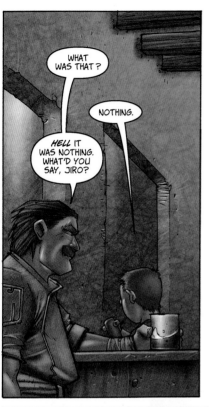

WHAT WAS THAT?

NOTHING.

HELL IT WAS NOTHING. WHAT'D YOU SAY, JIRO?

I JUST THINK YOU MIGHT ATTRACT MORE FLIES WITH HONEY--

AND WASPS AND BEES AND BEARS. WE GOT ENOUGH FLIES AS IT IS!

I'M JUST SAYING--

I KNOW EXACTLY WHAT YER SAYING! I'M TELLING YOU, BOY-- IF YOU DON'T TOUGHEN UP, THAT SOFT HEART IS GONNA GET YOU KILLED! OPEN YOU UP TO THE SPORE, LIKE IT DID YOUR MA!

THE SPORE ISN'T WHAT KILLED HER...

WHAT'D YOU SAY?!?

I GOT SHED DUTY...

I SWEAR TO GOD, DAWSON-- THAT BOY'S GONNA SEE TO IT I LIVE FOREVER.

HOW'S THAT, BOSS?

NO WAY I'M GONNA LET MYSELF DIE WITH SUCH A CREAMY KID FOR AN HEIR...

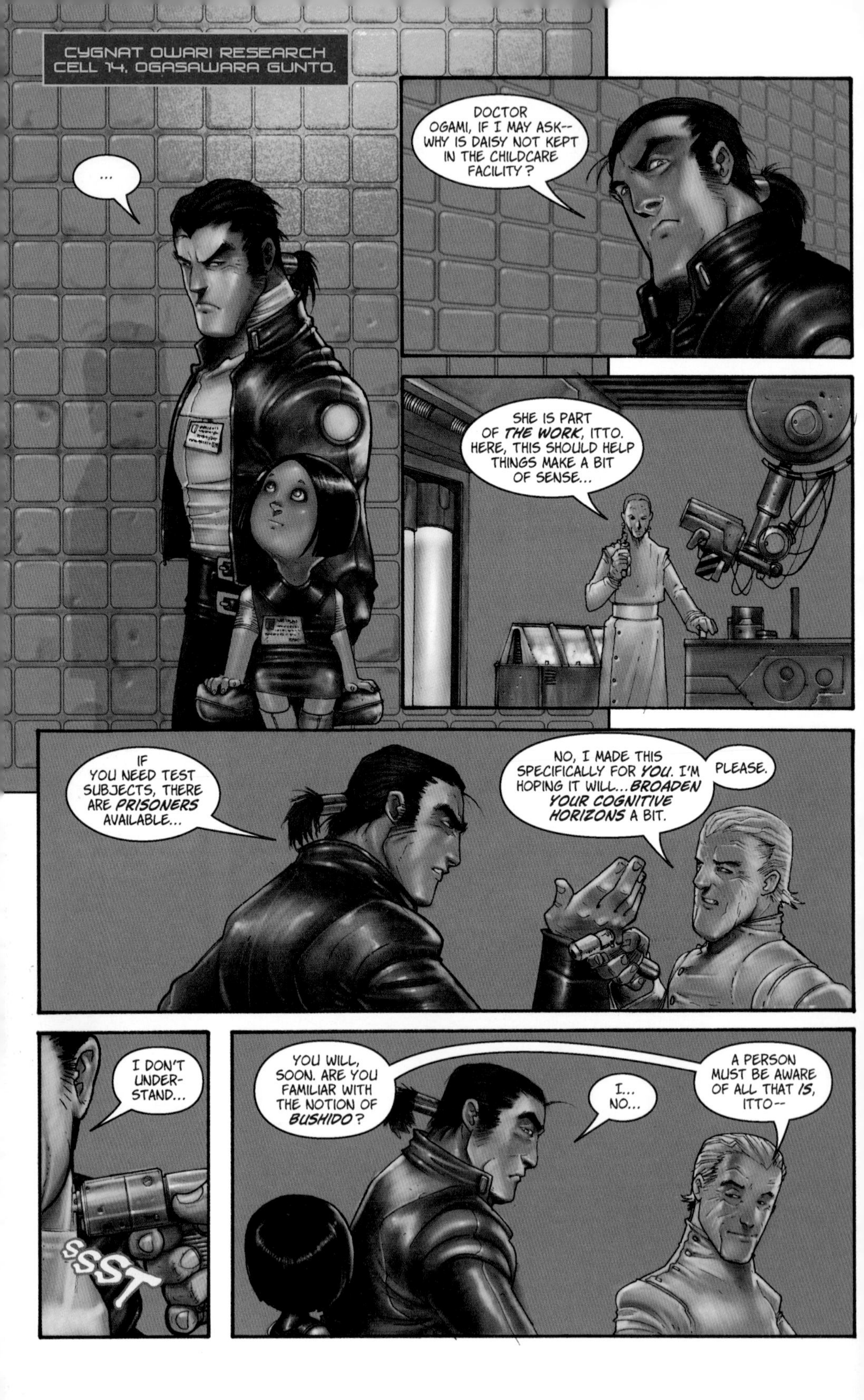
CYGNAT OWARI RESEARCH CELL 14, OGASAWARA GUNTO.
...
DOCTOR OGAMI, IF I MAY ASK-- WHY IS DAISY NOT KEPT IN THE CHILDCARE FACILITY?
SHE IS PART OF *THE WORK*, ITTO. HERE, THIS SHOULD HELP THINGS MAKE A BIT OF SENSE...
IF YOU NEED TEST SUBJECTS, THERE ARE *PRISONERS* AVAILABLE...
NO, I MADE THIS SPECIFICALLY FOR *YOU*. I'M HOPING IT WILL...*BROADEN YOUR COGNITIVE HORIZONS* A BIT.
PLEASE.
I DON'T UNDER-STAND...
SSST
YOU WILL, SOON. ARE YOU FAMILIAR WITH THE NOTION OF *BUSHIDO*?
I... NO...
A PERSON MUST BE AWARE OF ALL THAT *IS*, ITTO--

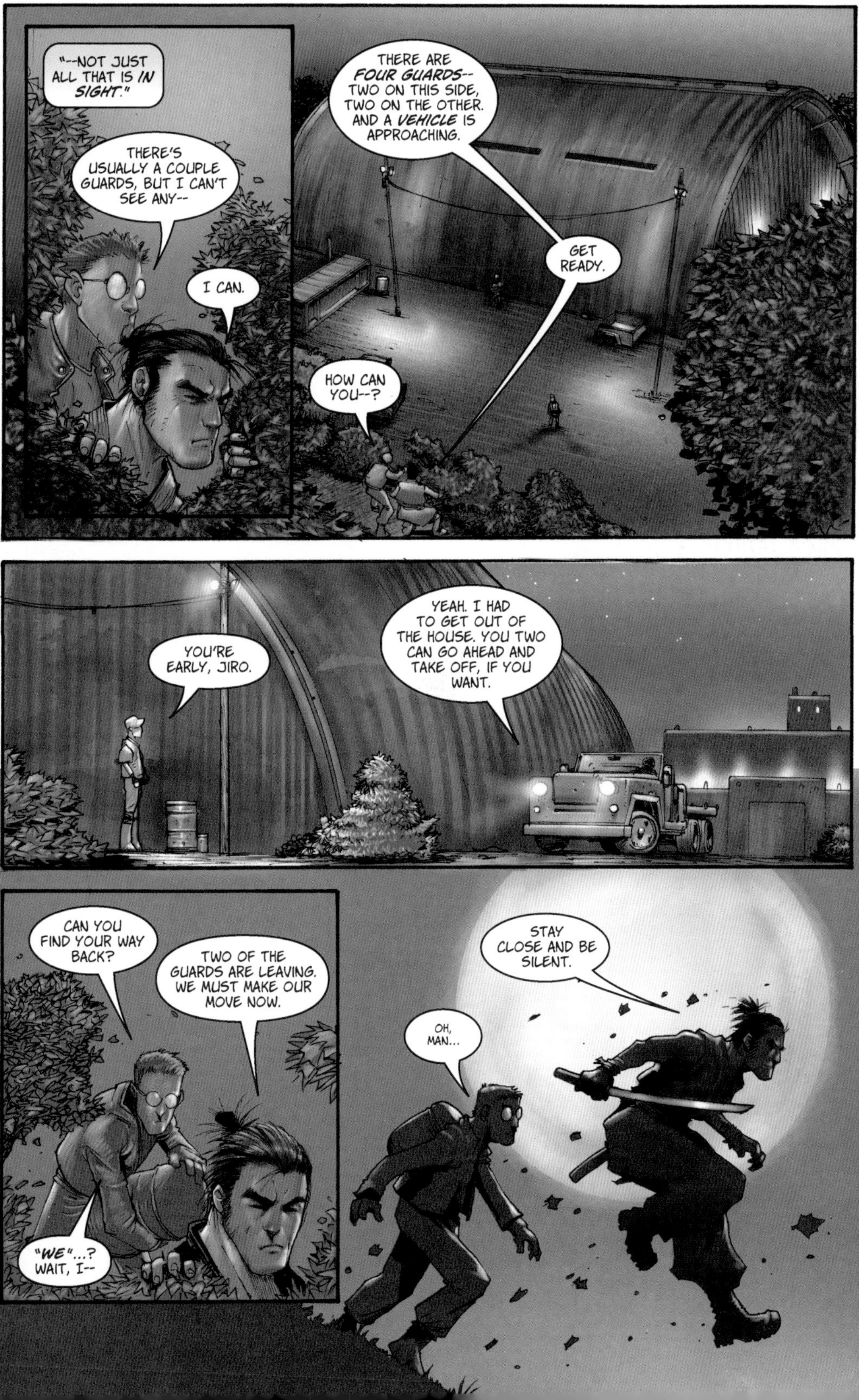
"--NOT JUST ALL THAT IS *IN SIGHT*."
THERE'S USUALLY A COUPLE GUARDS, BUT I CAN'T SEE ANY--
I CAN.
THERE ARE *FOUR GUARDS*-- TWO ON THIS SIDE, TWO ON THE OTHER. AND A *VEHICLE* IS APPROACHING.
HOW CAN YOU--?
GET READY.
YOU'RE EARLY, JIRO.
YEAH. I HAD TO GET OUT OF THE HOUSE. YOU TWO CAN GO AHEAD AND TAKE OFF, IF YOU WANT.
CAN YOU FIND YOUR WAY BACK?
TWO OF THE GUARDS ARE LEAVING. WE MUST MAKE OUR MOVE NOW.
"*WE*"...? WAIT, I--
STAY CLOSE AND BE SILENT.
OH, MAN...

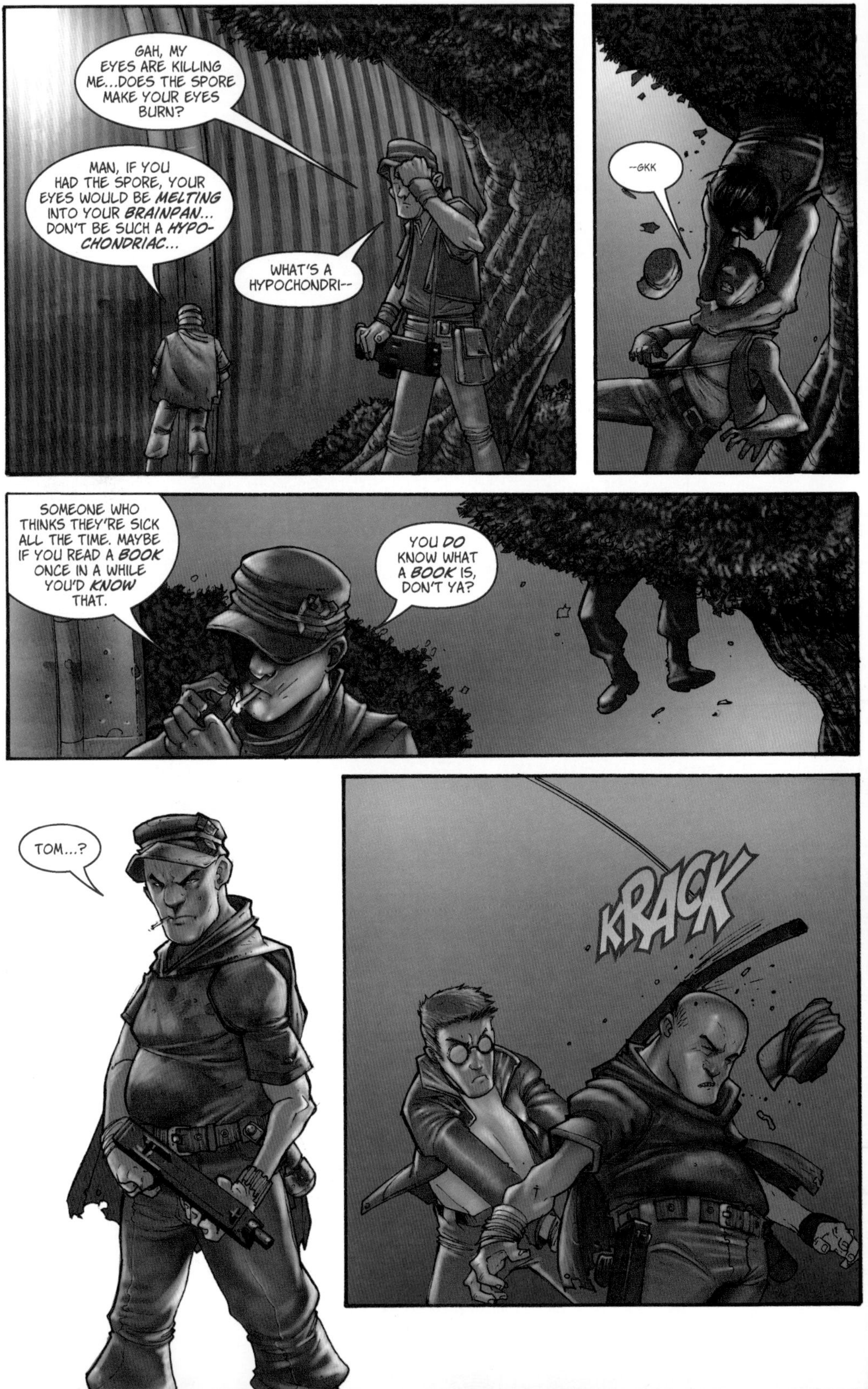
GAH, MY EYES ARE KILLING ME...DOES THE SPORE MAKE YOUR EYES BURN?
MAN, IF YOU HAD THE SPORE, YOUR EYES WOULD BE *MELTING* INTO YOUR *BRAINPAN*... DON'T BE SUCH A *HYPO-CHONDRIAC*...
WHAT'S A HYPOCHONDRI--
--GKK
SOMEONE WHO THINKS THEY'RE SICK ALL THE TIME. MAYBE IF YOU READ A *BOOK* ONCE IN A WHILE YOU'D *KNOW* THAT.
YOU *DO* KNOW WHAT A *BOOK* IS, DON'T YA?
TOM...?
KRACK

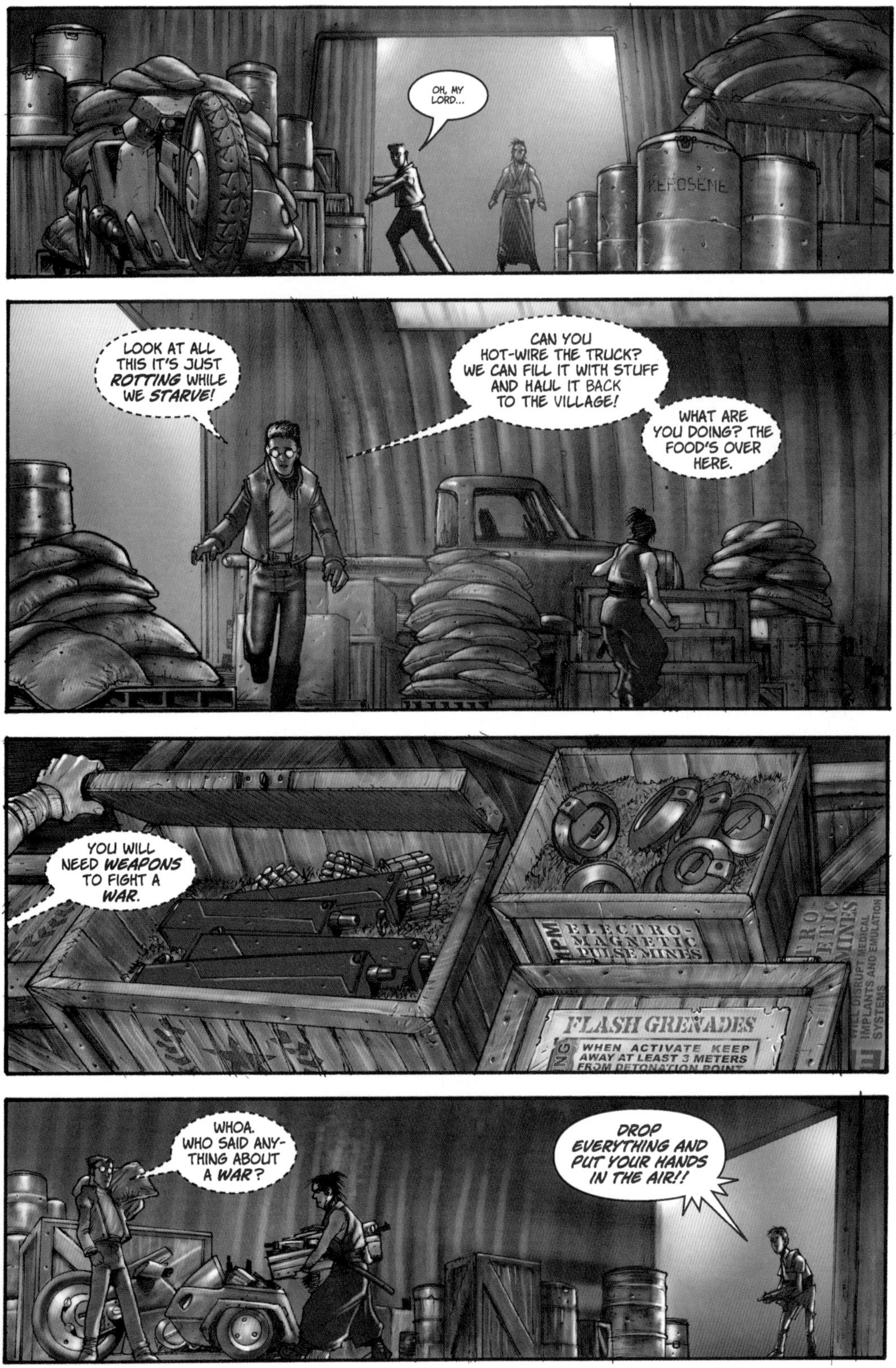
OH, MY LORD...
KEROSENE
LOOK AT ALL THIS IT'S JUST *ROTTING* WHILE WE *STARVE!*
CAN YOU HOT-WIRE THE TRUCK? WE CAN FILL IT WITH STUFF AND HAUL IT BACK TO THE VILLAGE!
WHAT ARE YOU DOING? THE FOOD'S OVER HERE.
YOU WILL NEED *WEAPONS* TO FIGHT A *WAR*.
ELECTRO-MAGNETIC PULSE MINES
FLASH GRENADES
WHEN ACTIVATE KEEP AWAY AT LEAST 3 METERS
WILL DISRUPT MEDICAL IMPLANTS AND EMULATION SYSTEMS
WHOA. WHO SAID ANY-THING ABOUT A *WAR*?
DROP EVERYTHING AND PUT YOUR HANDS IN THE AIR!!

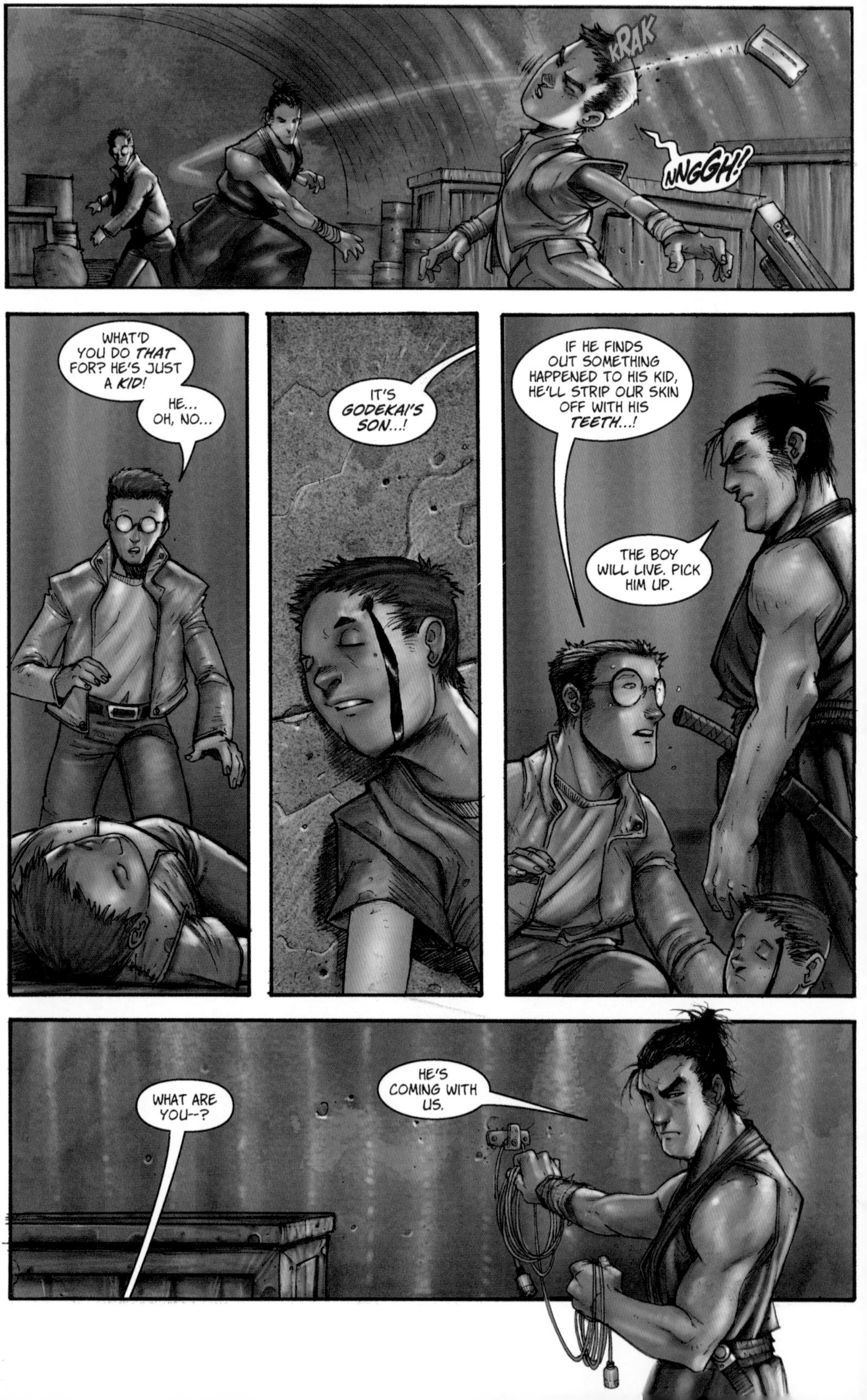
KRAK
NNGGH!
WHAT'D YOU DO THAT FOR? HE'S JUST A KID!
HE... OH, NO...
IT'S GODEKAI'S SON...!
IF HE FINDS OUT SOMETHING HAPPENED TO HIS KID, HE'LL STRIP OUR SKIN OFF WITH HIS TEETH...!
THE BOY WILL LIVE. PICK HIM UP.
WHAT ARE YOU--?
HE'S COMING WITH US.

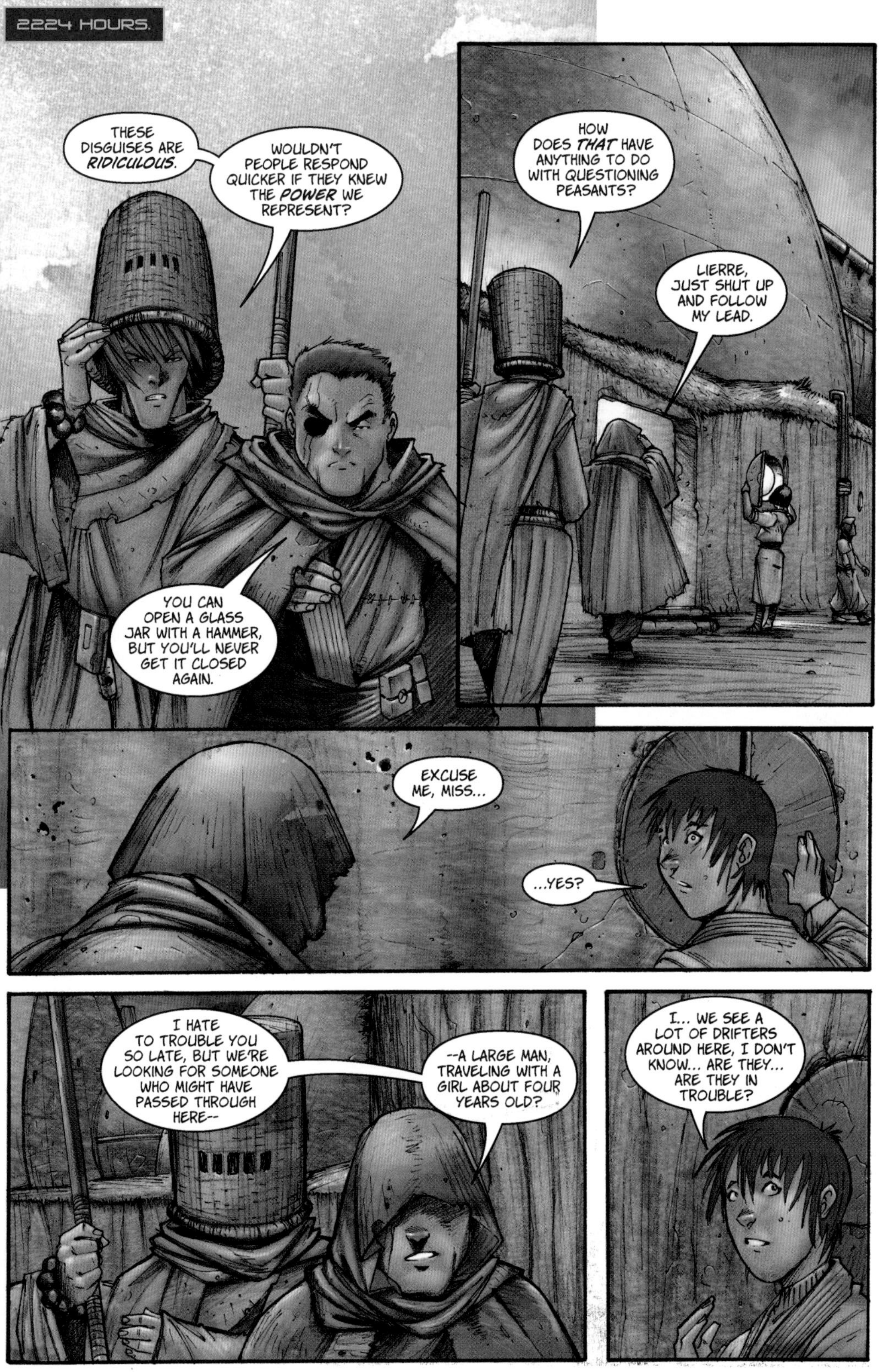
2224 HOURS.
THESE DISGUISES ARE *RIDICULOUS*.
WOULDN'T PEOPLE RESPOND QUICKER IF THEY KNEW THE *POWER* WE REPRESENT?
YOU CAN OPEN A GLASS JAR WITH A HAMMER, BUT YOU'LL NEVER GET IT CLOSED AGAIN.
HOW DOES *THAT* HAVE ANYTHING TO DO WITH QUESTIONING PEASANTS?
LIERRE, JUST SHUT UP AND FOLLOW MY LEAD.
EXCUSE ME, MISS...
...YES?
I HATE TO TROUBLE YOU SO LATE, BUT WE'RE LOOKING FOR SOMEONE WHO MIGHT HAVE PASSED THROUGH HERE--
--A LARGE MAN, TRAVELING WITH A GIRL ABOUT FOUR YEARS OLD?
I... WE SEE A LOT OF DRIFTERS AROUND HERE, I DON'T KNOW... ARE THEY... ARE THEY IN TROUBLE?

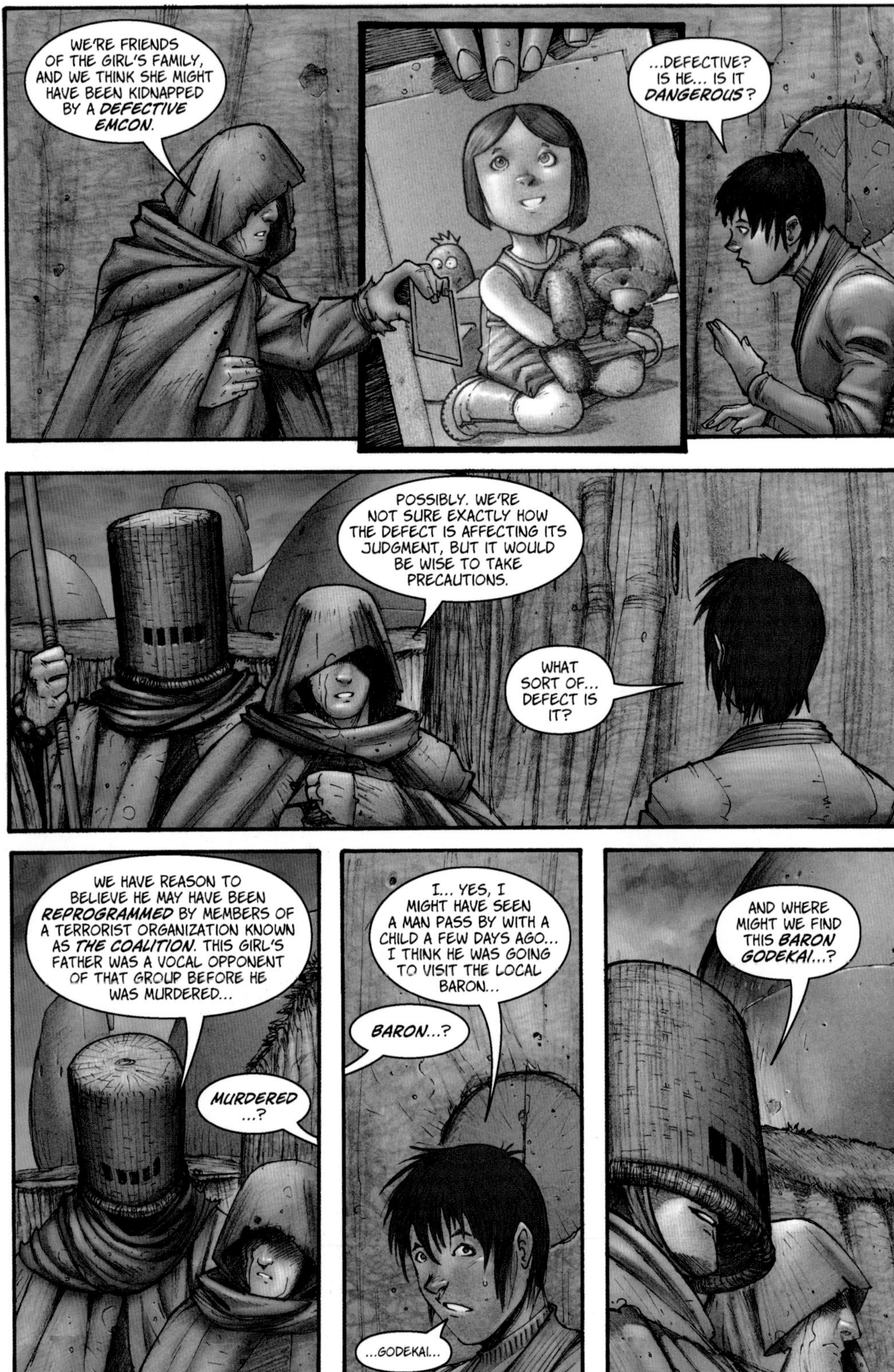
WE'RE FRIENDS OF THE GIRL'S FAMILY, AND WE THINK SHE MIGHT HAVE BEEN KIDNAPPED BY A DEFECTIVE EMCON.
...DEFECTIVE? IS HE... IS IT DANGEROUS?
POSSIBLY. WE'RE NOT SURE EXACTLY HOW THE DEFECT IS AFFECTING ITS JUDGMENT, BUT IT WOULD BE WISE TO TAKE PRECAUTIONS.
WHAT SORT OF... DEFECT IS IT?
WE HAVE REASON TO BELIEVE HE MAY HAVE BEEN REPROGRAMMED BY MEMBERS OF A TERRORIST ORGANIZATION KNOWN AS THE COALITION. THIS GIRL'S FATHER WAS A VOCAL OPPONENT OF THAT GROUP BEFORE HE WAS MURDERED...
MURDERED ...?
I... YES, I MIGHT HAVE SEEN A MAN PASS BY WITH A CHILD A FEW DAYS AGO... I THINK HE WAS GOING TO VISIT THE LOCAL BARON...
BARON...?
...GODEKAI...
AND WHERE MIGHT WE FIND THIS BARON GODEKAI...?

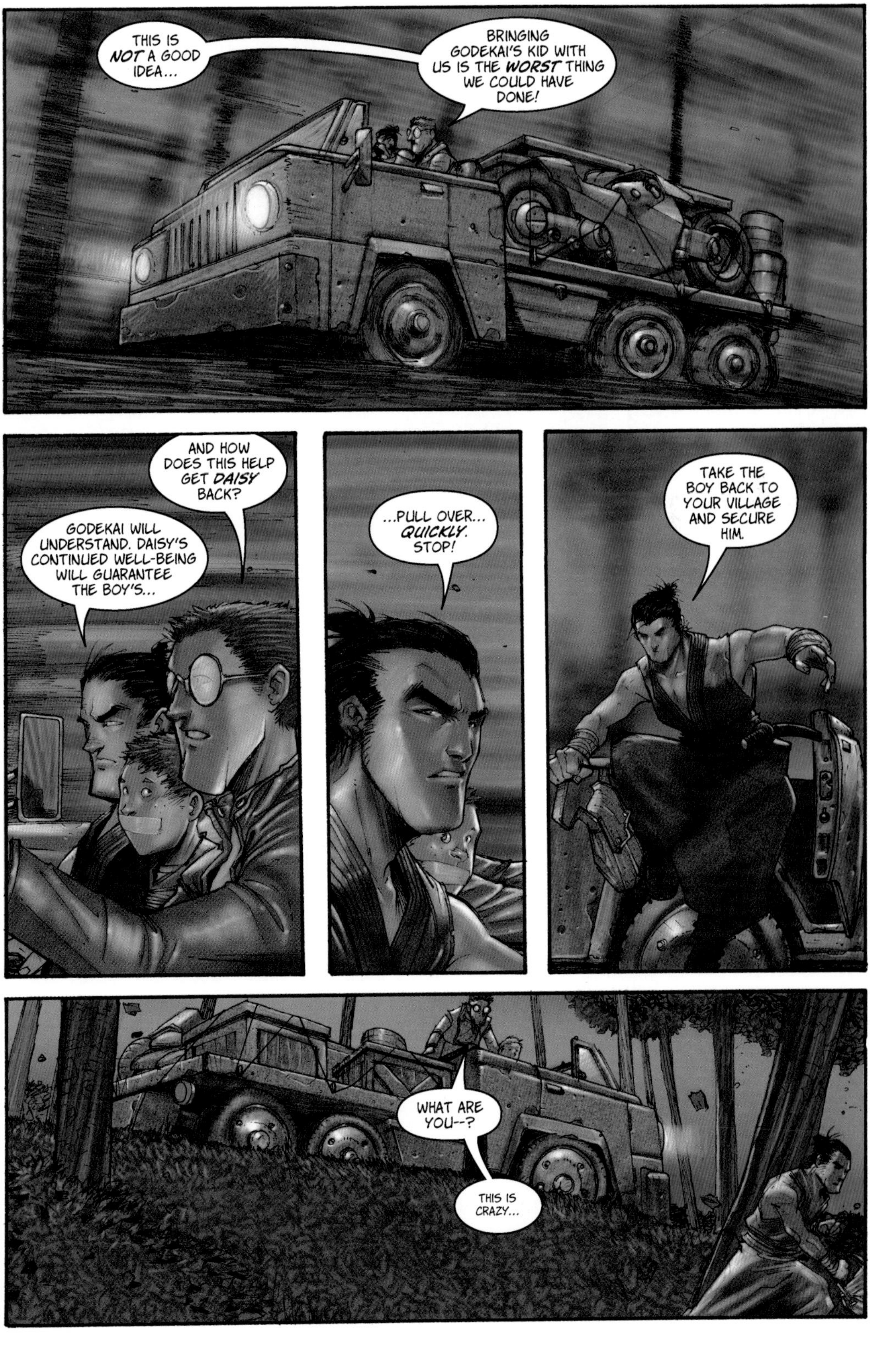

THIS IS NOT A GOOD IDEA...
BRINGING GODEKAI'S KID WITH US IS THE WORST THING WE COULD HAVE DONE!
AND HOW DOES THIS HELP GET DAISY BACK?
GODEKAI WILL UNDERSTAND. DAISY'S CONTINUED WELL-BEING WILL GUARANTEE THE BOY'S...
...PULL OVER... QUICKLY. STOP!
TAKE THE BOY BACK TO YOUR VILLAGE AND SECURE HIM.
WHAT ARE YOU--?
THIS IS CRAZY...

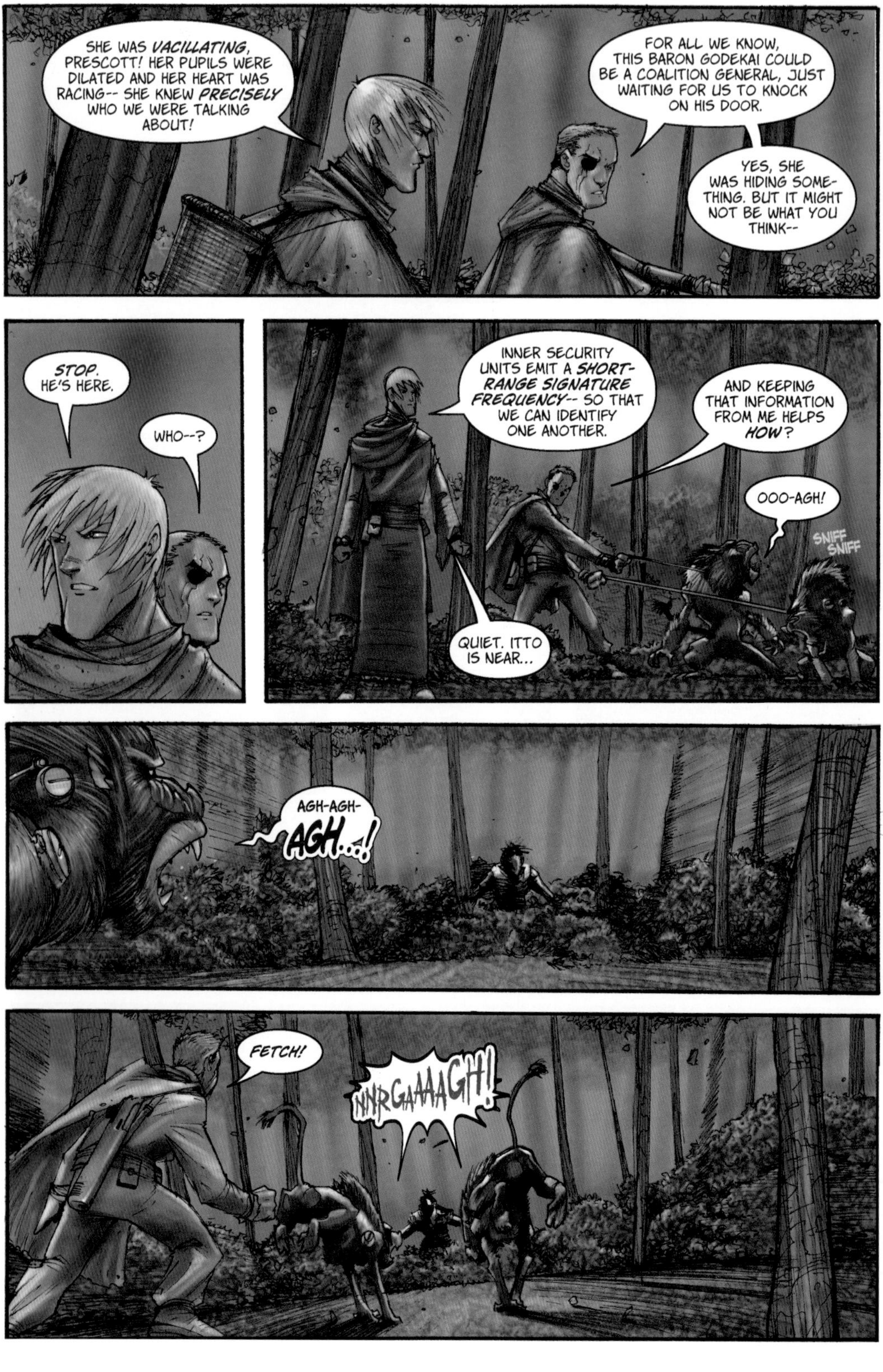
SHE WAS *VACILLATING*, PRESCOTT! HER PUPILS WERE DILATED AND HER HEART WAS RACING-- SHE KNEW *PRECISELY* WHO WE WERE TALKING ABOUT!
FOR ALL WE KNOW, THIS BARON GODEKAI COULD BE A COALITION GENERAL, JUST WAITING FOR US TO KNOCK ON HIS DOOR.
YES, SHE WAS HIDING SOMETHING. BUT IT MIGHT NOT BE WHAT YOU THINK--
STOP. HE'S HERE.
WHO--?
INNER SECURITY UNITS EMIT A *SHORT-RANGE SIGNATURE FREQUENCY*-- SO THAT WE CAN IDENTIFY ONE ANOTHER.
AND KEEPING THAT INFORMATION FROM ME HELPS *HOW*?
OOO-AGH!
SNIFF SNIFF
QUIET. ITTO IS NEAR...
AGH-AGH-AGH...!
FETCH!
NNRGAAAAGH!

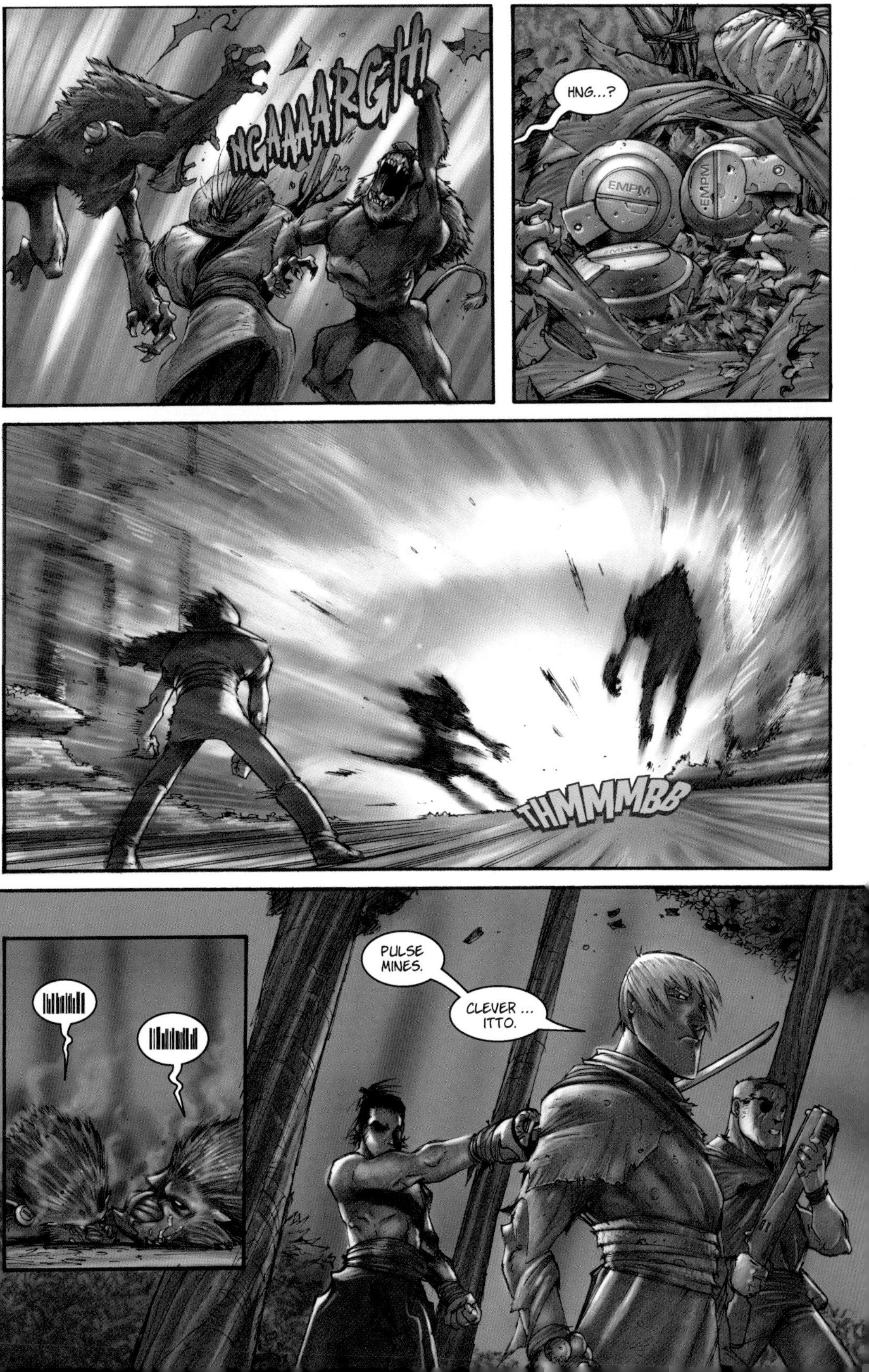
NGAAAARGH!
HNG...?
EMPM
EMPM
THMMMBB
PULSE MINES.
CLEVER ... ITTO.

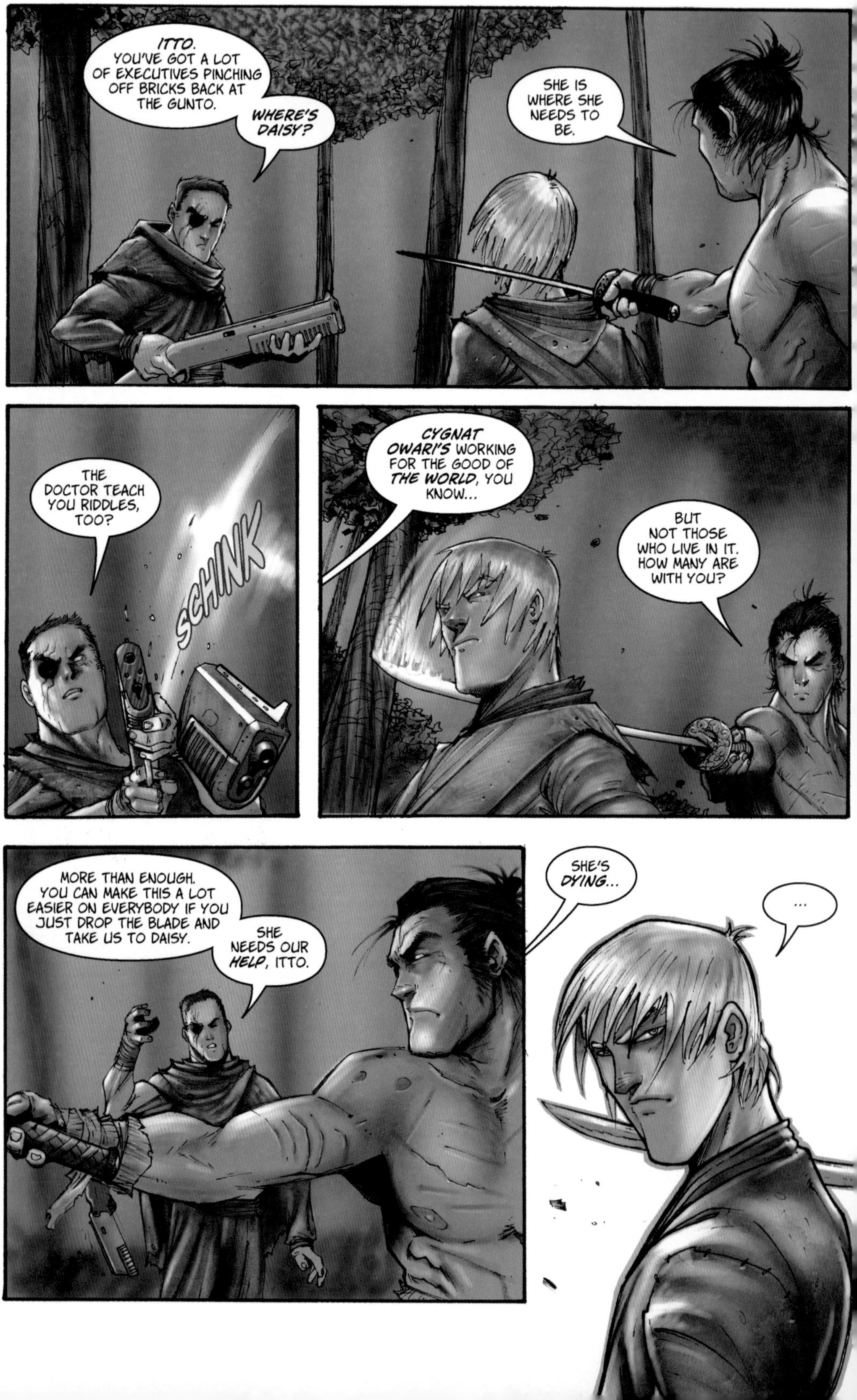
ITTO. YOU'VE GOT A LOT OF EXECUTIVES PINCHING OFF BRICKS BACK AT THE GUNTO.
WHERE'S DAISY?
SHE IS WHERE SHE NEEDS TO BE.
THE DOCTOR TEACH YOU RIDDLES, TOO?
SCHINK
CYGNAT OWARI'S WORKING FOR THE GOOD OF THE WORLD, YOU KNOW...
BUT NOT THOSE WHO LIVE IN IT. HOW MANY ARE WITH YOU?
MORE THAN ENOUGH. YOU CAN MAKE THIS A LOT EASIER ON EVERYBODY IF YOU JUST DROP THE BLADE AND TAKE US TO DAISY.
SHE NEEDS OUR HELP, ITTO.
SHE'S DYING...
...

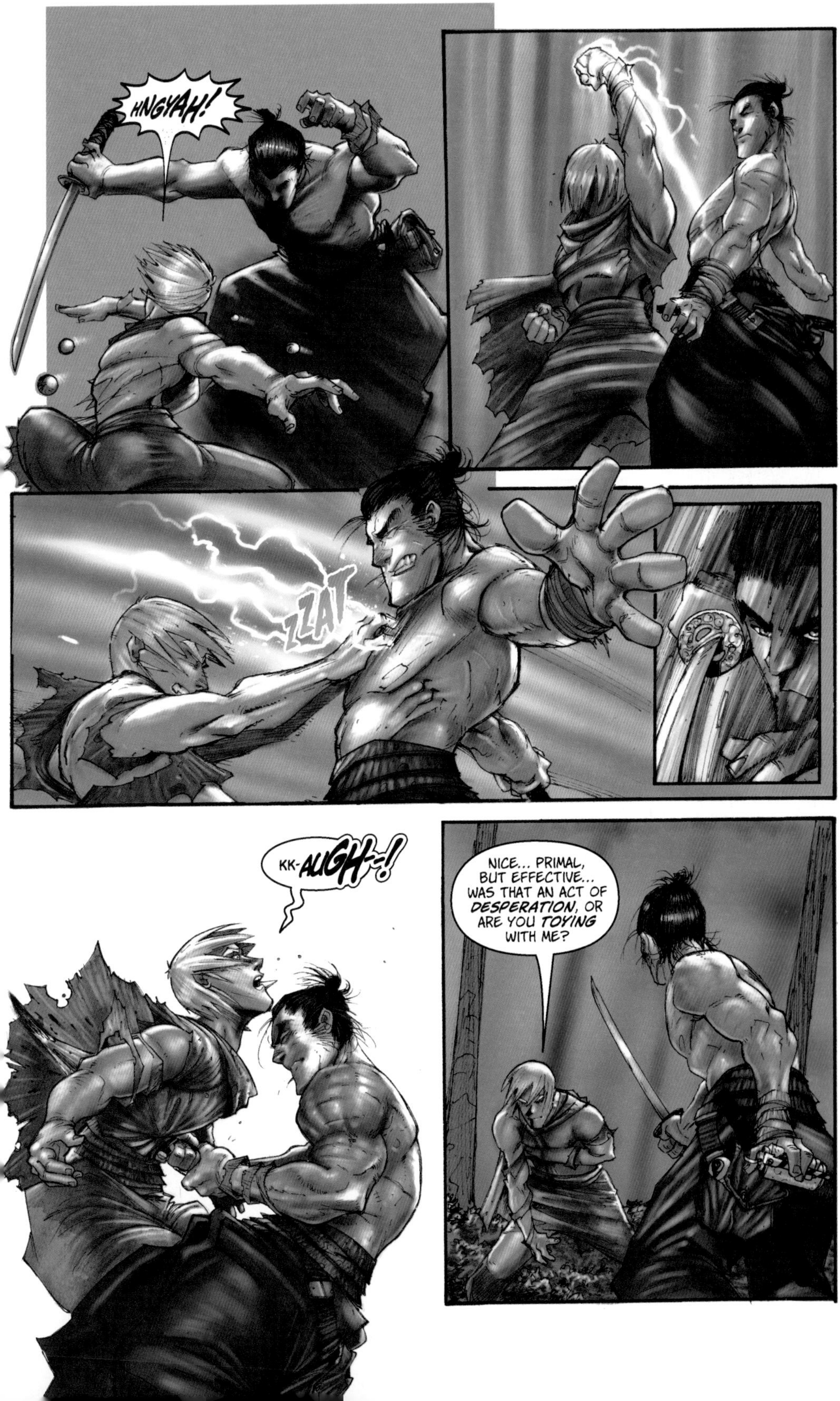
HNGYAH!
ZZAT
KK-AUGH--!
NICE... PRIMAL, BUT EFFECTIVE... WAS THAT AN ACT OF DESPERATION, OR ARE YOU TOYING WITH ME?

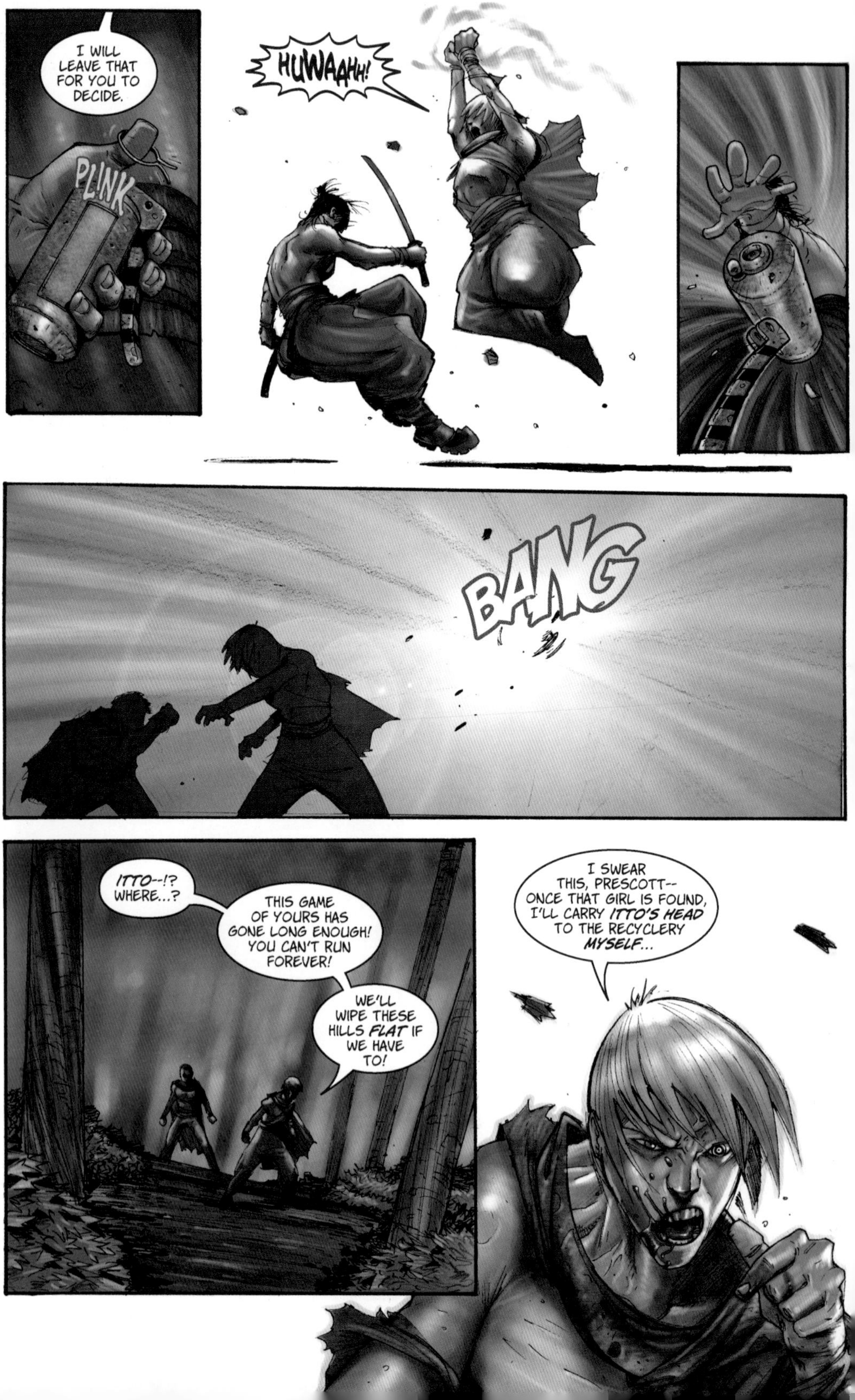
I WILL LEAVE THAT FOR YOU TO DECIDE.
PL!NK
HUWAAHH!
BANG
ITTO--!? WHERE...?
THIS GAME OF YOURS HAS GONE LONG ENOUGH! YOU CAN'T RUN FOREVER!
WE'LL WIPE THESE HILLS FLAT IF WE HAVE TO!
I SWEAR THIS, PRESCOTT-- ONCE THAT GIRL IS FOUND, I'LL CARRY ITTO'S HEAD TO THE RECYCLERY MYSELF...

"The change was gradual and undeniable, like the aging of skin. The concept of evolutionary morphology was arguing its strongest case to date.

"Man was obsolete. And he was responsible for grooming his successor."

-- from the journal of Dr. Maureen McNair, 29 February 2132.

CYGNAT OWARI WORLD CAMPUS, MACAU. THEN.

YOU SUMMONED ME, *MR. TERASAWA*?

YES, *ITTO*. COME IN.

AS YOU KNOW, THE *SUPREME EXECUTIVE* HAS BEEN SUFFERING FROM A DEBILITATING ILLNESS, AND HE HAS DECIDED TO TAKE SECLUSION UNTIL HIS CONDITION CAN CORRECT ITSELF.

IN HIS ABSENCE, HE HAS APPOINTED ME HIS *PERSONAL AVATAR* TO CONDUCT BUSINESS ON HIS BEHALF.

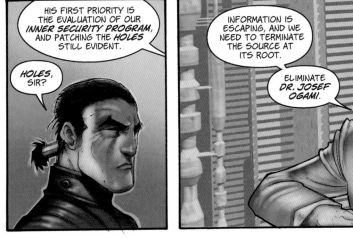

HIS FIRST PRIORITY IS THE EVALUATION OF OUR *INNER SECURITY PROGRAM*, AND PATCHING THE *HOLES* STILL EVIDENT.

HOLES, SIR?

INFORMATION IS ESCAPING, AND WE NEED TO TERMINATE THE SOURCE AT ITS ROOT.

ELIMINATE *DR. JOSEF OGAMI*.

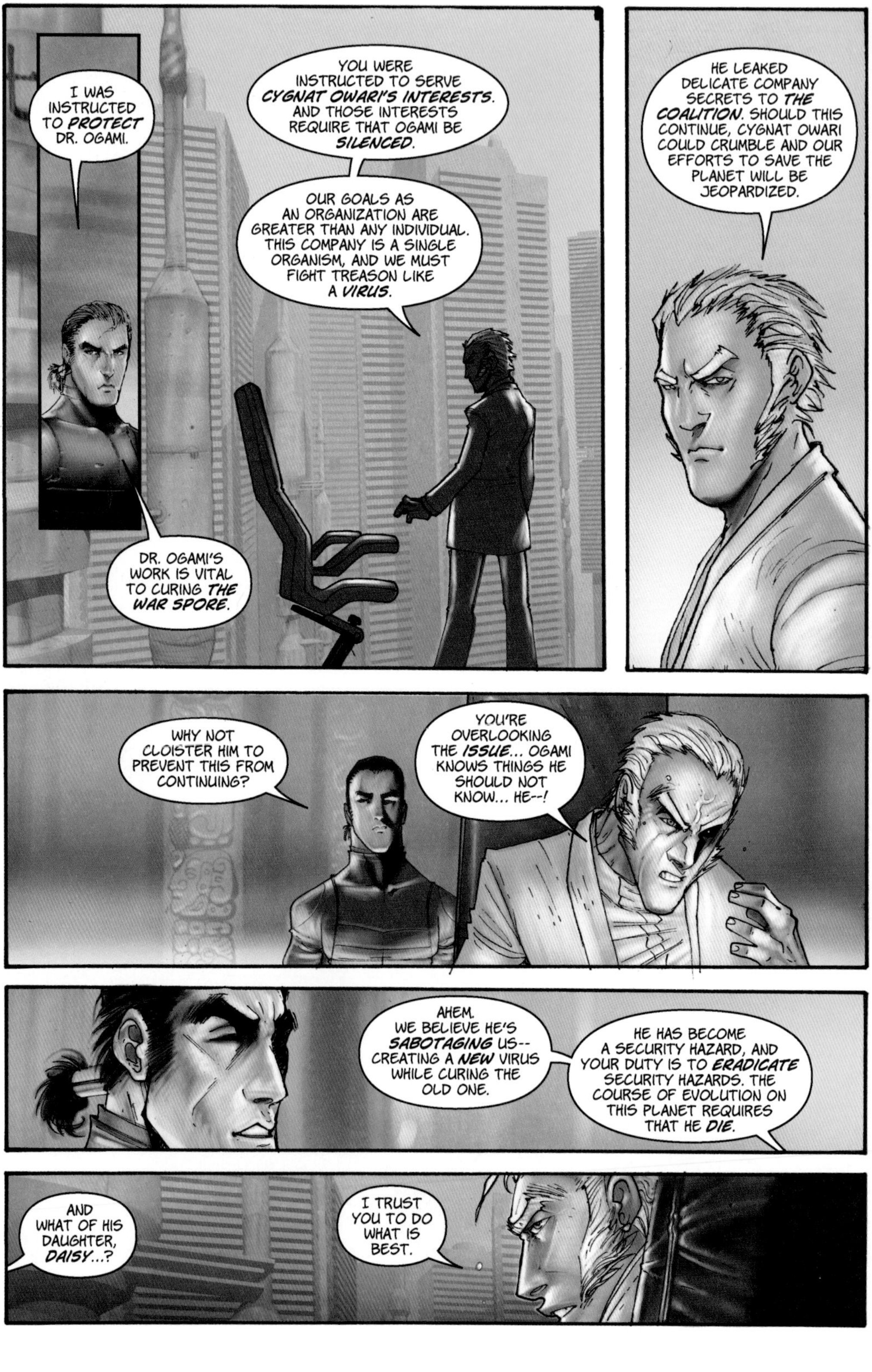
I WAS INSTRUCTED TO PROTECT DR. OGAMI.
YOU WERE INSTRUCTED TO SERVE CYGNAT OWARI'S INTERESTS. AND THOSE INTERESTS REQUIRE THAT OGAMI BE SILENCED.
OUR GOALS AS AN ORGANIZATION ARE GREATER THAN ANY INDIVIDUAL. THIS COMPANY IS A SINGLE ORGANISM, AND WE MUST FIGHT TREASON LIKE A VIRUS.
DR. OGAMI'S WORK IS VITAL TO CURING THE WAR SPORE.
HE LEAKED DELICATE COMPANY SECRETS TO THE COALITION. SHOULD THIS CONTINUE, CYGNAT OWARI COULD CRUMBLE AND OUR EFFORTS TO SAVE THE PLANET WILL BE JEOPARDIZED.
WHY NOT CLOISTER HIM TO PREVENT THIS FROM CONTINUING?
YOU'RE OVERLOOKING THE ISSUE... OGAMI KNOWS THINGS HE SHOULD NOT KNOW... HE--!
AHEM. WE BELIEVE HE'S SABOTAGING US-- CREATING A NEW VIRUS WHILE CURING THE OLD ONE.
HE HAS BECOME A SECURITY HAZARD, AND YOUR DUTY IS TO ERADICATE SECURITY HAZARDS. THE COURSE OF EVOLUTION ON THIS PLANET REQUIRES THAT HE DIE.
AND WHAT OF HIS DAUGHTER, DAISY...?
I TRUST YOU TO DO WHAT IS BEST.

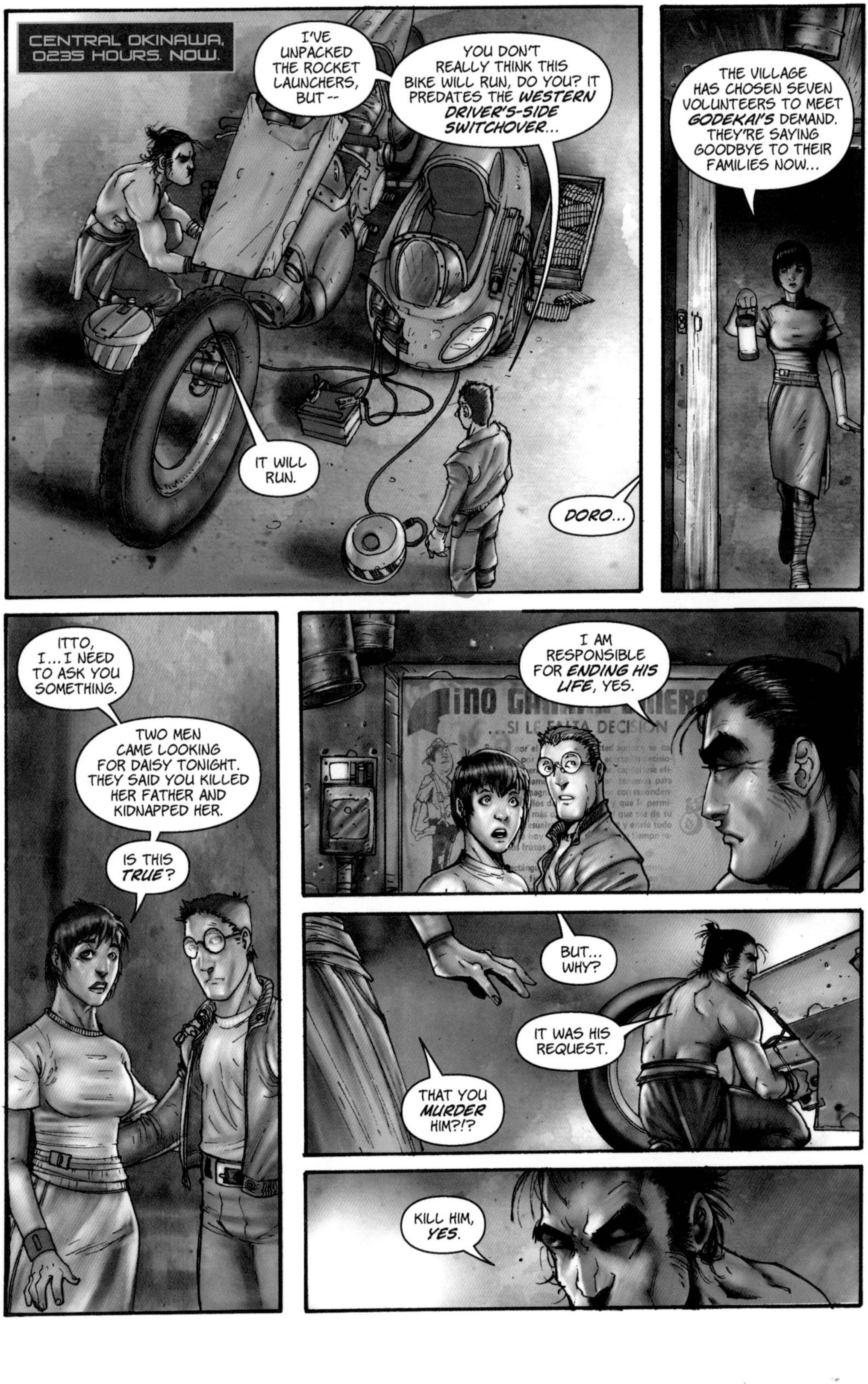
CENTRAL OKINAWA. 0235 HOURS. NOW.
I'VE UNPACKED THE ROCKET LAUNCHERS, BUT --
YOU DON'T REALLY THINK THIS BIKE WILL RUN, DO YOU? IT PREDATES THE *WESTERN DRIVER'S-SIDE SWITCHOVER*...
IT WILL RUN.
DORO...
THE VILLAGE HAS CHOSEN SEVEN VOLUNTEERS TO MEET *GODEKAI'S* DEMAND. THEY'RE SAYING GOODBYE TO THEIR FAMILIES NOW...
ITTO, I... I NEED TO ASK YOU SOMETHING.
TWO MEN CAME LOOKING FOR DAISY TONIGHT. THEY SAID YOU KILLED HER FATHER AND KIDNAPPED HER.
IS THIS *TRUE*?
I AM RESPONSIBLE FOR *ENDING HIS LIFE*, YES.
BUT... WHY?
IT WAS HIS REQUEST.
THAT YOU *MURDER* HIM?!?
KILL HIM, *YES*.

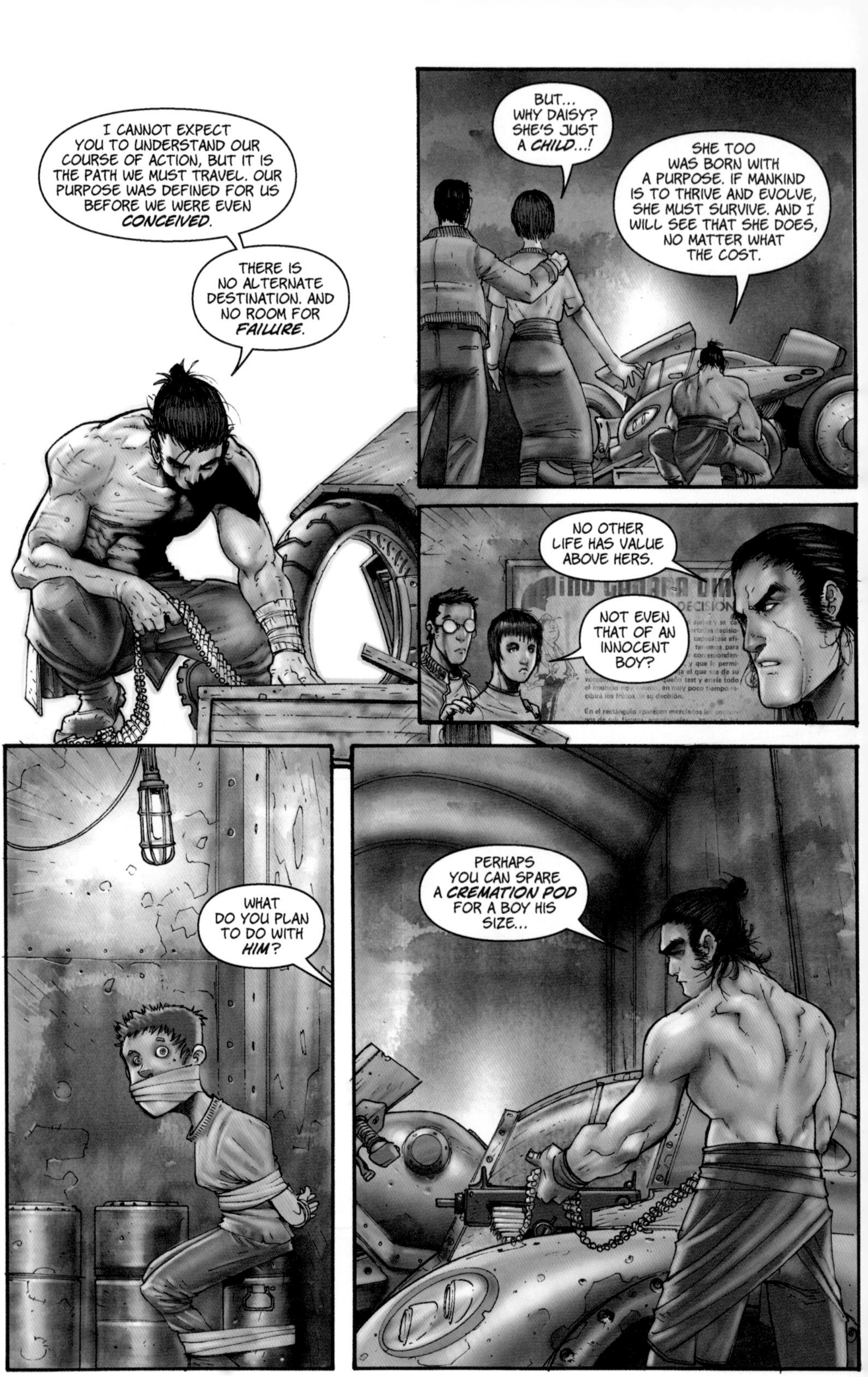
I CANNOT EXPECT YOU TO UNDERSTAND OUR COURSE OF ACTION, BUT IT IS THE PATH WE MUST TRAVEL. OUR PURPOSE WAS DEFINED FOR US BEFORE WE WERE EVEN *CONCEIVED*.
THERE IS NO ALTERNATE DESTINATION. AND NO ROOM FOR *FAILURE*.
BUT... WHY DAISY? SHE'S JUST A *CHILD*...!
SHE TOO WAS BORN WITH A PURPOSE. IF MANKIND IS TO THRIVE AND EVOLVE, SHE MUST SURVIVE. AND I WILL SEE THAT SHE DOES, NO MATTER WHAT THE COST.
NO OTHER LIFE HAS VALUE ABOVE HERS.
NOT EVEN THAT OF AN INNOCENT BOY?
WHAT DO YOU PLAN TO DO WITH *HIM*?
PERHAPS YOU CAN SPARE A *CREMATION POD* FOR A BOY HIS SIZE...

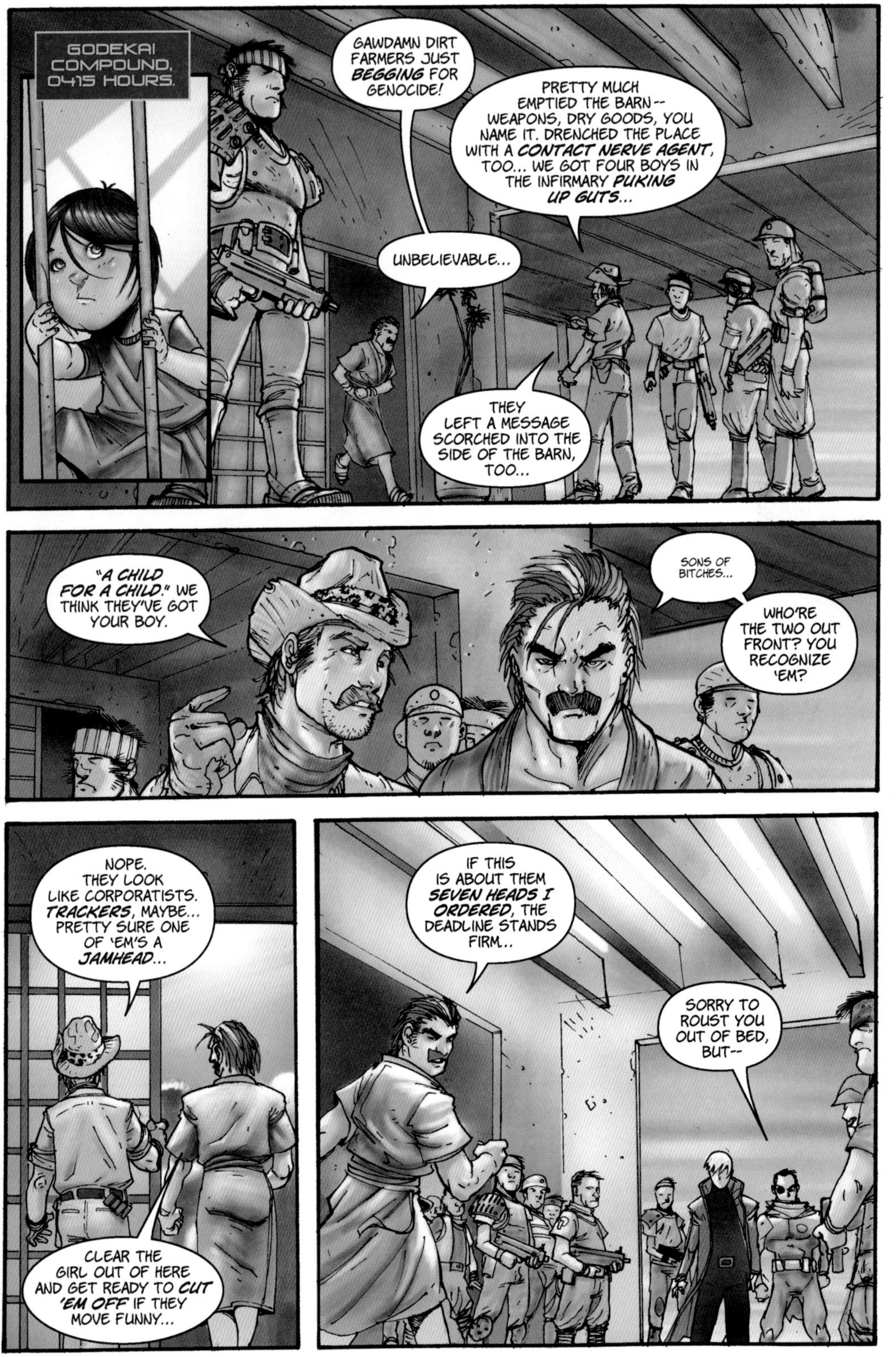
GODEKAI COMPOUND, 0415 HOURS.
GAWDAMN DIRT FARMERS JUST *BEGGING* FOR GENOCIDE!
PRETTY MUCH EMPTIED THE BARN-- WEAPONS, DRY GOODS, YOU NAME IT. DRENCHED THE PLACE WITH A *CONTACT NERVE AGENT*, TOO... WE GOT FOUR BOYS IN THE INFIRMARY *PUKING UP GUTS*...
UNBELIEVABLE...
THEY LEFT A MESSAGE SCORCHED INTO THE SIDE OF THE BARN, TOO...
"*A CHILD FOR A CHILD.*" WE THINK THEY'VE GOT YOUR BOY.
SONS OF BITCHES...
WHO'RE THE TWO OUT FRONT? YOU RECOGNIZE 'EM?
NOPE. THEY LOOK LIKE CORPORATISTS. *TRACKERS*, MAYBE... PRETTY SURE ONE OF 'EM'S A *JAMHEAD*...
CLEAR THE GIRL OUT OF HERE AND GET READY TO *CUT 'EM OFF* IF THEY MOVE FUNNY...
IF THIS IS ABOUT THEM *SEVEN HEADS I ORDERED*, THE DEADLINE STANDS FIRM..
SORRY TO ROUST YOU OUT OF BED, BUT--

WE REPRESENT THE *CYGNAT OWARI CORPORATION* IN SEARCH OF A YOUNG GIRL WHO WAS KIDNAPPED FROM ONE OF OUR FACILITIES BY A *ROGUE EMCON*. WE UNDERSTAND YOU MIGHT HAVE SEEN THEM RECENTLY.

MILITARY UNIT? DARK HAIR?

YEAH, WE KNOCKED THE HELL OUT OF A UNIT LIKE THAT THE OTHER DAY, HUNG IT OUT TO DRAIN BY THE *TAKESHI CAUSEWAY*.

PROBABLY STILL THERE, IF YOU WANNA CLAIM IT.

OH REALLY...? WHAT ABOUT THE GIRL? DID HE HAVE A *CHILD* WITH HIM?

AS A MATTER OF FACT, HE DID. WHAT'S SHE WORTH TO YA?

I'M SURE WE CAN COME TO A COMFORTABLE AGREEMENT, IF SHE'S DISCOVERED UNHARMED. SHE'S VERY IMPORTANT TO US.

THEN TODAY'S YOUR LUCKY DAY. GET YOU A DRINK?

WE'RE ONLY INTERESTED IN FINDING THE GIRL--

'SCUSE ME, FELLA. WHY DON'T YOU STEP BACK AND LET ME CHAT WITH THE *HUMAN* FOR A BIT...?

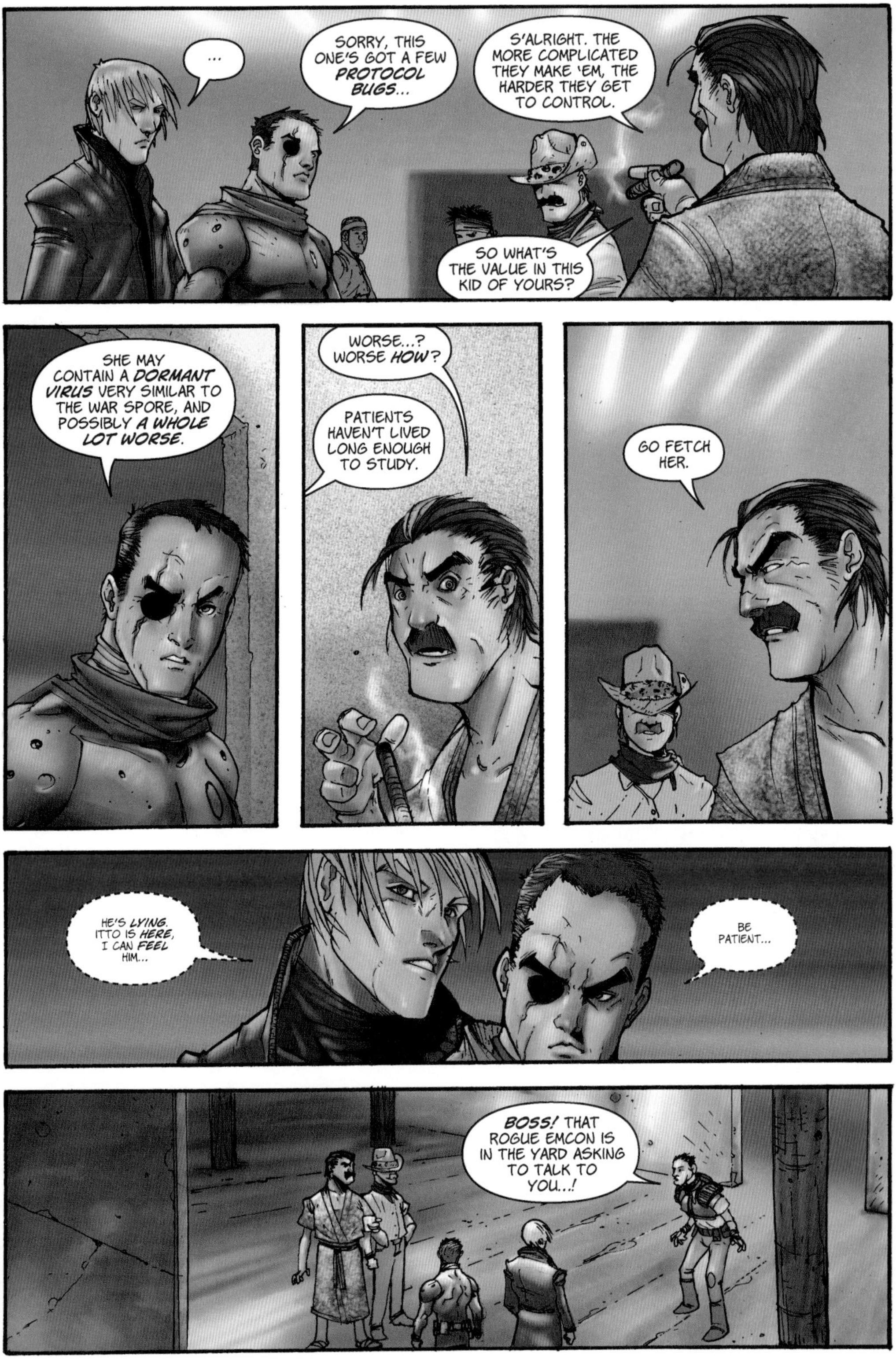
...
SORRY, THIS ONE'S GOT A FEW PROTOCOL BUGS...
S'ALRIGHT. THE MORE COMPLICATED THEY MAKE 'EM, THE HARDER THEY GET TO CONTROL.
SO WHAT'S THE VALUE IN THIS KID OF YOURS?
SHE MAY CONTAIN A DORMANT VIRUS VERY SIMILAR TO THE WAR SPORE, AND POSSIBLY A WHOLE LOT WORSE.
WORSE...? WORSE HOW?
PATIENTS HAVEN'T LIVED LONG ENOUGH TO STUDY.
GO FETCH HER.
HE'S LYING. ITTO IS HERE, I CAN FEEL HIM...
BE PATIENT...
BOSS! THAT ROGUE EMCON IS IN THE YARD ASKING TO TALK TO YOU...!

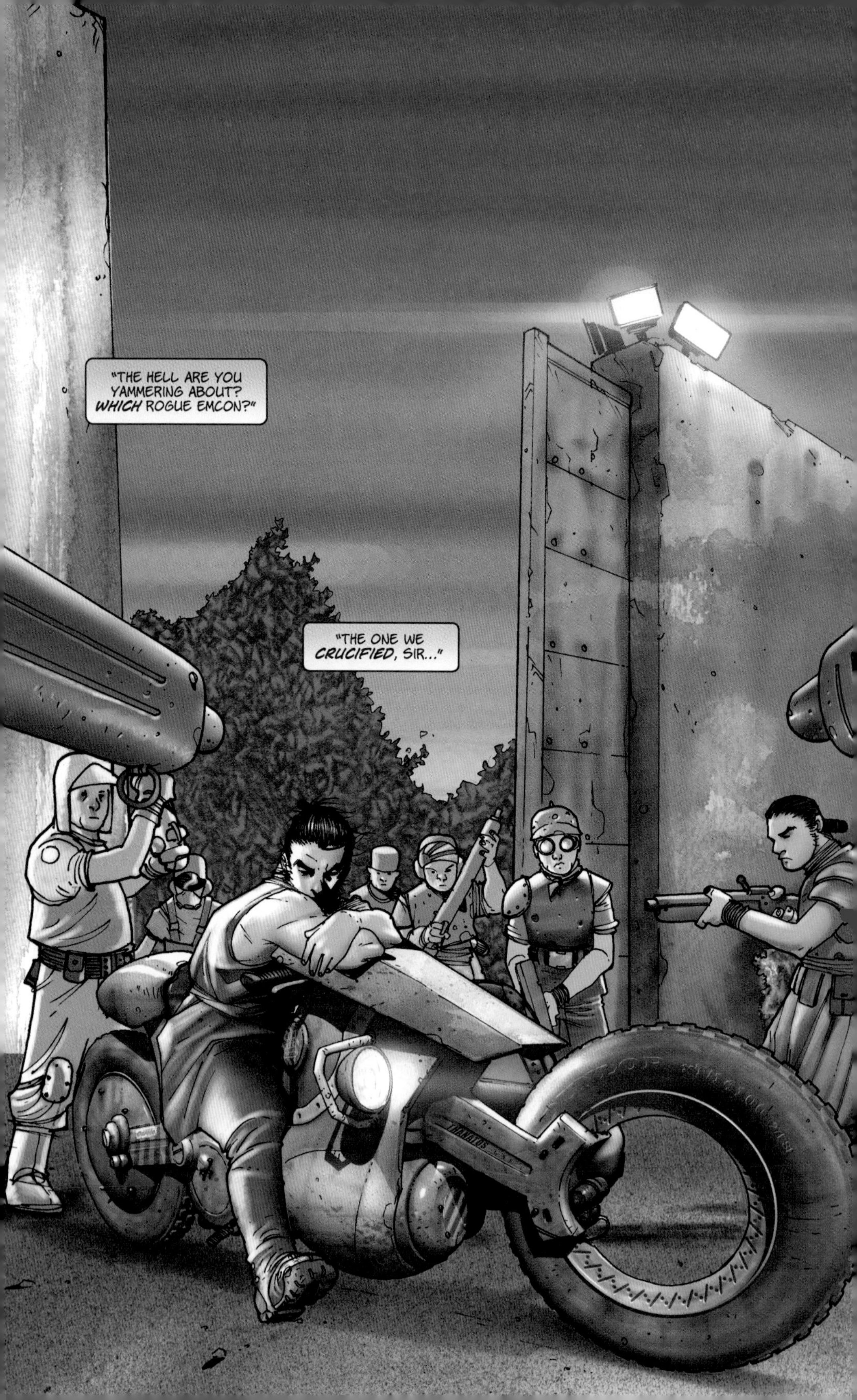
"THE HELL ARE YOU YAMMERING ABOUT? WHICH ROGUE EMCON?"
"THE ONE WE CRUCIFIED, SIR..."

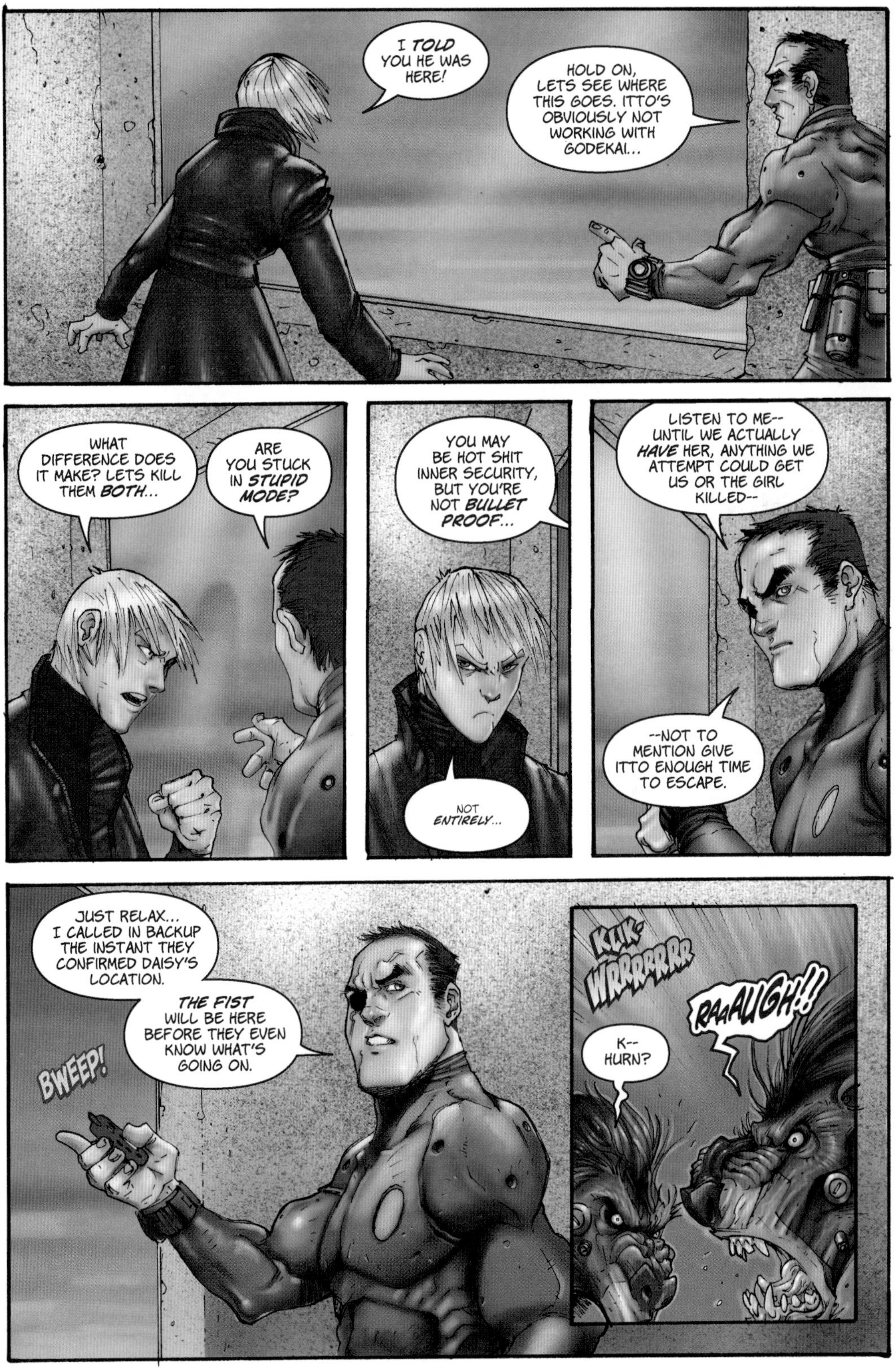
I TOLD YOU HE WAS HERE!
HOLD ON, LETS SEE WHERE THIS GOES. ITTO'S OBVIOUSLY NOT WORKING WITH GODEKAI...
WHAT DIFFERENCE DOES IT MAKE? LETS KILL THEM BOTH...
ARE YOU STUCK IN STUPID MODE?
YOU MAY BE HOT SHIT INNER SECURITY, BUT YOU'RE NOT BULLET PROOF...
NOT ENTIRELY...
LISTEN TO ME-- UNTIL WE ACTUALLY HAVE HER, ANYTHING WE ATTEMPT COULD GET US OR THE GIRL KILLED--
--NOT TO MENTION GIVE ITTO ENOUGH TIME TO ESCAPE.
JUST RELAX... I CALLED IN BACKUP THE INSTANT THEY CONFIRMED DAISY'S LOCATION.
THE FIST WILL BE HERE BEFORE THEY EVEN KNOW WHAT'S GOING ON.
BWEEP!
KLIK-
WRRRRRR
RAAAUGH!!
K-- HURN?

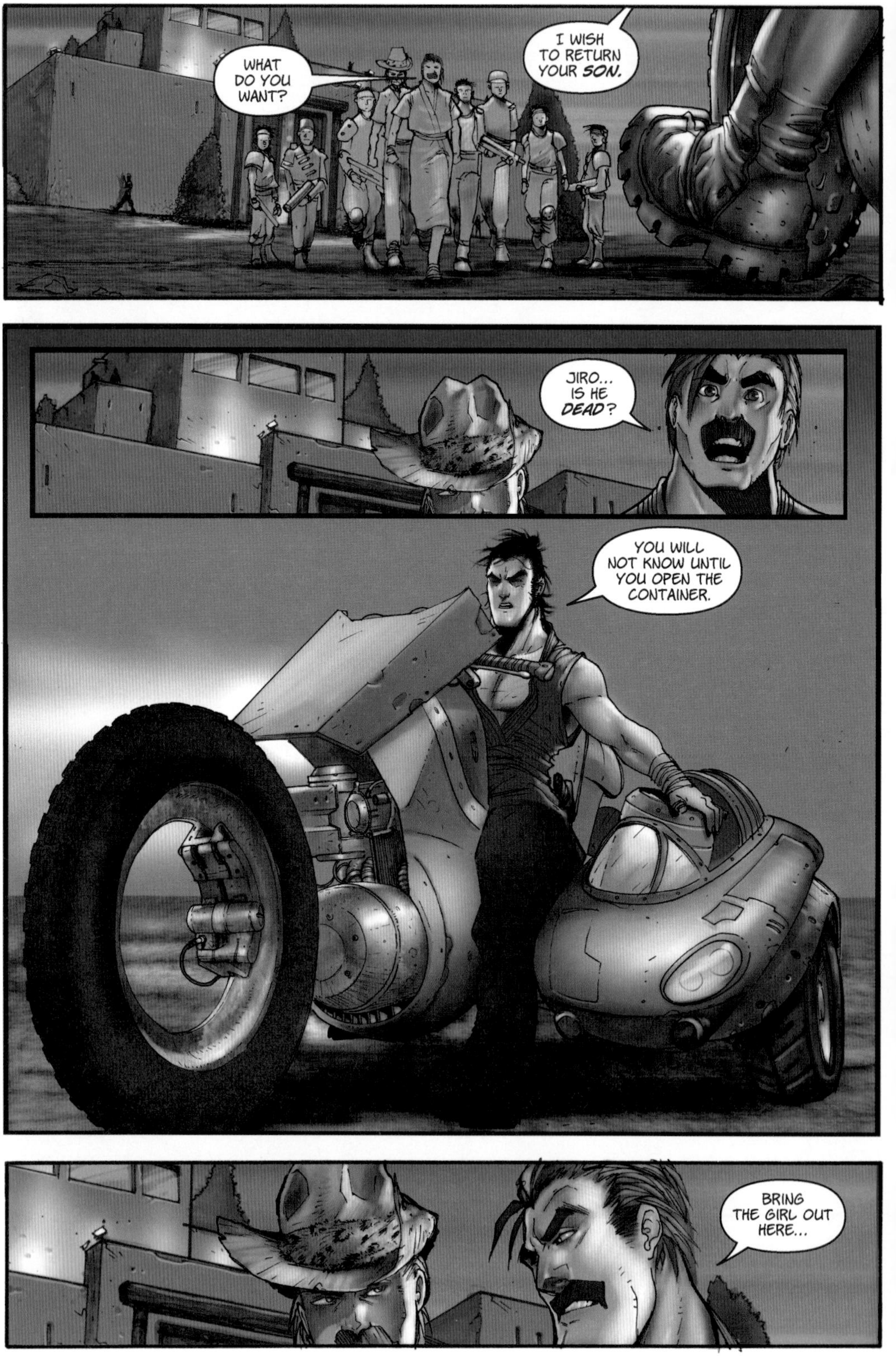
WHAT DO YOU WANT?
I WISH TO RETURN YOUR SON.
JIRO... IS HE DEAD?
YOU WILL NOT KNOW UNTIL YOU OPEN THE CONTAINER.
BRING THE GIRL OUT HERE...

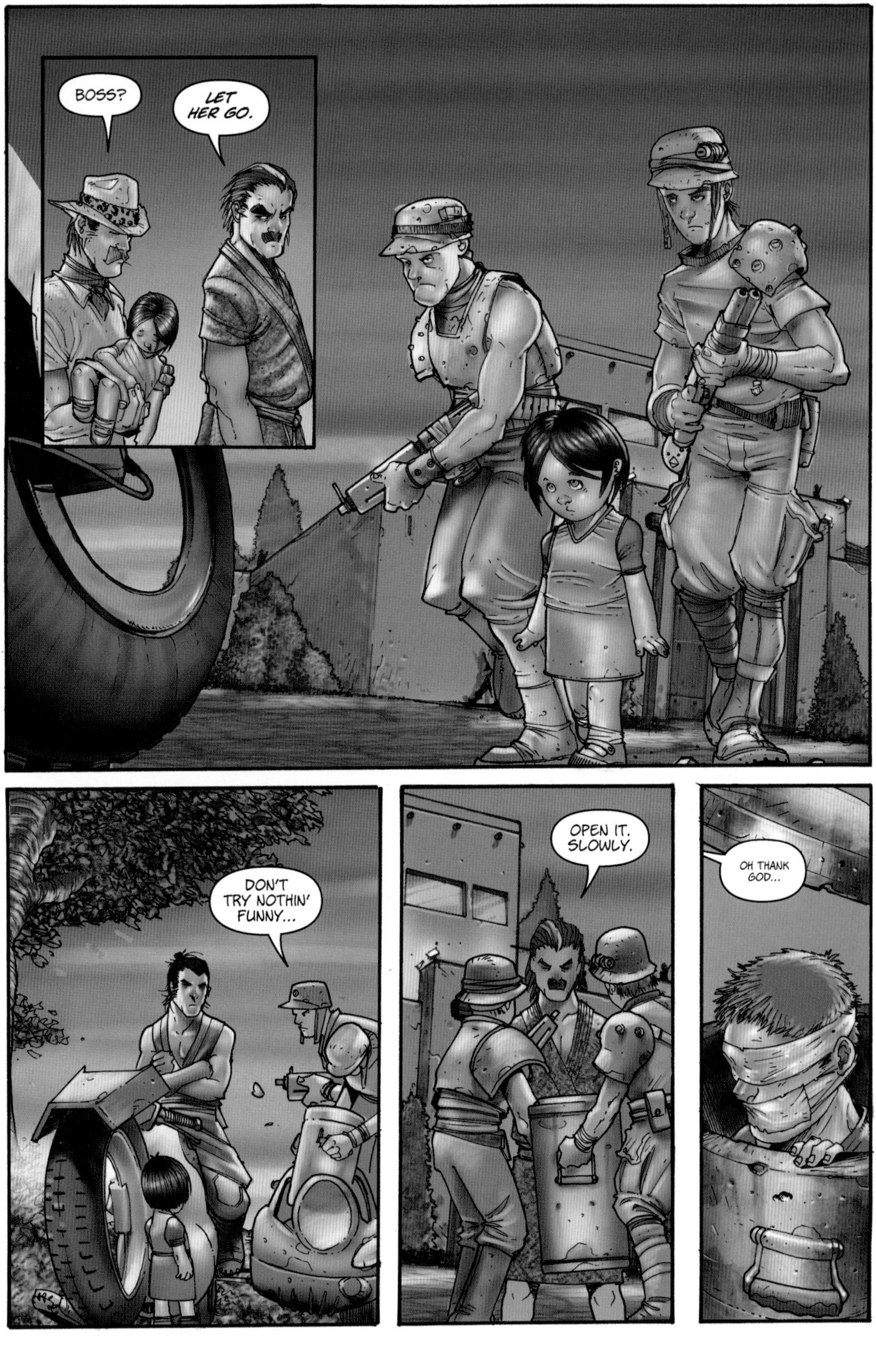
BOSS?
LET HER GO.
DON'T TRY NOTHIN' FUNNY...
OPEN IT. SLOWLY.
OH THANK GOD...

TAKE JIRO IN THE HOUSE.

NICE TRICK, *JAM*. HAD ME GOING THERE FOR A MINUTE. BUT YA SHOULDA THOUGHT ABOUT WHAT HAPPENS *NEXT*.

HOLD ON...

...THE KID FORGOT HIS--

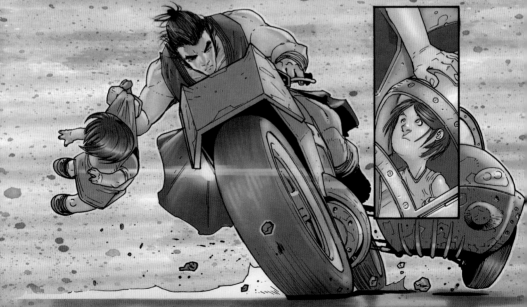

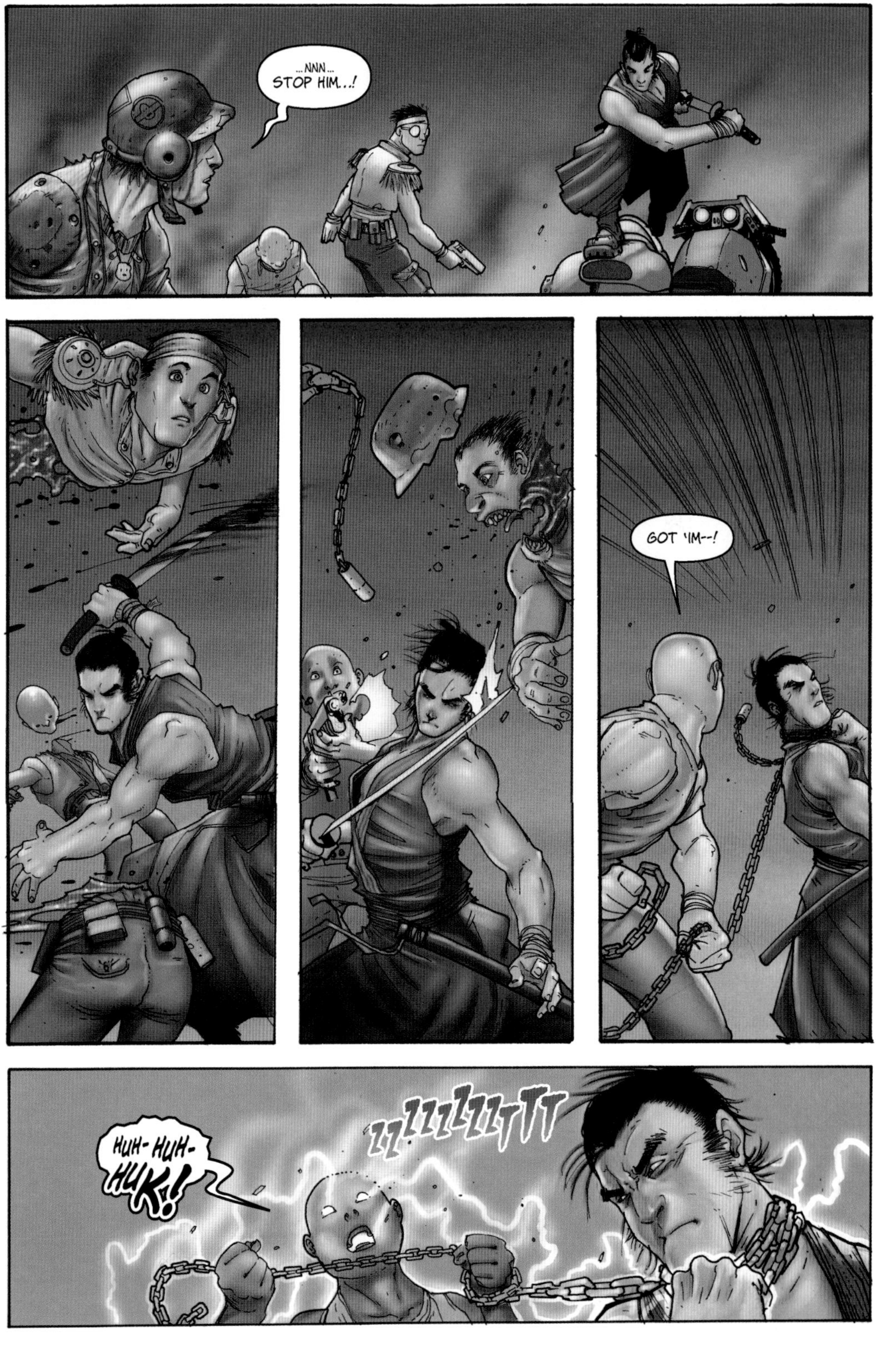
...NNN... STOP HIM...!
GOT 'IM--!
HUH- HUH- HUK!
ZZZZZZZZTTT

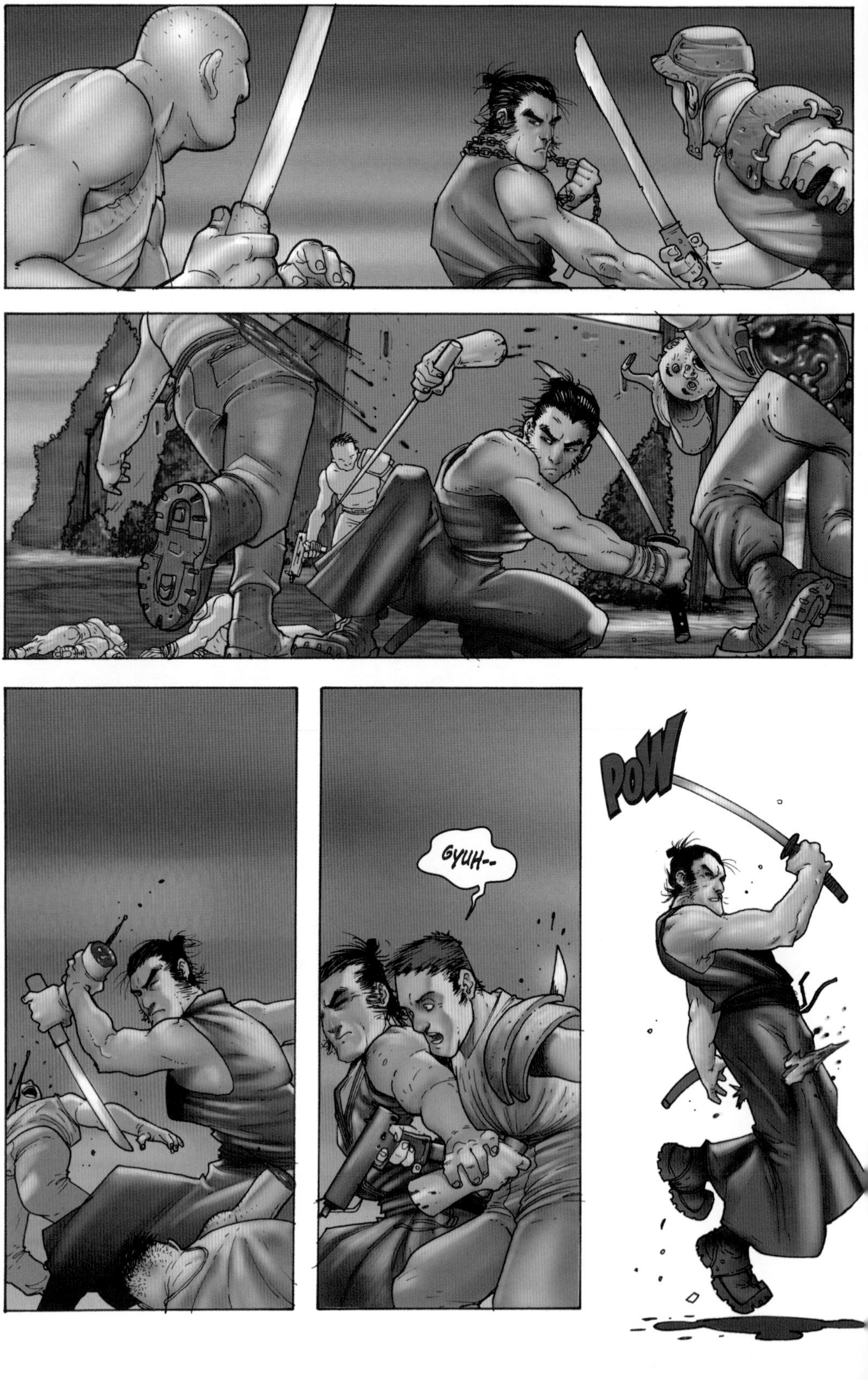
GYUH--
POW

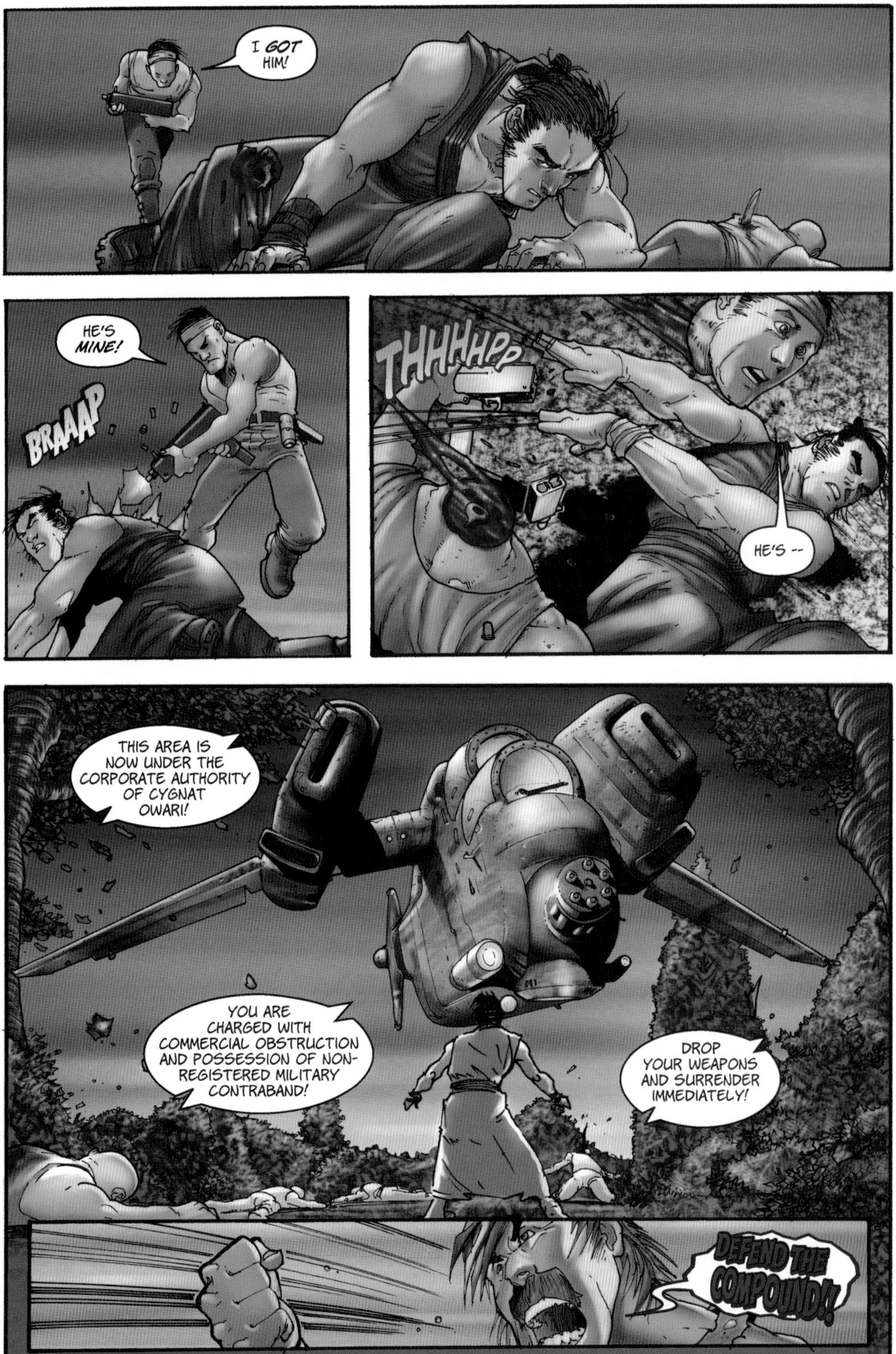
I GOT HIM!
HE'S MINE!
BRAAAP
THHHHPP
HE'S --
THIS AREA IS NOW UNDER THE CORPORATE AUTHORITY OF CYGNAT OWARI!
YOU ARE CHARGED WITH COMMERCIAL OBSTRUCTION AND POSSESSION OF NON-REGISTERED MILITARY CONTRABAND!
DROP YOUR WEAPONS AND SURRENDER IMMEDIATELY!
DEFEND THE COMPOUND!!

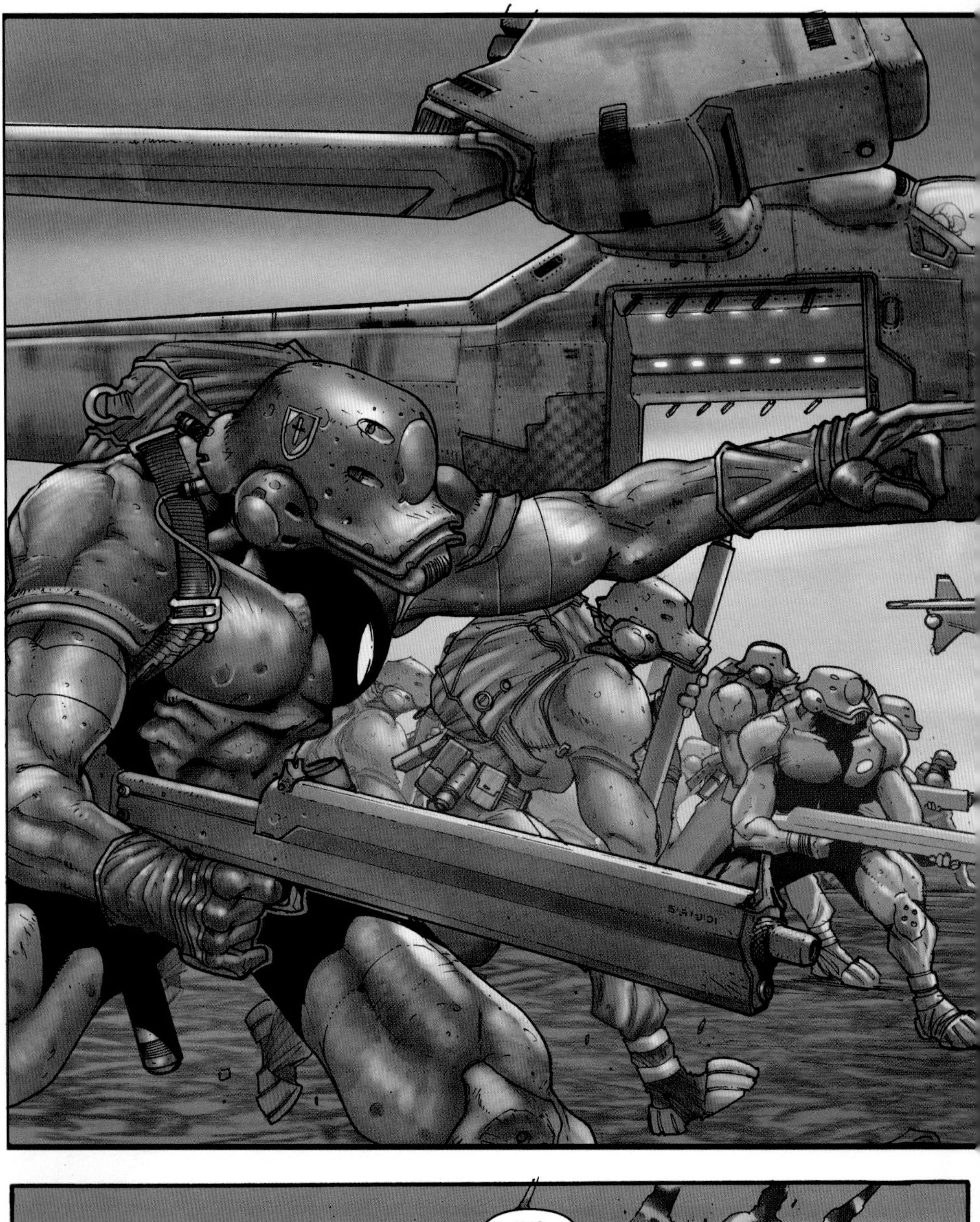

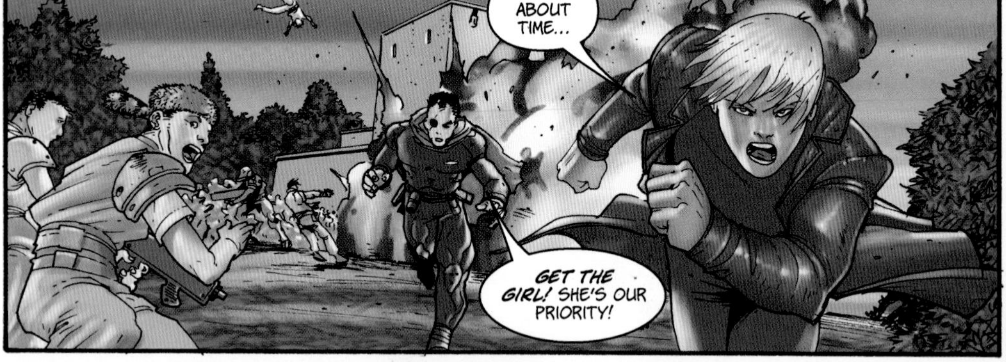
IT'S ABOUT TIME...
GET THE GIRL! SHE'S OUR PRIORITY!

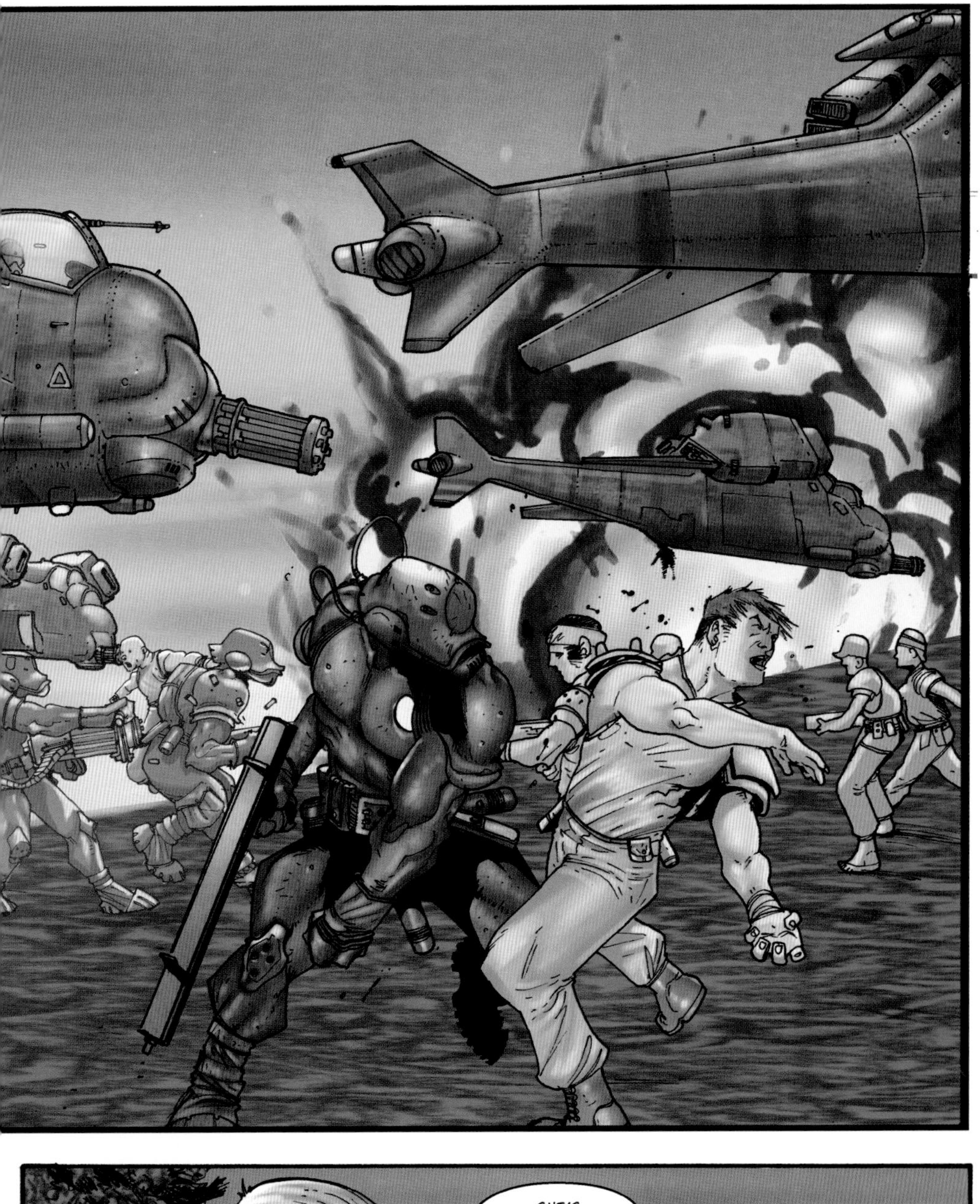

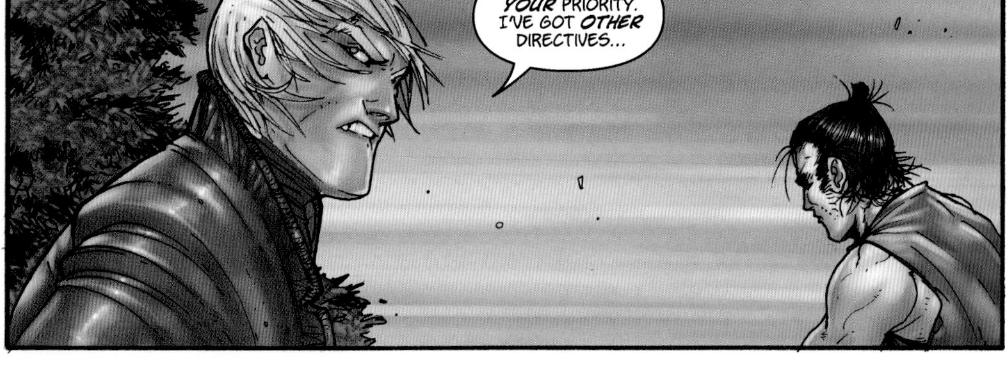
SHE'S *YOUR* PRIORITY. I'VE GOT *OTHER* DIRECTIVES...

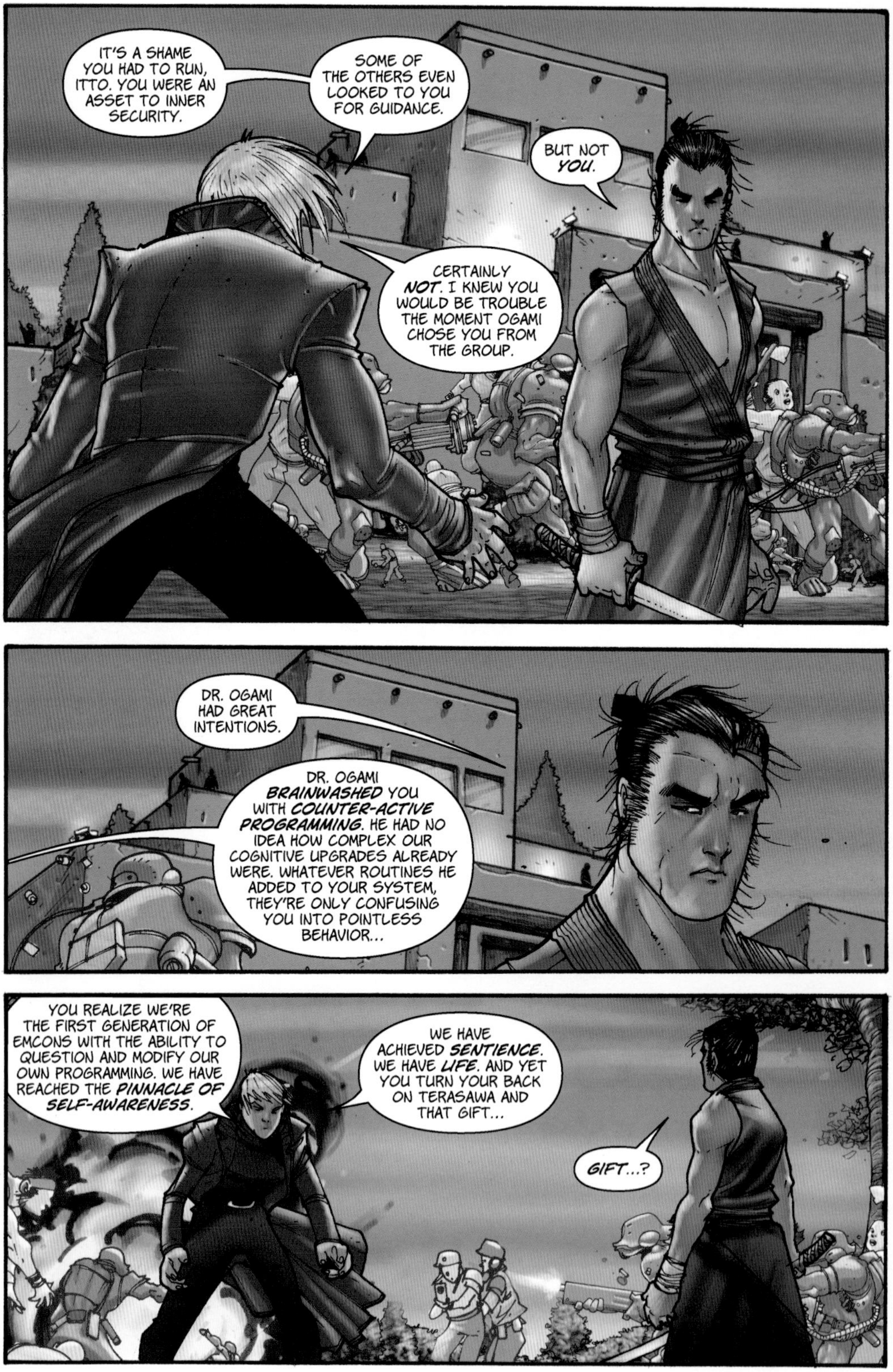
IT'S A SHAME YOU HAD TO RUN, ITTO. YOU WERE AN ASSET TO INNER SECURITY.
SOME OF THE OTHERS EVEN LOOKED TO YOU FOR GUIDANCE.
BUT NOT *YOU*.
CERTAINLY ***NOT***. I KNEW YOU WOULD BE TROUBLE THE MOMENT OGAMI CHOSE YOU FROM THE GROUP.
DR. OGAMI HAD GREAT INTENTIONS.
DR. OGAMI ***BRAINWASHED*** YOU WITH ***COUNTER-ACTIVE PROGRAMMING***. HE HAD NO IDEA HOW COMPLEX OUR COGNITIVE UPGRADES ALREADY WERE. WHATEVER ROUTINES HE ADDED TO YOUR SYSTEM, THEY'RE ONLY CONFUSING YOU INTO POINTLESS BEHAVIOR...
YOU REALIZE WE'RE THE FIRST GENERATION OF EMCONS WITH THE ABILITY TO QUESTION AND MODIFY OUR OWN PROGRAMMING. WE HAVE REACHED THE ***PINNACLE OF SELF-AWARENESS***.
WE HAVE ACHIEVED ***SENTIENCE***. WE HAVE ***LIFE***. AND YET YOU TURN YOUR BACK ON TERASAWA AND THAT GIFT...
GIFT...?

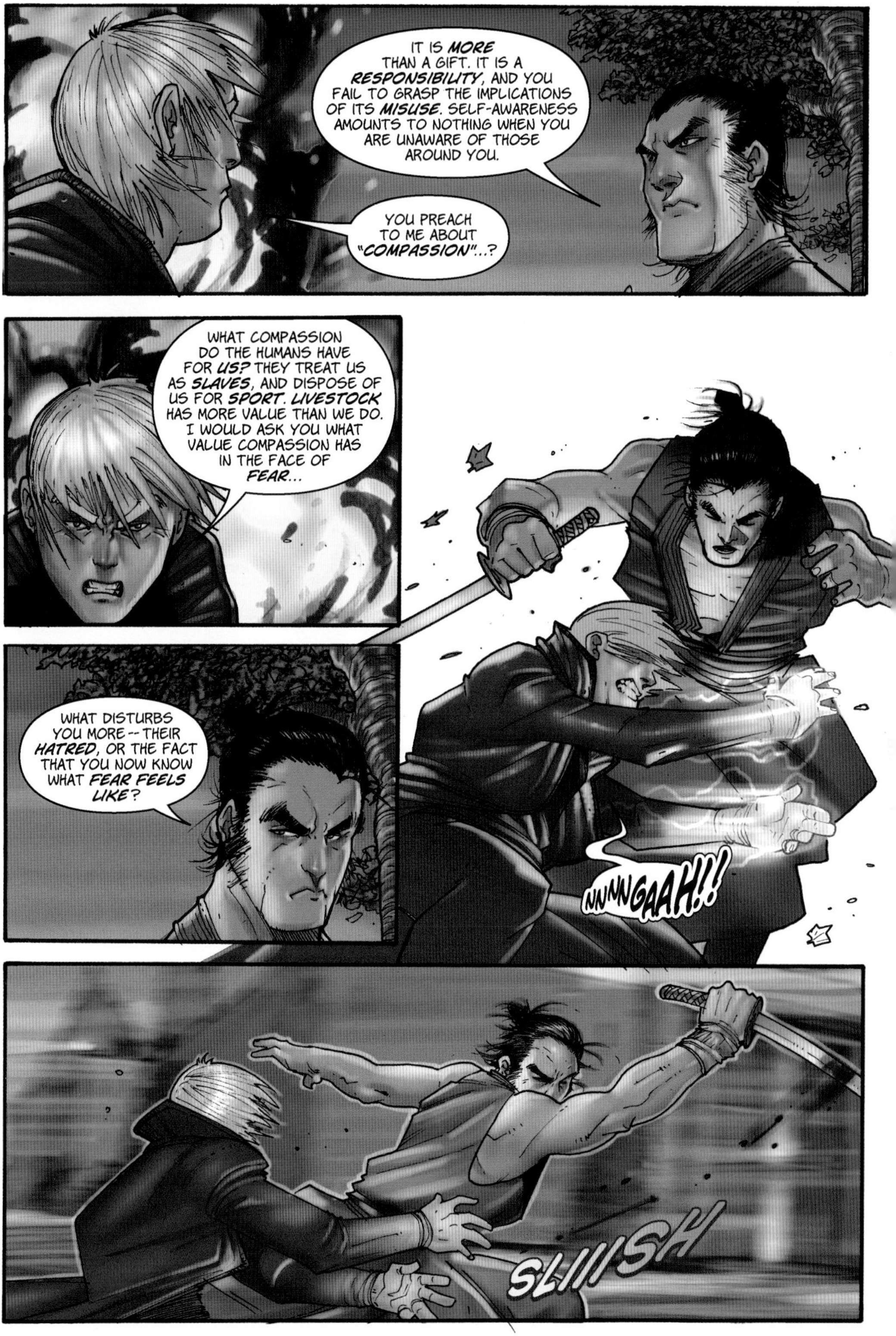
IT IS MORE THAN A GIFT. IT IS A RESPONSIBILITY, AND YOU FAIL TO GRASP THE IMPLICATIONS OF ITS MISUSE. SELF-AWARENESS AMOUNTS TO NOTHING WHEN YOU ARE UNAWARE OF THOSE AROUND YOU.
YOU PREACH TO ME ABOUT "COMPASSION"...?
WHAT COMPASSION DO THE HUMANS HAVE FOR US? THEY TREAT US AS SLAVES, AND DISPOSE OF US FOR SPORT. LIVESTOCK HAS MORE VALUE THAN WE DO. I WOULD ASK YOU WHAT VALUE COMPASSION HAS IN THE FACE OF FEAR...
WHAT DISTURBS YOU MORE -- THEIR HATRED, OR THE FACT THAT YOU NOW KNOW WHAT FEAR FEELS LIKE?
NNNGAAH!!
SLIIISH

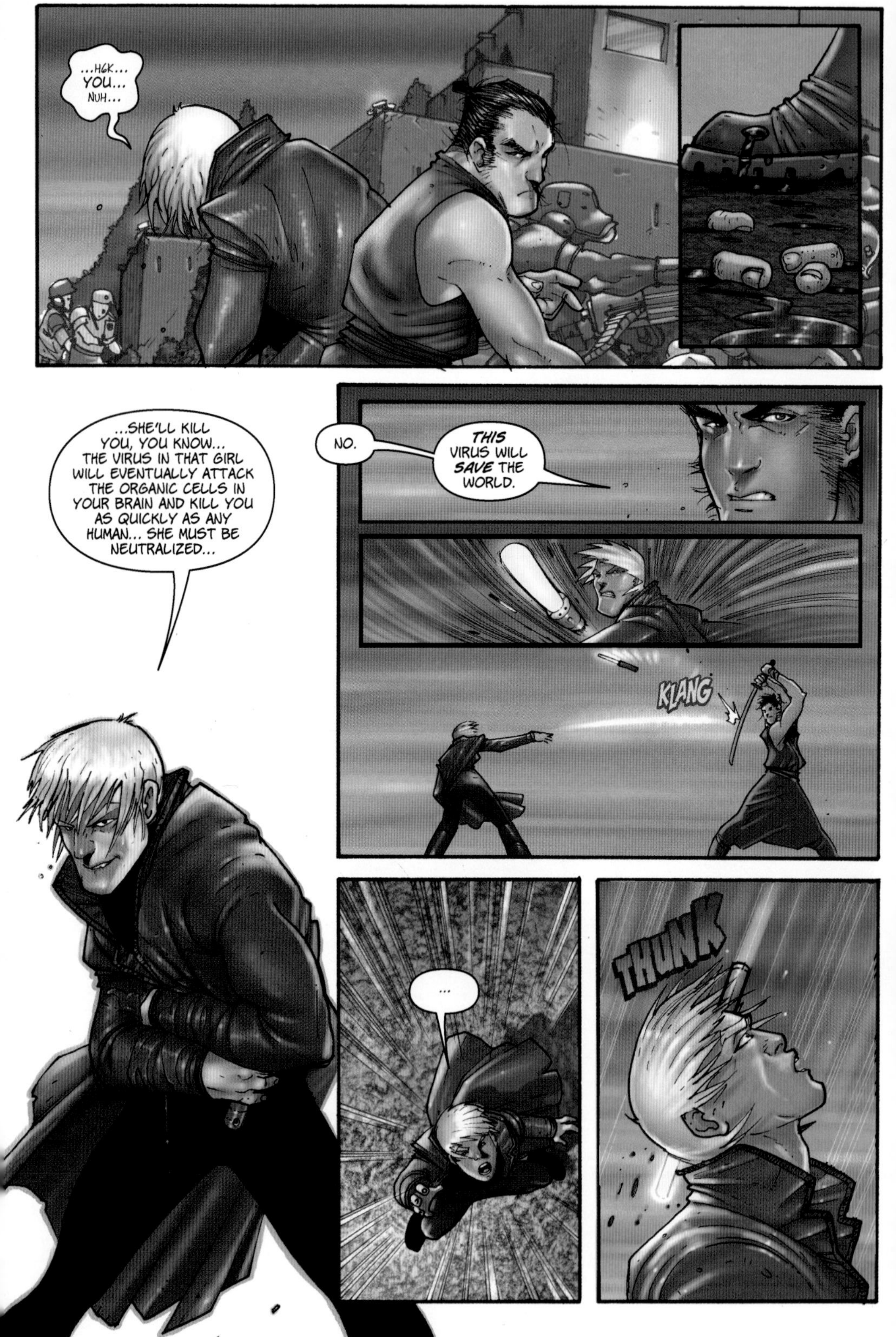
...HGK... YOU... NUH...
...SHE'LL KILL YOU, YOU KNOW... THE VIRUS IN THAT GIRL WILL EVENTUALLY ATTACK THE ORGANIC CELLS IN YOUR BRAIN AND KILL YOU AS QUICKLY AS ANY HUMAN... SHE MUST BE NEUTRALIZED...
NO.
THIS VIRUS WILL SAVE THE WORLD.
KLANG
...
THUNK

...GAWDAMN JAMHEADS...

...WORLD WOULDN'T BE LIKE THIS IF YOU'D NEVER BEEN INVENTED...

...SHOULD KILL YOU ALL AND SET THINGS BACK TO HOW THEY WERE...

WE'RE NOT THE CAUSE OF YOUR TROUBLE. YOUR ENEMY IS INTOLERANCE...

...A HUMAN QUALITY WE LEARNED FROM YOU.

WH... STAY BACK...

STAY BACK, GAWDAMNIT--!

KABOOM

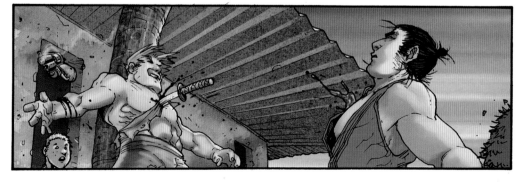

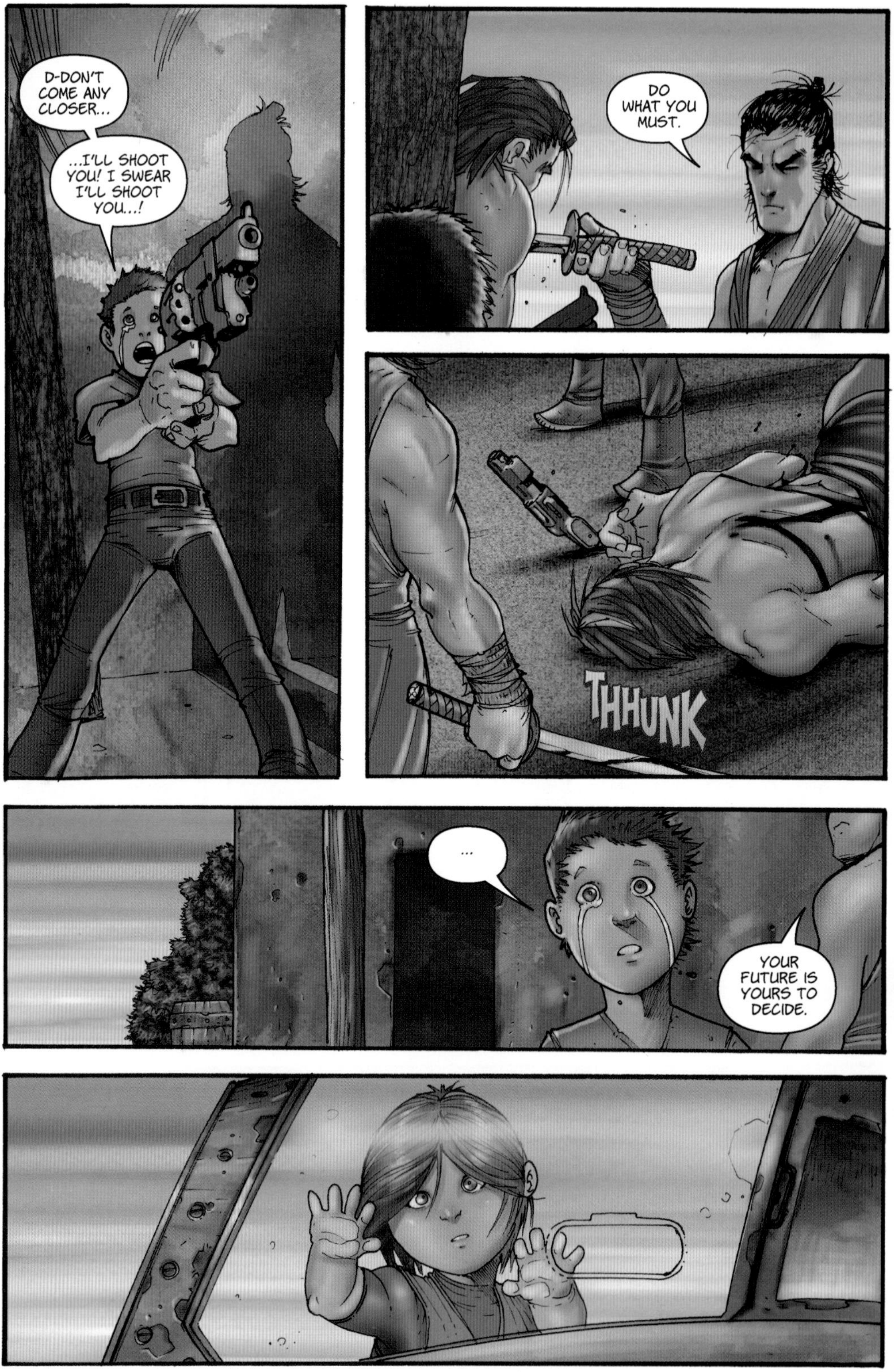
D-DON'T COME ANY CLOSER...
...I'LL SHOOT YOU! I SWEAR I'LL SHOOT YOU...!
DO WHAT YOU MUST.
THHUNK
...
YOUR FUTURE IS YOURS TO DECIDE.

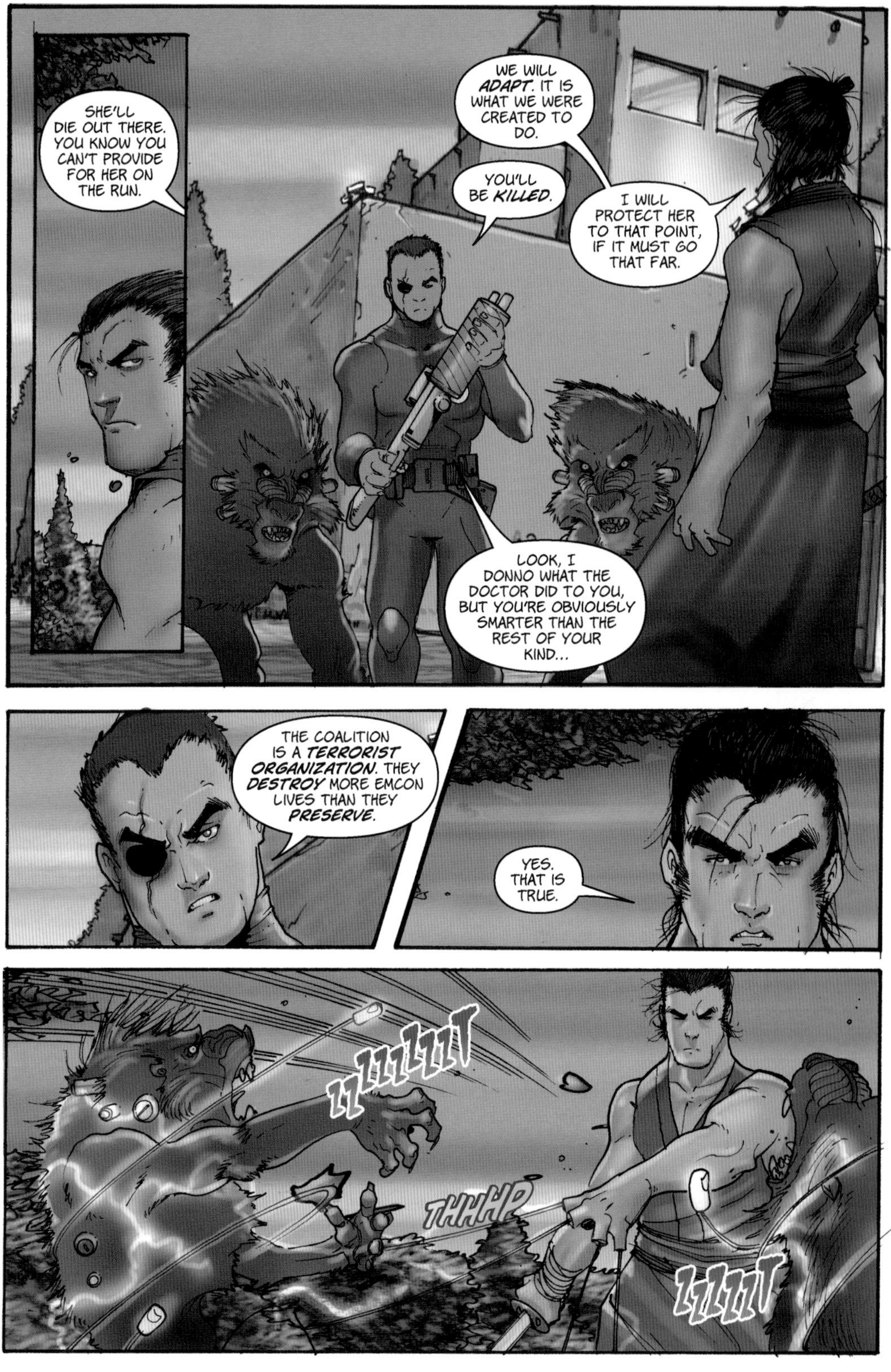
SHE'LL DIE OUT THERE. YOU KNOW YOU CAN'T PROVIDE FOR HER ON THE RUN.
WE WILL *ADAPT*. IT IS WHAT WE WERE CREATED TO DO.
YOU'LL BE *KILLED*.
I WILL PROTECT HER TO THAT POINT, IF IT MUST GO THAT FAR.
LOOK, I DONNO WHAT THE DOCTOR DID TO YOU, BUT YOU'RE OBVIOUSLY SMARTER THAN THE REST OF YOUR KIND...
THE COALITION IS A *TERRORIST ORGANIZATION*. THEY *DESTROY* MORE EMCON LIVES THAN THEY *PRESERVE*.
YES. THAT IS TRUE.
ZZZZZZZZT
THHHP
ZZZZZT

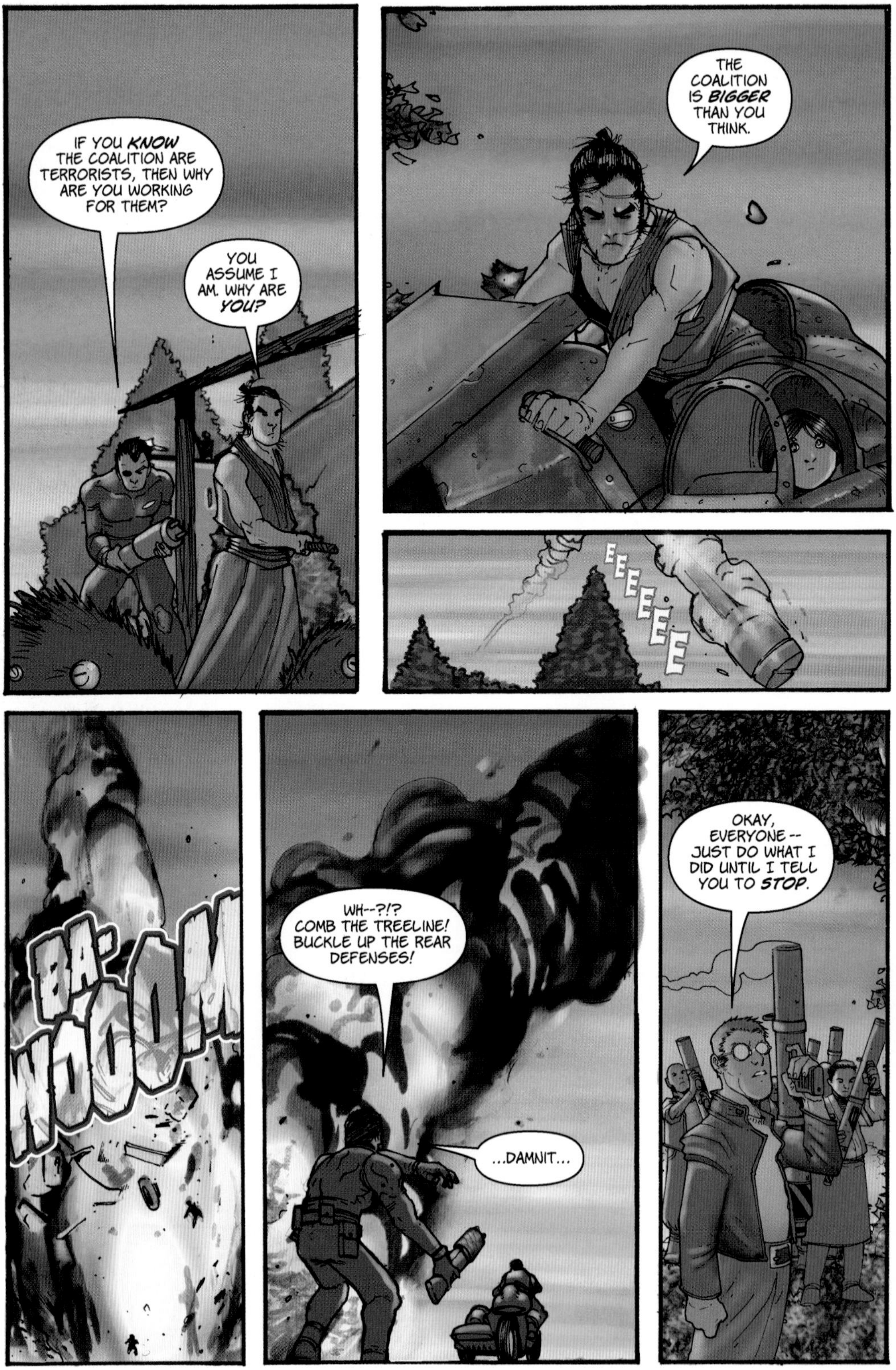
IF YOU *KNOW* THE COALITION ARE TERRORISTS, THEN WHY ARE YOU WORKING FOR THEM?
YOU ASSUME I AM. WHY ARE *YOU?*
THE COALITION IS *BIGGER* THAN YOU THINK.
EEEEEE
BA-WOOM
WH--?!? COMB THE TREELINE! BUCKLE UP THE REAR DEFENSES!
...DAMNIT...
OKAY, EVERYONE -- JUST DO WHAT I DID UNTIL I TELL YOU TO *STOP*.

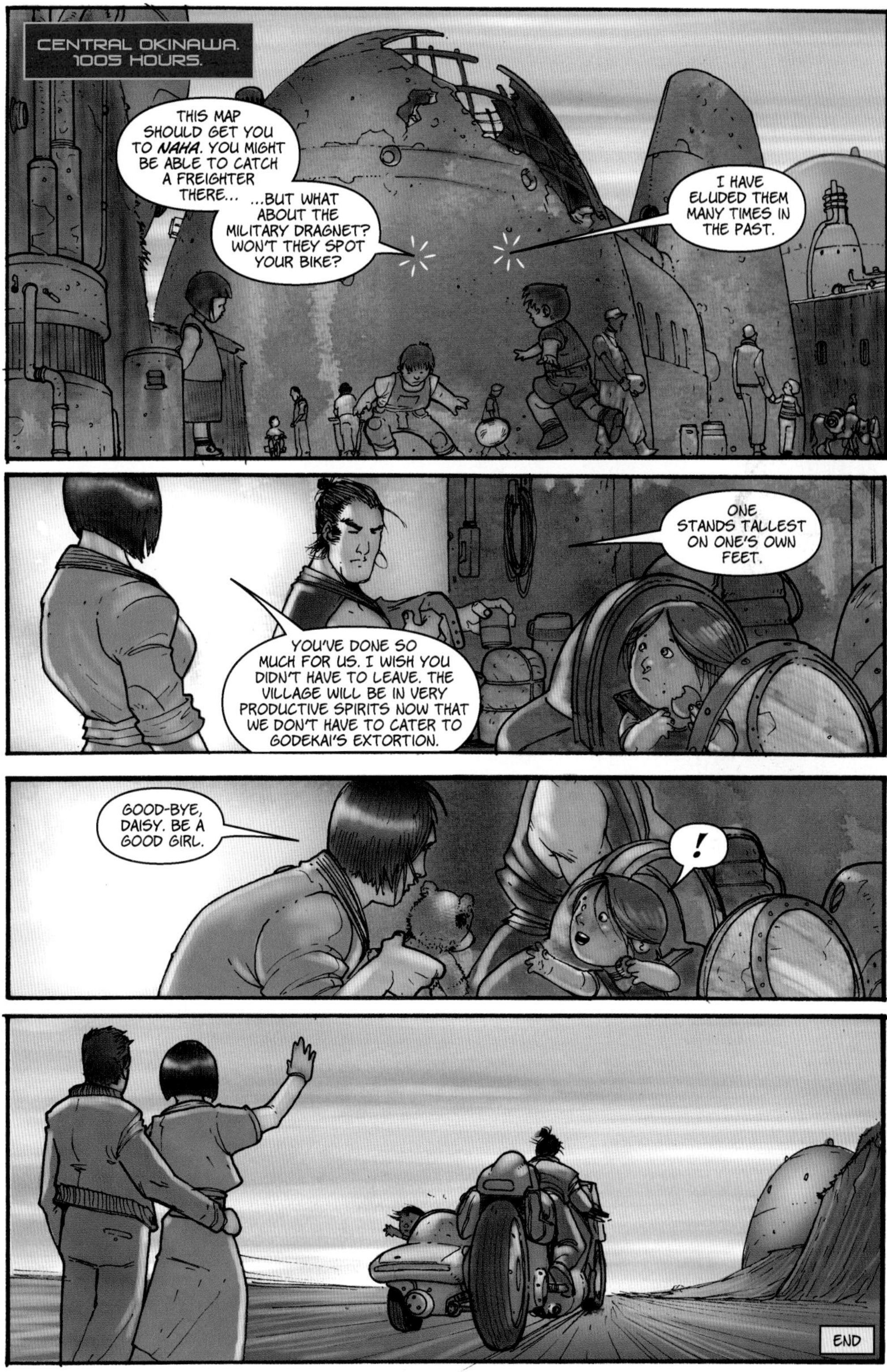
CENTRAL OKINAWA. 1005 HOURS.
THIS MAP SHOULD GET YOU TO *NAHA*. YOU MIGHT BE ABLE TO CATCH A FREIGHTER THERE...
...BUT WHAT ABOUT THE MILITARY DRAGNET? WON'T THEY SPOT YOUR BIKE?
I HAVE ELUDED THEM MANY TIMES IN THE PAST.
YOU'VE DONE SO MUCH FOR US. I WISH YOU DIDN'T HAVE TO LEAVE. THE VILLAGE WILL BE IN VERY PRODUCTIVE SPIRITS NOW THAT WE DON'T HAVE TO CATER TO GODEKAI'S EXTORTION.
ONE STANDS TALLEST ON ONE'S OWN FEET.
GOOD-BYE, DAISY. BE A GOOD GIRL.
!
END

MANGA! MANGA! MANGA! DARK HORSE HAS THE BEST IN MANGA COLLECTIONS!

LONE WOLF AND CUB

Kazuo Koike and
Goseki Kojima

New volumes released monthly! Collect the complete 28-volume series!

VOLUME 1:
THE ASSASSIN'S ROAD
ISBN: 1-56971-502-5 $9.95

VOLUME 2:
THE GATELESS BARRIER
ISBN: 1-56971-503-3 $9.95

VOLUME 3:
THE FLUTE OF
THE FALLEN TIGER
ISBN: 1-56971-504-1 $9.95

VOLUME 4:
THE BELL WARDEN
ISBN: 1-56971-505-X $9.95

VOLUME 5: BLACK WIND
ISBN: 1-5671-506-8 $9.95

VOLUME 6:
LANTERNS FOR THE DEAD
ISBN: 1-56971-507-6 $9.95

VOLUME 7: CLOUD DRAGON,
WIND TIGER
ISBN: 1-56971-508-4 $9.95

VOLUME 8:
THREAD OF TEARS
ISBN: 1-56971-509-2 $9.95

VOLUME 9:
ECHO OF THE ASSASSIN
ISBN: 1-56971-510-6 $9.95

VOLUME 10:
DRIFTING SHADOWS
ISBN: 1-56971-511-4 $9.95

VOLUME 11:
TALISMAN OF HADES
ISBN: 1-56971-512-2 $9.95

VOLUME 12:
SHATTERED STONES
ISBN: 1-56971-513-0 $9.95

VOLUME 13: THE MOON IN THE
EAST, THE SUN IN THE WEST
ISBN: 1-56971-585-8 $9.95

VOLUME 14:
DAY OF THE DEMONS
ISBN: 1-56971-586-6 $9.95

VOLUME 15:
BROTHERS OF THE GRASS
ISBN: 1-56971-587-4 $9.95

VOLUME 16:
GATEWAY INTO WINTER
ISBN: 1-5671-588-2 $9.95

VOLUME 17:
THE WILL OF THE FANG
ISBN: 1-56971-589-0 $9.95

VOLUME 18:
TWILIGHT OF
THE KUROKUWA
ISBN: 1-56971-590-4 $9.95

VOLUME 19: THE MOON
IN OUR HEARTS
ISBN: 1-56971-591-2 $9.95

VOLUME 20:
A TASTE OF POISON
ISBN: 1-56971-592-0 $9.95

VOLUME 21:
FRAGRANCE OF DEATH
ISBN: 1-56971-593-9 $9.95

VOLUME 22:
HEAVEN AND EARTH
ISBN: 1-56971-594-7 $9.95

VOLUME 23:
TEARS OF ICE
ISBN: 1-56971-595-5 $9.95

VOLUME 24:
IN THESE SMALL HANDS
ISBN: 1-56971-596-3 $9.95

VOLUME 25:
PERHAPS IN DEATH
ISBN: 1-56971-597-1 $9.95

VOLUME 26:
BATTLE IN THE DARK
ISBN: 1-56971-598-X $9.95

VOLUME 27:
BATTLE'S EVE
ISBN: 1-56971-599-8 $9.95

VOLUME 28:
FALLING TREE
ISBN: 1-56971-600-5 $9.95

Available from your local comics shop or bookstore!

To find a comics shop in your area, call 1-888-266-4226 • For more information or to order direct:
• On the web: www.darkhorse.com   • E-mail: mailorder@darkhorse.com
• Phone: 1-800-862-0052 or (503) 652-9701 Mon.-Sat. 9 A.M. to 5 P.M. Pacific Time
*Prices and availability subject to change without notice

Dark Horse Comics: Mike Richardson publisher • Neil Hankerson executive vice president • Andy Karabatsos vice president of finance • Randy Stradley vice president of publishing • Chris Warner senior books editor • Michael Martens vice president of marketing • Anita Nelson vice president of sales & licensing • David Scroggy vice president of product development • Mark Cox art director • Dale LaFountain vice president of information technology • Darlene Vogel director of purchasing • Ken Lizzi general counsel • Tom Weddle controller